NO 11 '13

NORTHWEST
MISSOURI
■ St. Joseph

Hannibal ■

NORTHEAST
MISSOURI

■ Kansas City

■ Columbia

St. Louis ■

CENTRAL
MISSOURI

Jefferson City

SOUTHEAST
MISSOURI

■ Springfield

SOUTHWEST MISSOURI

TENTH EDITION

OFF THE BEATEN PATH®
MISSOURI →

A GUIDE TO UNIQUE PLACES

PATTI DeLANO

gpp®
travel

Guilford, Connecticut

All the information in this guidebook is subject to change. We recommend that you call ahead to obtain current information before traveling.

Copyright © 2013 by Patti A. DeLano

Editor: Amy Lyons
Project Editor: Lynn Zelem
Text design by Linda R. Loiewski
Maps by Equator Graphics © Morris Book Publishing, LLC

ISSN 1539-8129
ISBN 978-0-7627-8649-7

Printed in the United States of America
10 9 8 7 6 5 4 3 2 1

Contents

About the Author

Patti DeLano is a travel writer and photographer from the Kansas City area who has lived in the Ozarks of Missouri and vacationed across the borders in Arkansas and Kansas for more than 40 years. She has also written *Arkansas Off the Beaten Path* and *Kansas Off the Beaten Path* for Globe Pequot Press. She lives on the island of Venice, Florida, where she now travels by sailboat as crew aboard *S/V Didgeridoo* with Captain David McKie.

In memory of my daddy, John Randazzo,
and his 90 years of life with me in Missouri,
and to my mom, Sally Randazzo, who at age 95
finally left Missouri to come live near me in Florida.
With love.

Acknowledgments

No book comes easily, but a sense of humor helps. It's especially true of a book of this sort, which requires so many hours of research and fine-tuning. And so, the sense of humor and the camaraderie of my Missouri friends were essential to this 10th edition.

Thank you to William Jewell College in Liberty, Missouri, where as a "reentry student" scholar with some, shall we say, maturity, I learned the art and craft of writing.

The Missouri Tourism Bureau and the Missouri Departments of Conservation and Natural Resources, not to mention all the visitors' bureaus and chambers of commerce I contacted in hundreds of little towns, made it easier. I want to offer special thanks to the hundreds of people around the state who sent me new information and helped make the 10th edition even more fun.

It's impossible to include all the wonderful, quirky places I discovered in the course of researching this book—it would weigh five pounds. Others I simply did not know about; still others have recently appeared or, sadly, have gone out of business. If you know of a special place, or a change in an existing listing, please write me or the publisher so that I can add this information when I next update the book. We would love to hear from you concerning your experiences with this guide and how you feel it could be improved and be kept up to date. Please send your comments and suggestions to: Globe Pequot Press, Reader Response/Editorial Department, PO Box 480, Guilford, CT 06437. Or e-mail: editorial@GlobePequot.com.

Introduction

Think of Missouri and a hundred images tumble forward like candy from a piñata. The Pony Express. The Santa Fe Trail. Lewis and Clark. The Civil War. Frank and Jesse James. Mark Twain (who once said that he was born here because "Missouri was an unknown new state and needed attractions"; we certainly got one in Samuel Clemens).

But all of the images are not from the distant past, flickering like a silent movie through the veil of time. There's Branson, now threatening Nashville as the country music capital of the country, with countless entertainment palaces boasting big-name stars of everything from music to magic. There's even a rodeo restaurant! (I'll tell you how to beat the crowds and traffic and help you find a quiet bed-and-breakfast instead of a computer-located motel.) There's also Kansas City's Country Club Plaza, the world's first shopping center. Kansas City steaks. Charlie Parker and jazz. General John J. Pershing. The Gateway Arch. Barbecue. Writers Calvin Trillin and Richard Rhodes. The founder of Hallmark Cards, Joyce Hall, built an empire, with the international headquarters in Kansas City. Actors Brad Pitt, Kathleen Turner, Bob Cummings, John Goodman, and Don Johnson, as well as Walt Disney, all have ties to Missouri. And, of course, our own Harry S Truman. Now you're on a roll.

What you may not think of immediately are the things I will show you in *Missouri: Off the Beaten Path*. Did you know that J. C. Penney got his start here? There's a museum to honor his modest beginnings in Hamilton. And Jacques Cousteau—

harrystruman

Just for the record: Harry S Truman had no middle name. Just the S. Consequently, there is no period after the S, in Harry S Truman, because it is not an abbreviation. Only sticklers and people from Missouri notice this, and the author is a stickler from Missouri. However, the controversy goes both ways at the Truman Library and even Harry himself used a period after the S in his signature—occasionally.

when you think of the man, you imagine oceanic dives in faraway places, right? Not always. Cousteau filmed a "deep-earth dive" right here in Bonne Terre and explored his way up the Mississippi and Missouri Rivers as well. Then there's the Kingdom of Callaway, with its postwar ties to none other than Winston Churchill. There are wineries and breweries and distilleries, and there are elegant restaurants and comfort-food cafes that range from fine French to fire-breathing Cajun, with home-style cooking settled somewhere in between.

What we are not is flat farmland, empty prairie, or wall-to-wall cows (or cowboys and Indians, for that matter). There's a rich diversity of landscape here.

Missouri is covered with forests and rolling hills. It boasts more than 5,000 caves, and those are only the ones I know about. The rugged white bluffs along the rivers (the rocky remains of a prehistoric inland sea) and the volcanic formations and underground streams and caverns in the Lake of the Ozarks area are among the most beautiful in the country. The rivers that sculpted all this spectacular scenery are magnets for exploration; the Jacks Fork, Eleven Point, and Current Rivers are designated National Scenic Riverways. Remnant prairies still beckon—patchwork bits and pieces left over from presettlement days, when the big bluestem and gayfeather grasses were tall enough to hide a man on horseback, and the wind-driven waves imitated a sea of grass.

In 1673 Marquette and Joliet came down the Mississippi River and saw the land that is now called Missouri. The Jesuit missionaries (the Mission of St. Francis Xavier) established the first white settlement in Missouri near the present site of St. Louis around 1700. The Mississippi River, which forms the eastern boundary of the state, is still one of the busiest shipping lanes in the world and has been flowing here since before the dawn of time. The upstart Missouri River, on the other hand, was the gift of a departing glacier a short half million years ago; it simply wasn't there before that time. The division between the glaciated plains to the north (rolling and covered with a generous layer of topsoil, also a legacy of the wall of ice, which stole the soil from points north) and the bony Ozark region to the south (rough and hilly with valleys cut deep into rock) is the river that bisects the state from Kansas City to St. Louis. Missouri is where old prairie runs up against the oldest mountain range in the country—a fitting symbol for one of the most historically divided states in the Union.

It was in Missouri that the Civil War was most brutal, issuing as it did from tension that had been building for decades. This pre–Civil War strife between free-state Kansas and the Southern-leaning Missouri was bloody, especially because many Missourians believed that slavery was wrong and worked with the Underground Railroad to help slaves to freedom.

After the Civil War Quantrill's Raiders and such legendary outlaws as Cole Younger and the James brothers continued the bloodshed. The state bears the reminders to this day. Civil War battlefields and tiny cemeteries, with their solemn testimony of the losses of the war, embody the lingering dichotomy between Northern and Southern sensibilities.

Before the Civil War and for some years afterward, the two rivers—the Missouri and the Mississippi—were main arteries of commerce. All of Missouri's large cities began as river ports, with a lively competition between them for business and settlers. Kansas City and its popular hot spot, Westport (formerly Westport Landing); St. Joseph, Lexington, Boonville, and Jefferson City, the capital; and Hermann, Washington, and St. Charles, the first capital, all began as ports on the Missouri. Hannibal, St. Louis, Ste. Genevieve, Cape Girardeau, and New Madrid were ports of call on the Mississippi.

In 1870 national attention focused on the great steamship race from New Orleans to St. Louis. Two boats, the *Natchez* and the *Robert E. Lee,* chugged up the Mississippi and drew crowds all along the way. Today the big rivers and their connecting waterway system make a 22,000-mile navigable network. Almost all year the tugs and barges can be seen wherever public and private docks allow commodities to be moved inexpensively by water. Only winter's ice jams stop the flow of traffic.

Kansas City, Missouri's second-largest city (now outgrowing St. Louis, much to the pride of the western part of the state), had its beginnings as a shipping point on the Kansas (then called the Kaw) River bend of the Muddy Mo, where the river turns sharply east on its trek across the state's midriff. The region known by early explorers as the Big Blue Country was occupied by the Kanza (Kansas) Indians, whose name means "people of the south wind." The peaceful Kanza engaged in farming, fishing, and trapping; they were quickly displaced when settlers began to move in.

Missouri was once as far off the beaten path as one could get, the jumping- off point to the trackless West; beyond was the great unknown. You can still see the tracks of the wagon wheels etched deeply into our soil on the Santa Fe, California, and Oregon Trails.

Now everything's up to date in Kansas City, as the lyrics to a song once told us. A beautifully modern metropolis, Kansas City has more fountains than any city except Rome and more miles of tree-lined boulevards than any other American city. The Nelson-Atkins Museum of Art owns one of the finest collections of Oriental art in the country.

westwardbound supplyline

To supply settlers moving west, packet boats departed from St. Louis and traveled to Kansas City and westward on the wide Missouri River. More than 20 steamboats a day docked at the wharf facilities in St. Joseph, carrying all types of homesteading materials, beads to trade with the Indians, tools, staple goods—everything the growing nation needed as the westward expansion continued.

St. Louis, on the other side of the state, has a world-class botanical garden and a rich cultural heritage that rivals any big city in the East. Not surprisingly, St. Louis is proud of its French legacy, a gift of the early explorers.

The KATY Trail (its name is derived from MKT, the Missouri-Kansas-Texas Railroad) begins nearby in Machens, just north of St. Louis. This bicycle and hiking trail follows the old MKT railroad route to Clinton, 75 miles southeast of Kansas City. It covers more than 237 miles of river bluffs, forests, and farmlands with cafes and shops along its route to cater to trail buffs. The KATY is the longest completed rails-to-trails project in the nation. There are so many fun things to do at the recently resurrected towns of bygone days. The scenery along the trail is breathtaking.

The word *Missouri* first appeared on maps made by French explorers in the 1600s. It was the name of a group of Indians living near the mouth of a large river. *Pekketanoui,* roughly its Indian name, means "river of the big canoes," and the Missouri would have required them—it was big, swift, and tricky to navigate before the locks and dams of the US Army Corps of Engineers tamed it, or attempted to.

We don't know how the Native Americans pronounced *Missouri,* and it is about a 50-50 split between the state's current residents. In a recent survey a little more than half the population, most in western Missouri, pronounced the name "Missour-uh." The eastern half of the state favored "Missour-ee."

The "Show-Me State" carries its nickname proudly. We have a reputation as stubborn individualists, as hardheaded as our own Missouri mules—or so they say—and we won't believe something until you show us. It's not such a bad way to be. Our people, like our agrarian ancestors, want concrete proof—we'll change, all right, but only when we're fully convinced that change is synonymous with progress and that progress is indeed an improvement. The past is definitely worth preserving when it is as colorful as ours.

So I will show you parts of the Show-Me State that are tucked away off the beaten path. Some are in the middle of farmland, some are in national forests, and some are in our largest cities. There will be no Worlds of Fun or Six Flags over Mid-America or Kauffman Stadium plugs in this book; such places are definitely on the path, and you can find them on your own. What this book does have is something for everyone, as out of the way—and "far from the madding crowd"—as you could wish.

Restaurant cost categories refer to prices of entrees without beverages, desserts, taxes, or tips. Those listed as inexpensive are $10 or less; moderate, between $10 and $20; and expensive, $21 and over. Places to stay listed as inexpensive are up to $100 per double per night; moderate, $101 to $200 per night; and expensive, $201 and up per night.

trivia

What's in a symbol? From early civilizations, humans have used symbols to tell the story of what is important in their lives. Missouri has had a unique history, and each of the state symbols carries a poignant message of the state and its people. As times change, groups propose symbols to represent products or causes that have evolved and that they believe should be recognized. The newest state symbol is the state grape, which was approved by Governor Bob Holden on July 11, 2003. The state's winemaking industry has grown and prospered, leading to the desire for a new symbol.

No matter where you're from, whether you love a fine Bordeaux or a fine bourbon, whether you like to go in a sports car dressed to the nines or in a pickup truck wearing an old pair of jeans, you will feel at home in Missouri.

Missouri Information

State flag: The field is made up of three horizontal bands—red, white, and blue—of equal width. The state coat of arms appears in the center. It is encircled by a band of blue bearing 24 white stars.

Capital: Jefferson City

Statehood: August 10, 1821, the 24th state

State bird: Bluebird

State tree: Flowering dogwood

State flower: Hawthorn

State insect: Honeybee

State tree nut: Black walnut

State animal: Mule

State horse: Missouri Foxtrotter

State fish: Channel catfish

State aquatic animal: Paddlefish

State musical instrument: Fiddle

State American folk dance: Square dance

State mineral: Galena

State rock: Mozarkite

State fossil: Crinoid

State grape: Norton/Cynthiana

Missouri Day: Third Wednesday in October. The day is used to encourage students to study Missouri history and to celebrate the accomplishments of Missouri citizens.

Origin of name: From Native American sounds meaning "owners of big canoes." First applied to the river, then to the land.

Nickname: The Show-Me State

State song: "Missouri Waltz," by J. R. Shannon, music arranged by Frederick Logan from a melody by John Valentine Eppel.

State seal: A coat of arms appears on the seal. The shield in the center of the seal is divided into two parts. One half shows a bear and a crescent, representing Missouri. The other half shows the eagle of the United States. The two halves are bound together, or united, by a band ending in a belt buckle. The words in the band—"United we stand; divided we fall"—reflect the need for all the states to be united. Two bears support the shield and stand on a streamer on which the state motto is inscribed. A helmet appears above the shield; the 24 stars above the helmet indicate that Missouri was the 24th state. The date at the bottom in Roman numerals (1820) is the date of the Missouri Compromise.

SOUTHEAST MISSOURI

To call southeast Missouri the most beautiful part of the state wouldn't be fair; beauty is a mysterious commodity based on personal definition, as intangible as smoke. But the region has plenty to offer. There is natural beauty—dappled shade of the national forests, cascades of clear blue springs and rivers, and white river bluffs and volcanic rock formations of the Johnson's Shut-ins—that meets everyone's definition of beauty. Antebellum and Victorian homes on wide boulevards grace the oldest cities west of the Mississippi. Both beautiful and historic, southeast Missouri will appeal to all your senses with its food, wine, scenery, and rich and varied past.

When the river was the frontier to the American West, thousands crossed it in search of land, freedom, and a new life. Trappers, traders, explorers, and settlers joined Native Americans in the fertile river valleys and rich prairies.

Enter the state from the east, and you will encounter the St. Louis area, the big city/small town that spreads west on I-70 and south on I-55. Sneak off of these two freeways, and the many small highways branching off from them, to find some of the most charming towns in

Missouri R.

GATEWAY
TO THE
WEST

Jefferson
City

Union

St. Louis

WINE
COUNTRY

Mississippi R.

Rolla

Park
Hills

WILD LANDS

ILL.
MO.

RIVER
HERITAGE
AREA

Cape
Girardeau

OLD MOUNTAIN
REGION

Charleston

MO.
KY.

Poplar Bluff

MO.
ARK.

BOOTHEEL
REGION

Kennett

MO.
TENN.

N

0   40 mi
0   40 km

the state, towns that date from the beginning of the westward expansion of the country.

Here you have a choice of crowded festivals and busy public camp-grounds or the isolation and peace deep in the national forests and wildlife preserves. Missouri in winter is quietly beautiful and secluded; in summer, it is lively and fun. Adventures here range from scuba diving (yes! deep-earth diving in Missouri!) and whitewater canoeing to wine tasting and genealogi-cal searches in the oldest records in the American West. Whether you want to party or to get away from it all, you can wander off the beaten path into southeast Missouri.

Gateway to the West

The bustling **St. Louis** area is still the best place to begin westward explora-tion. Located on a shelf of riverfront under a bluff, the original city spread to the prairies surrounding it. It was the starting point for the Meriwether Lewis and William Clark expedition in 1804. The history of western expansion begins here, where the Missouri and the Mississippi Rivers meet.

St. Louis, founded in 1764, boasts the oldest park west of the Mississippi (Lafayette Park), the second-oldest symphony orchestra in the nation, the world's largest collection of mosaic art at the Cathedral of St. Louis, and one of the finest botanical gardens in the world. The graceful Italianate mansion **Tower Grove House** at the **Missouri Botanical Garden** (800-642-8842 or 314-577-5150; mobot.org) is a more than 150-year-old wonder that blooms with color each Christmas season. Local garden clubs, the Herb Society of St. Louis, and others bathe the house in wreaths, seasonal flowers, and greens. Candlelight tours and teas and holiday luncheons are the special events. The home and 79-acre garden are open for tours every day except Christmas from 9 a.m. to 5 p.m. For nonresidents of St. Louis County, admission is $8 for adults, children younger than age 12 free. (In the Children's Garden, kids can climb tree houses and play in water jets.) For residents of St. Louis County, admission is $4 for adults, $3 for seniors; children younger than age 12 and members free. There is also an additional charge of $4 for a narrated tram ride; children younger than age 2 ride free.

Also in St. Louis are the futuristic Climatron and the country's tallest man-made monument, the **Gateway Arch,** which is also the world's third

TOP RECOMMENDATIONS IN SOUTHEAST MISSOURI

most popular tourist attraction (but we're talking beaten path here, aren't we?).

It's also a city of firsts. The first Olympiad in the US was held here in 1904; the first hot dog, ice-cream cone, and iced tea were all introduced at the 1904 World's Fair. Remember "Meet me in St. Louie, Louie, meet me at the fair?" For more information about the city, look for the St. Louis website at stlouis.missouri.org.

The Gateway to the West (or to the East, if you are traveling the other way) was fed by train travel beginning in the early 1800s. More than 100,000 passengers have passed through *Union Station* each day since it was built in 1896. (Actually, it sounds more like a revolving door than a gateway.)

This is a two-block-long gray limestone fortress with a red-tile roof that features a clock tower that looms 230 feet in the air. When the last train left the station in 1978, the city had a white elephant of gargantuan proportions on its hands. Union Station was too historic to tear down, too expensive to keep up. So, it received a new identity: It is a retail, restaurant, and entertainment complex whose 100 shops, cinema, restaurants, and nightclubs have drawn tourists downtown again and sparked a revival of the area. There's even a virtual-reality

graduate education

The oldest university west of the Mississippi River is St. Louis University, which began as an academy in 1818.

mini-arcade, called Virtuality, where you can slip on a helmet and join the cyber world of Zone Hunter.

The Grand Hall, once the waiting room, is now the lobby of the 546-room Hyatt Regency Hotel (800-233-1234). Room rates are from $149. Look up at the 65-foot barrel-vaulted ceilings and finely decorated walls. Arches and columns abound. The famous "whispering arch" allows you to whisper to a friend 40 feet away. Sculpted maidens holding gilded torches, floral flourishes, and scroll work entice the eye. Most impressive is the glowing stained-glass window depicting three women representing New York, San Francisco, and—the one in the middle—St. Louis, the crossroads of America.

Downstairs is the Midway and cavernous Train Shed. More than 80 shops, cafes, and restaurants surrounded by walkways, bridges, fountains, and flowers fill the space. On most weekends strolling mimes and jugglers entertain shoppers. Boats cruise on a man-made lake next to an open-air *biergarten.* And although the trains don't stop here anymore, you can grab the MetroLink public rail system (314-421-6655) right outside for a ride to the Gateway Arch or Busch Stadium. The station can be reached from the airport, so if you are stuck at Lambert Field, you can get on the train and spend a couple hours enjoying a good meal or just doodling around at Union Station. Stop at the sculpture fountain across the street from the station. It's called *Meeting of the Waters* and it symbolizes the confluence of the Missouri and Mississippi Rivers.

First, though, get a map of St. Louis. Although its many interesting little neighborhoods make the city charming, they also make it difficult for visitors to find their way.

The **Gateway Arch,** Eero Saarinen's 630-foot architectural marvel that commemorates Thomas Jefferson and the nation's westward expansion, may not be exactly off the beaten path—after all, it's one of the most-visited tourist destinations in the country—but did you know there's a wonderful museum tucked away underground beneath the Arch in the Jefferson National Expansion Memorial? It's the **Museum of Westward Expansion,** which documents our irrepressible urge to explore and settle lands ever farther westward. We didn't stop until we reached the Pacific Ocean; the museum makes you feel you were along for the trip. You'll see artifacts and displays that relate to the Lewis and Clark expedition, which was intended not only to find a trade route to the West but also to discover the natural

TOP ANNUAL EVENTS IN SOUTHEAST MISSOURI

MAY

Gypsy Caravan Memorial Day
More than 20,000 shoppers stream into the University of Missouri at St. Louis campus to buy wares from exhibitors.
Admission charged.
(314) 286-4452
stlsymphony.org/gypsycaravan

Bluegrass Pickin Time Music Show
Dixon
(573) 579-3574

JULY

Soulard Bastille Day Celebration
St. Louis
(314) 773-6767
soulardthecity.com

Annual Jaycee Bootheel Rodeo and Redneck Barbecue Cook-off
A world-championship event with top Nashville recording artists performing nightly.
Sikeston
(800) 455-BULL
sikestonrodeo.com

Jour De Fete
A large craft fair.
Ste. Genevieve
(573) 883-7097 or (800) 373-7007

SEPTEMBER

St. James Annual Grape and Fall Festival
St. James
(573) 265-3899
grapeandfallfestival.com

Mosaics
An upscale yet affordable showcase of fine artisans from across the state.
St. Charles
(636) 946-7776
historicstcharles.com

OCTOBER

Oktoberfest
Citywide
First four full weekends in October.
Hermann
hermannmissouri.com

Milo's Annual Risotto Cook-Off
St. Louis
On the Hill at Milo's Bocce Garden.

Oktoberfest,
Second full weekend in October, with craftspeople in traditional dress, bluegrass music.
Black Forest Village (an 1870s replica village)
Cape Girardeau
(573) 335-0899

DECEMBER

Kimmswick Historical Society's Annual Christmas Tour of historic homes
Each home has a different theme.
Kimmswick
(636) 675-9592
visitkimmswick.com

Las Posadas
A lighted Christmas walk with Mary and Joseph, the first Sat night in Dec.
St. Charles
(636) 946-7776
historicstcharles.com

history of this new land encompassed by the Louisiana Purchase. You'll find Native American and pioneer artifacts as well, and when you come back out blinking into the sunshine, you'll experience a moment of disorientation as you reenter the 21st century.

Hours are Memorial Day through Labor Day 8 a.m. to 10 p.m. and in winter from 9 a.m. to 6 p.m. Also under the Arch are a fine bookstore and gift shop run by the National Park Service; be prepared to take a bit of history home with you.

Just south of the Arch the *Tom Sawyer* and *Becky Thatcher* riverboats provide one-hour cruises of St. Louis Harbor. Call **Gateway Riverboat Cruises** (800-878-7411) for times and prices. Gateway descends from Streckfus Steamers, which was established in 1884. Captain John Streckfus ran steamboats from New Orleans to St. Paul, Minnesota, and stopped in towns along the way. There was live music aboard, and Streckfus would comb the clubs in New Orleans looking for good musicians. One day in 1918 he found a musician who was fresh out of reform school. His name was Louis Armstrong, and he would work the riverboats *Sidney* and *Capital* until 1922. Legend has it, believe this or not, that the musicians called the new kind of music they played on the Streckfus riverboats "J.S." (for John Streckfus) and that eventually became the word *jazz*.

While you history-minded folk are in the neighborhood of the Arch, don't miss the **Old Cathedral Museum,** visible just to the west and still in the Gateway Arch Park. Here you'll find some of the finest (and oldest) ecclesiastical art in the country, with works by the Old Masters not uncommon. Documents dating from the beginning of the cathedral as well as photographs on the building of the Arch are all part of the museum. If it's

The Loop Area

The Loop area is fun to visit—the musicians playing on the street, the stars on the sidewalk, and the ambience. Your only regret is that your time here is too short. Even in the middle of the day, the place is alive. What must it be like at night when Chuck Berry is in town? You can stay at *Moonrise Hotel* (314-721-1111), a boutique hotel in the heart of the Loop. A big cratered moon spins atop the hotel, and there is a collection of lunar art in the lobby and large rooms.

Sunday evening, you can attend Mass at the cathedral at 5 p.m. The Old Cathedral Museum (314-231-3251) at 209 Walnut in St. Louis is open daily from 9:30 a.m. to 3:30 p.m. Donation only.

While you are down on the riverfront, you can even take a five-minute helicopter tour of downtown. Everything you want to know about the Arch is at (877) 982-1410; gatewayarch.com.

If you visit the **St. Louis Cathedral** on Lindell in the Central West End, built in 1907, look up to the heavens, or the ceiling in this case, and you will see the largest collection of mosaic art in the world.

bellefontaine cemetery

Calvary Cemetery and Bellefontaine Cemetery (bellefontainecemetery.org) are next to each other in north St. Louis. Here lie the bodies of Civil War General William Tecumseh Sherman; author Kate Chopin; playwright Tennessee Williams; Dred Scott, the slave who sued unsuccessfully for his freedom; and Madame Pelagie Aillotte Rutgers (a woman of color who was one of the wealthiest property owners in the early city). And a monument to the memory of four Nez Perce warriors who died while visiting General William Clark of Lewis and Clark fame. Clark is buried at Bellefontaine, along with Beat Generation author William Burroughs, brewery magnate Adolphus Busch, and Pulitzer Prize–winning poet Sara Teasdale.

The oak doors lead into a sanctuary decorated in the Byzantine tradition of beautiful domes, arches, and mosaics. The mosaics are made with over 41 million glass tesserae tiles with more than 8,000 shades of color; they tell the stories of faith throughout history. You will see Christ's 12 apostles, the Last Supper, and scenes of Old Testament prophesies of Christ's coming. Areas throughout the cathedral contain more mosaic panels. Tiffany's of New York created the panels in the Blessed Virgin's Chapel of the Cathedral in the Italian style from Mary's Presentation to her Assumption. Panels also depict the life of Saint Louis IX, king of France and namesake of the city.

Bailey's Chocolate Bar (1915 Park Ave.; 314-241-8100; baileyschocolatebar.com) in St. Louis is the go-to place for chocolate lovers everywhere. David Bailey not only has a full bar with more than 60 different beers, martinis, and champagne, but he also turns out desserts using chocolate from around the world. Truffles, ice-cream desserts, and luscious

chocolate drinks for those cool Missouri days. (Ah, yes, try "La Morte"—
Death—a blend of chocolate, vanilla, and cream.) If you don't like chocolate
but your sweet tooth demands something else, there is always a changing
palate of whimsical goodies from which to choose. No sweets for you? Then
look at the mix-and-match cheese menu and have several types of cheese
with the fresh house-made bread, fruit, and nuts. The Chocolate Bar is
open 7 days a week, Mon through Sat from 4 p.m. to 1 a.m. and Sun from
4 p.m. to midnight. Also in the downtown area is the ***St. Louis Mercantile Library Association Art Museum*** at 510 Locust. If you admire the
works of Missouri artist George Caleb Bingham, who captured our history
on canvas; if you're awed by the accomplishments of George Catlin as he
traveled among the tribes of Native Americans and painted them one by
one; if you've wished you could see a painting by one of the famous Peale
family of 19th-century artists (portrait painter Sarah Peale, in this case, who
supported herself for many years here in the past century), you won't want
to miss this place.

This is the oldest circulating library west of the Mississippi, and in addition to art, you can find rare books: Americana, westward expansion, river
transportation, and so on. Admission is free.

The name doesn't tell you the reason for searching out this place, but
once you know, you will be a regular at the ***Crown Candy Kitchen*** (1401
St. Louis Ave.; 314-621-9650; crowncandykitchen.net), just 1¼ miles north
of the Arch, where wonderful chocolate candy has been made since 1913.
The main attraction here, however, is the city's oldest soda fountain. The
business was founded in 1913 by the current owners' grandfather. Their
father, George, inherited the business and the three current owners, Andy,
Mike, and Tom Karandzieff, grew up here. Nothing much has changed in
their world-class milk shakes: homemade ice cream, milk, and your choice
of syrup. If you want a "malted," you can have that, too. Of course, what is
a milk shake without a chili dog? Andy and Mike can fix that up for you, no
problem. The malted has 1,100 calories in it, so what difference will a little
chili dog make in the big scheme of things, right? Oh yes, they still make
fresh chocolate candy in the winter. Truth be told, they make chicken salad
to die for and a great BLT if you want to be sensible about lunch. Hours are
Mon through Thurs from 10:30 a.m. to 8 p.m., Fri and Sat from 10:30 a.m.
to 9 p.m., and Sun from 11 a.m. to 5 p.m.

The Mother Road

Getting your kicks on Route 66 is still possible in Missouri. As the famous high-way "winds from Chicago to LA," you "go through St. Louis, and Joplin, Missouri" along the Mother Road. In St. Louis, Drewes Frozen Custard has been a stopping place on old Route 66 since 1929. Farther on you can still see the distinctive art deco tile front from the Coral Court Motel at the Museum of Transportation. Next is Route 66 State Park, where the state is creating a museum devoted to road-side Americana. You can walk among Missouri's wildflowers at the Shaw Arboretum of the Missouri Botanical Garden at Gray Summit and visit Meramec Caverns at Stanton as people have been doing since 1933. Spend the night at the circa 1930 Wagon Wheel Motel, which still stands in Cuba.

Perhaps the most beautiful spot on Missouri's portion of Route 66 is Devil's Elbow along the bluffs over the Big Piney River. The 1940s Munger-Moss Motel is in Lebanon, where you can rest up for the drive through Springfield. Be sure to watch for the Shrine Mosque, an *Arabian Nights*–style edifice that has hosted concerts since the 1950s. On to Carthage's magnificent Victorian homes and the Route 66 Drive-In Theatre. The new highway created some havoc. Spencer is a ghost town now but some of the original roadway remains from when the town was bypassed.

Joplin, the western end of Route 66 in Missouri, is one of the dozen towns named in the famous song immortalizing the more-than-1,000-mile route that winds from Chicago to Los Angeles through the heart of Missouri.

As long as we are talking about ice cream, it's only fair to tell you about another favorite. This is the old 1950s walk-up kind of place with a packed parking lot. See a lot of people in bright yellow T-shirts? Lucky you; you have found **Ted Drewes Frozen Custard** (6726 Chippewa St.; 314-481-2652; teddrewes.com). This place has been a St. Louis favorite since 1929 when Ted's father started the business. Drewes is known for the thickest shake anywhere (you can hold it upside down and the spoon and straw stay put), so thick ("how thick is it?") he calls it a "concrete," because it just won't shake. So thick the server wears a hard hat. These thick—very thick—shakes have mysterious names such as the Cardinal Sin, named for the baseball team (fudge sauce and red cherries), or the All Shook Up (Elvis's favorite snack: peanut-butter cookies and banana). But the straw-berry shortcake is the best thing on the menu. Hours are from 11 a.m. until a little after midnight 7 days a week. There's a second location at 4224 S. Grand, St. Louis (314-352-7376), if one wasn't enough. This time order the Abaco Mocha, a tropical treat, or a Foxtreat with fudge sauce, raspberries, and macadamia nuts.

A few blocks away is another favorite with the Sweet Tooth (Sweet Tooths? Sweet teeth? Oh, dear . . .) in your family. ***Gooey Louie's*** at 6483 Chippewa (314-352-CAKE; gooeylouiecake.com) is famous for the gooey butter cake everyone loves. Everything is baked from scratch in this family-owned bakery that uses an old family recipe with real farm-fresh butter, eggs, cream cheese . . . well, you get the picture. The Gooey Butter Bites are a good place to start to just try them out, not that there is any chance you won't love them. Then you can try the Hwy 40: Driving Me Nuts, or Let's Go Blueberries, or a personal favorite, the Red Velvet Gooey Butter. Food Network loves 'em—what's not to love?

Circus Flora (314-289-4040; circusflora.org) is a one-ring circus under the big top in Grand Center. It relives the days before the Civil War when Floating Palace circus traveled the Mississippi. The box office is at Centene Center for the Arts, 3547 Olive St., 2nd floor.

Sweetie Pie's (4270 Manchester; 314-371-0304; sweetiepieskitchen .com) puts the *soul* in soul food. Robbie Montgomery and her son Tim Norman began cooking here in 1997, and Sweetie Pie's has been a success ever since. Everyone's favorite is the

trivia

If you are doing St. Louis on the cheap, you will be glad to find St. Louis's treasured **Forest Park** and the St. Louis Zoo (314-367-2224; forestparkforever.org), where many of the attractions are free. You can see a Broadway-type musical that is locally produced at the outdoor Muny Opera, the oldest and largest outdoor musical theater (constructed in 1917) at no charge. Just show up early and bring a picnic because 1,620 of the 9,000 seats in this urban hillside outdoor theater are set aside as free on a first-come basis. Check the schedule at (314) 361-1900; muny.org. You can take a boat ride around the Grand Basin and have lunch at the Boathouse, a waterside cafe. Trails, bicycling, golf and tennis, hay rides, ice skating, tobogganing, and cross-country skiing are also available. There's also the zoo, art museum, science center, and the Missouri History Museum.

And if there is a free Live on the Levee concert, you can join the crowd at the riverfront (celebratest-louis.org).

homemade mac and cheese, probably, but of course there are those who favor the Smothered Pork, deep-fried pork steaks covered with gravy made from the delicious roux at the bottom of the pan, or the fried chicken in corn-breading like mama used to make. What else but sweet potatoes, greens, and corn bread could accompany that? Robbie used to be a singer; pictures of her and Ike and Tina Turner adorn the walls. She cooked on the road for the musicians because due to segregation the black performers could not eat in most restaurants. Open Tues through Sun from 11:30 a.m. till 8 p.m.

The *Loop* area of St. Louis has been evolving into one of the most exciting and entertaining neighborhoods in the metro area. There has been a renaissance in this neighborhood between the 6000 and 6600 blocks of Delmar Boulevard. This area is close to Washington University and is a shining example of urban revitalization. There are more than 30 international and American restaurants offering Ethiopian, Lebanese, European, Persian, Italian, Nigerian, Greek, Japanese, Thai, Mexican, Korean, and Chinese cuisine. There are also barbecue, deli, fondue, and contemporary and classic American selections. The renaissance continues in the area of entertainment with sidewalk performers and live music. Almost every genre of music can be found in the many clubs along the boulevard. Make sure that you look down at the sidewalk stars, where the nonprofit *St. Louis Walk of Fame* is a shining tribute of more than 100 stars honoring famous St. Louisians. There are also plaques listing their many achievements, which make this pleasant stroll educational as well as enjoyable. Also impressive and inviting are the many and diverse boutiques. *Pin-Up Bowl* (6191 Delmar Blvd.; 314-727-5555; pinupbowl.com) is St. Louis's original bowling and martini lounge. Above 8 bowling lanes are 4 projection screens showing music videos and cartoons. If you are a "pinup connoisseur," you will love this place. Many pinups are from original calendars and *Esquire* magazine centerfolds from the 1940s. The menu features Campbell's soup, fresh pizza, and many appetizers, sandwiches, and desserts. The alley is open until 3 a.m. and becomes a party as much as a bowling experience after midnight, with crazy drinks in unusual colors and a mostly yuppie crowd.

Seven galleries and the *Tivoli Theatre* are located at 6350 Delmar (314-727-7271; landmarktheatres.com). The Tivoli, restored to its original 1924 splendor, has 3 screens and shows a variety of independent films. Memorabilia makes this a walk down movie-memory lane.

St. Louis is the hometown of Chuck Berry, and located at 6504 Delmar in the Loop is ***Blueberry Hill*** (314-727-4444; blueberryhill.com). Owner Joe Edwards describes this St. Louis landmark as being filled with pop culture memorabilia, including Chuck Berry's guitar and a plethora of vintage 45-rpm jukeboxes. A wide variety of items are available on the menu. There are darts, video games, pinball games, and even a photo booth. The Duck Room features live touring bands, and don't miss the Elvis Room, which features karaoke on Thurs and Fri night. The restaurant is open from 11 a.m. daily.

If hotels and motels are not to your taste, call Lori and Dean Murray to join them in their home at 703 N. Kirkwood Rd., St. Louis. ***The Eastlake Inn Bed and Breakfast*** (314-965-0066) is a 1920s colonial inn comfortably set on a wide green lawn surrounded by flowering catalpa, magnolia, and dogwood trees. As the name suggests, the home is filled with original Eastlake furnishings. After a full breakfast you can walk to antiques shops and restaurants for dinner. You'll feel like a St. Louis native. Rooms are $115 to $250.

The Laumeier Sculpture Park (12580 Rott Rd.; 314-821-1209; laumeier.org) is located about 12 miles southwest of downtown St. Louis. The artwork here is grand and huge. Artist Alexander Liberman's *The Way* is made of steel cylinders intended for use as underground storage tanks. He arranged them in bent piles and welded them together. The whole thing was painted bright red. In June and July sculptors work for weeks on detailed sand castles; in winter a fire-and-ice sculpture made of giant ice blocks glows amid roaring bonfires. The 98-acre park has more than 60 pieces. The wooded path hides human-size sheet-metal figures by Ernest Trova. Special events—symphony, dance, ballet, and theater productions—and a gallery full of indoor art are there, too. A cafe and a museum shop are inside, but outdoors is more fun. Take I-44 to Lindbergh Boulevard, go south ½ mile, and turn right onto Rott Road; the park entrance is ½ mile on the left. It is open daily from 8 a.m. until a half hour after sunset. Gallery hours are 10 a.m. to 5 p.m. Tues through Sat and noon to 5 p.m. Sun. Admission is free.

You should not go to St. Louis without visiting The Hill, southwest of the city, an Italian neighborhood famous for its restaurants. There is no favorite, because it depends on the type of ambience you seek. The best bargain is probably ***Cunetto's House of Pasta*** (5452 Magnolia Ave.; 314-781-1135; cunetto.com). It's a good place to take the family, prices are moderate, and the atmosphere is Continental—tablecloths, wine, no bright lights, and a full-service bar. Owner Frank Cunetto calls it gourmet Italian with good prices. His dad and uncle opened the doors more than 30 years ago, and it has been a popular spot ever since. Hours for lunch are Mon through Fri from 11 a.m. to 2 p.m. Dinner is served Mon through Thurs from 4:45 to 10 p.m. and on Fri and Sat until 11 p.m.

But more interesting is **Charlie Gitto's on the Hill** (5226 Shaw Ave.; 314-772-8898; charliegittos.com) because this is where one of the best-loved Italian dishes—toasted ravioli—was invented in 1947. It was a lucky accident that Charlie's father was the maitre d' at this very spot when it was called Angelo's. He and Angelo were messing around with different ravioli recipes and dropped the little stuffed pillows into oil instead of water. Now they are dusted with fresh Parmesan and served with marinara sauce for the perfect appetizer. If you can't decide what to order, ask for the trio of the day, smaller portions of three menu items selected by the chef. Dessert must be tiramisu, Charlie's mama's family recipe made with cocoa, mascarpone cheese, and homemade cookies soaked in sambuca and espresso.

There are about 20 Italian eateries on the Hill, but if you want to take something home, run in to **Mama Toscano's** (2201 Macklind; 314-776-2926; mamatoscano.com) and carry out homemade ravioli (sold by the pound), cannelloni, meatballs, and sauce to go. Nick and Virginia Toscano make thousands of ravioli by hand, rolling out the pasta with a rolling pin. This will be much more appreciated than a T-shirt when you get home. Hours are Tues through Fri 7 a.m. to 4:30 p.m., Sat 7 a.m. to 4 p.m.

Locals all wind up at **Amighetti's Bakery and Cafe** (5141 Wilson; 314-776-2855; amighettis.com) for the sweet-pepper-laced subs. Then wipe the cannoli cream off your face and be sure to take the time to visit **St. Ambrose Church** (314-771-1228; stambroseonthehill.org), the Hill's centerpiece about 4 blocks from Cunetto's. It is Lombardy Romanesque and was the first acoustical plaster church in St. Louis. The columns of scagliola plaster look like marble and were made using plaster, ground gypsum, sponges, and polishing. The statues were donated by groups from different villages in Italy. Sunday Mass is at 7, 9, and 11 a.m. Across the street is **Milo's Bocce Garden,** where locals gather. When you settle in with one of the restaurant's Italian sausage sandwiches or anchovy pizzas to watch the bocce leagues play, it sounds—and feels—as though you have crossed the Atlantic. Of

'Sploding Cannoli

Speaking of cannoli, that ricotta/whipped cream treat that finishes a good Italian meal, it reminds me of a funny, call it "tradition" that has been in my Italian family for years. Who knows where it started or where it will end, but whenever a newcomer joins the family for a holiday meal for the first time—this means girlfriends, boyfriends, fiancées, visiting in-laws, whatever—we all begin to snicker and giggle when the cannoli are served after dinner. The plates are arranged so that the newcomers get a cannoli with cream filling plugging both ends while the center is filled with powdered sugar. (Don't try this at home.) Then everyone sits around waiting for the unfortunate person to bite into it and cause an explosion of powdered sugar that covers the face of the unsuspecting victim. I really thought the "tradition" would die with my generation, until my son's mother-in-law joined us for Thanksgiving dinner one year and my little granddaughter, bless her heart, came into the kitchen to whisper in my ear, "Gramma, are we going to do the 'sploding cannoli trick on Grammy?" Some traditions will never die as long as sons whisper into their children's ears. . . .

course, you must try for the annual Columbus Day Bocce Tournament for some serious players as well as Milo's annual Risotto Cook-Off in October.

Volpi's (5258 Dagget Ave.; 314-772-8550; volpifoods.com) is a family-owned maker of authentic Italian meats by third-generation salumieri. Family recipes have been handed down from Lorenza Pasetti and his father, Armando, for cure-dried Italian meats like prosciutto, pepperoni, rotola, and salami. There are no artificial ingredients, and the product is simple and good.

It's not all about food here on the Hill, though. St. Louis designer Nina Ganci imports yarn from Italy among other places and makes sweaters that are most unusual. In **Skif** (2008 Marconi Ave.; 314-773-4401; skifo.com) you will find sweaters that can be worn upside-down or inside-out, or held together with chopsticks. The yarns are hand-knit by freelance weavers and then stitched into works of art by a team of designers. They actually look good on anybody and every (real) body of any size, and the asymmetrical shapes can be draped to suit your moods or show off the parts of your body you like. The sweaters are not cheap, starting at over $200, but they are one of a kind and will be noticed for sure. This is a working sweater factory, not a storefront.

If you prefer to head south instead, you'll find St. Louis's own French Quarter in historic **Soulard,** 2 miles south of the Arch on Broadway. There's a dandy mix of period architecture and pubs, cafes, and shops for you to browse in. You can buy everything from turnips to live chickens on Saturday mornings in the busy farmers' market in this French/Irish neighborhood, and finish up at a well-stocked spice shop. Soulard is an old brewery neighborhood where rehabilitated row houses line the streets. The Anheuser-Busch brewery is nearby, and when the wind is right you can smell hops and barley cooking. Soulard also has a large collection of jazz and blues clubs.

For information on many bed-and-breakfasts in the state, you can contact the **Ozark Mountain Country Reservation Service** (800-933-8529 or 417-334-4720; ozarkbedandbreakfast.com). They are especially helpful if you are touring the Ozarks and are headed for Branson.

Antiques stores line both sides of Cherokee Street for 4 blocks in the funky antiques district south of downtown. Prices here are very affordable, and there are dusty treasures in dark corners and beautifully restored pieces as well. You will find rare books, antique linens and lace, and glassware; shop owners will still haggle on the price of more expensive items.

If you want to stay in the St. Louis area but not in the city itself, there is a cluster of suburban cities nearby. Many of them have bed-and-breakfast inns available. Check out the charming cobblestoned street of downtown St. Charles (800-366-2427 or 636-946-7776; historicstcharles.com), once Missouri's state capital and now home to specialty shops and restaurants housed in historic buildings. There are 7 B&Bs in St. Charles, located off I-70 west of St. Louis.

Now Kansas City isn't the only Missouri city with a dollhouse museum. The **Miniature Museum of Greater St. Louis** (4746 Gravois; 314-832-7790; miniaturemuseum.org) has a fine collection of dollhouses and miniatures, many of them painstakingly hand-crafted and donated by local miniaturists. The museum is a bit off the beaten path, but well worth the visit. Hours are Wed through Sat 11 a.m. until 4 p.m. and Sun 1 until 4 p.m. There is a small admission charge.

Okay, it's easy to make jokes about a dog museum, and everyone who writes for a living has given it a doggone good try. But man's best friend deserves to be celebrated, and this canine tribute, the **American Kennel Club Museum of the Dog** (1721 S. Mason Rd.; 314-821-DOGS;

museumofthedog.org), located in the 1853 Greek revival Jarville House in St. Louis County's Queeny Park, about 18 miles west of the St. Louis riverfront, is worth a visit if you are seeking the best art of dogdom. Begin with the oil-on-mahogany portrait of the ex-presidential pet Millie, the English springer spaniel who called the White House home for four years. See a sculpted bronze whippet, a massive wooden mastiff (once part of a carousel ride), and many works of art commissioned by breeders of show-winning dogs. Coonhounds, retrievers, and herders join Dalmatians, bloodhounds, and Afghans. Pekingese, wolfhounds, and dogs of every variety, including those of more mixed heritage, are celebrated in paintings, wood carvings, ceramic figurines, and photographs that show them doing what dogs do—sniffing, running, licking, sleeping, or just being. The gift shop will give you "paws" for thought with posters, stationery, and dozens of trinkets bearing likenesses of dogs and dog accessories (tie clasps made of tiny dog biscuits, for example).

On Sunday afternoons the popular "Dog of the Week" program features a guest breeder, trainer, or veterinarian and a dog for demonstration. A book-and-videotape library allows potential dog owners to judge the merits of various breeds. In the past well-mannered dogs were welcome to tour the gallery with their owners, but because of too many "accidents," that was stopped. The museum is open from 10 a.m. until 4 p.m. Tues through Sat and from 1 to 5 p.m. Sun. Take I-64/US 40 west past the I-270 loop, exit on Mason Road, and drive south. Watch for the signs. Admission is $5 for adults; $2.50 for ages 60 and older; and $1 for children ages 5 to 25. The program begins around 2 p.m.

The **Endangered Wolf Center** (636-938-5900; endangeredwolfcenter .org) offers an adults-only (that got your attention) Wine and Cheese Twilight Howl. Shall I go on? It begins indoors at 7 p.m. with wine and cheese and a talk by experts on wolf behavior (do they really howl at a full moon?), then moves outdoors near the wolf habitats for the wolf howl. They show you how to initiate a wolf howl and see if the wolves howl back. I doesn't take long to get the howling started. Then back inside for dessert and coffee and questions. The program is

it'selementary

The first public kindergarten in the country was opened in St. Louis in 1873.

offered year-round on the third Friday of the month. Advance reservations are required—it fills up fast. This is a 50-acre breeding area for red wolves, Mexican gray wolves, and other canids. The goal is the eventual reintroduction of these beautiful dog-like creatures, which are near extinction. The keepers here avoid touching them except for veterinary visits because it is essential to their survival to fear humans. But they do give them names: Anna and Rocky are two of fewer than 100 Mexican grays left in the world. They are big and strong and watch their puppies closely. Another pair, Alano and Frijole, prance with tails held high to show that this is, indeed, their territory. These canids are the species' last hope for survival. They are kept in fenced enclosures and can be seen from 9 a.m. to 5 p.m. daily. (Call in advance, because walk-ins are not permitted. Tours are by appointment only.) In May the center is closed for breeding.

Speaking of carnivores, St. Louis tries to keep up with Kansas City in the world of barbecue. Although admitting some prejudice on the KC side, there are those who say that *Phil's Bar-B-Q* (9205 Gravois Rd.; 314-638-1313) comes very close to great. So jump on I-55 to the Wilbur Park neighborhood and swing by Phil's, in a rustic shack decorated with bowling trophies. It started as a backyard barbecue run by the Polizzi family. Now, three generations later, it is still the place to have ribs. The sauce is sweet and tangy and very close to great on the pork shoulder sandwich.

The Richmond Heights neighborhood has won some national recognition on the Food Network and Travel Channel for a monster called the "Pointersarus" at *Pointer's Pizza* (1023 S. Big Bend Blvd.; 314-644-2000; pointersdelivery.com).

This creature is an 11½-pound, 28-inch meat-covered, cheese-laden pizza that they defy any two people to finish. In fact, there is a $500 reward if the two of you can wolf it down in an hour. It is made of 4½ pounds of dough, 36 ounces of sauce, 1 pound of cheese, and 2 pounds each of meat—that is a lot of pepperoni, my friend Travel Channel said, "It is built to taunt people with large eyes and little stomachs" and called it "a caloric nightmare." You think? But what the heck. Why not give it a try?

Florissant, just north of downtown St. Louis, is so called because the first inhabitants found it a beautiful, flowering valley. It still is—but that's not all the town has to offer. Jesuit father Pierre Jean DeSmet, champion of the Indian nations, founded the *Old St. Ferdinand's Shrine* (1 Rue St.

Francois; 314-837-2110), now open to the public. The cornerstone was laid in 1821 to replace the little log church destroyed by fire. Tours are available on Sun from Apr through Oct, 1 to 4 p.m. without an appointment. The shrine is open for tours any day by appointment.

If you just want to get out of St. Louis for a bit, here's a day trip an hour southwest of the city that you might enjoy. Take I-44 and get off on US 50 near **Union.** At **Junie Moon Cafe** (300 W. US 50; 636-584-0180), you can eat down-home comfort food for under 10 bucks. From breakfast to the Blu Cheese Burger with homemade chips, Philly wrap, or pulled pork, it is worth the trip. The town of **Rosebud** and a batch of antiques shops are on either side of the highway and, surprise, **Clancy's Irish Pub #2** (211 US 50; 573-764-9310) is open Mon through Sat from 11 a.m. until 1:30 p.m. serving traditional tavern food, corned beef and cabbage, a lunch special that is different every day, and, of course,

trivia

People streaking along US 40 near the Oakland Avenue exit are likely to hit the brakes when they see massive turtles sunning themselves on the banks of the road. These huge terrapins are not waiting to cross the road but are the creations of sculptor Robert Cassilly. If you look closely, the 40-foot-long snapping turtle, slick-shelled stinkpot, red-eared slider, Mississippi map, and soft-shelled turtle have children crawling inside their cavelike mouths, swinging from their necks, and grasping their eyeballs to climb up top their heads. A path leads to a sunken playground full of turtle eggs, some with freshly hatched crawlers emerging from the shells. Stop and visit the Turtles at Forest Park, Oakland Avenue, just off US 40 East anytime from sunrise to sunset.

a good selection of beers, Missouri wines, and Irish whiskeys. The owner is always there—he is the bartender, cook, and waiter—so everything is guaranteed good.

Advertising Icons Museum (4600 Madison Ave., Suite 1500; advertisingiconmuseum.org) is a 12,000-square-foot exhibit on the Country Club Plaza in the West Edge office building. This is *brand* new (pun intended). So far the museum is open by appointment only, but plans to open to the public soon. Go to the website for more information and dates. The museum will house a 3,000-piece icon collection that will be displayed in a larger-than-life home setting. The kitchen will include two iconic women:

Aunt Jemima and Betty Crocker. Both women are emblems of home cooking and have changed both symbolically and physically as society shifted its views on gender roles. Other brand names have made it into our language: Mr. Bubble, the Energizer Bunny, and the Jolly Green Giant. The museum will be the permanent home of the Madison Avenue Advertising Walk of Fame. Each year the public votes online for two icons and "taglines" that they believe should be inducted into the Hall of Fame. Out front, a 10-foot-tall California Raisin statue will be on permanent display.

Wine Country

Wine Country towns cluster along the riverbanks like hardy grapes on vines. The towns of Defiance, Augusta, Washington, Dutzow, Marthasville, New Haven, Berger, and Hermann all have wineries that produce a variety of wines, both dry and sweet. The Seyval makes a crisp medium-bodied wine similar to a Chenin Blanc. The Vidal, a full-bodied wine with fruity characteristics, is somewhat like an Italian dry white wine. The Vignole is more versatile and can range from the style of a German Riesling to a sweet, late-harvest dessert wine. The Norton (Cynthiana) grape produces rich, full-bodied red wines, the Chambourcin a medium-bodied red with a fruity aroma. The Concord and Catawba produce sweet wines.

Outside St. Louis on I-44 West is the town of *Eureka,* home to more than 60 antiques and craft shops. Pick up a complete list of shops at the first one you spot as you come off the interstate. This town could be a one-stop, shop-till-you-drop experience, but that would be crazy, because you are now heading into an antiques-hunter's heaven.

The *Eureka Antique Mall* (107 E. 5th St., N. Outer Road, West Eureka; 636-938-5600) is followed by *Wallach House Antiques* (510 West Ave., Eureka; 636-938-6633; wallachhouse.com), filled with old and new finds. There are several more antiques shops in town, so just ask around. Another fascinating stop is the *Firehouse Gallery and Antiques* (131 S. Central Ave., Eureka; 636-938-3303), which features limited-edition artwork.

Take I-44 West to US 109 at Eureka, Missouri. Head north on US 109 for about 2.5 miles until you reach Alt Road. Turn left onto Alt Road and travel for approximately 1 mile. Turn north at the first right, which will be Hidden Valley Drive. Keep to the right until you arrive at *Hidden Valley*

Resort, where you can, yes, ski! Everything from the beginners' Wonder Carpet on Easy Street, so called for obvious reasons—there isn't even a rope to get up the easy hill—to the Polar Plunge tubing area. There is real (man-made) snow, a 310-foot vertical drop, 2 triple chairlifts, and 2 rope tows. The Outlaw Terrain Park features rails, jumps, and more for expert boarders and skiers only. There is a rental shop for skis and boards and PSIA-certified instructors. It's fun and easy enough to get you ready someday for your bucket-list trip to Jackson Hole (named America's scariest ski slope). You can check out the live web cam at hiddenvalleyski.com.

Midwesterners seem to have a deeply rooted preference for all things smoked, probably from all those nights our ancestors spent around a camp-fire. Who can resist a terrific country ham, hickory-smoked bacon, or a ten-der slab of ribs? You won't have to if you pay a visit to the *Smoke House Market* (16806 Chesterfield Airport Rd., Chesterfield; 636-532-3314). Every-thing is smoked the natural way, with no preservatives and real hickory smoke. Smoked pork chops, lamb chops, Cajun sausage, along with ribs and bacon, are available in the shop. Owners Thom and Jane Sehnert planned it that way, and Jane's got the background for it; her folks had owned the business since 1952. Hours are Tues through Sun 9 a.m. to 8 p.m.

The Sehnerts branched out and opened *Annie Gunn's* next door, a grill with an Irish theme, complete with Irish potato soup and a menu of unusual sandwiches and meat from the smokehouse. The most popular is the Bour-sin burger, which is covered with highly spiced garlic and herb cheese. And there is the Braunschweiger sandwich, the Cajun sausage sandwich, fabulous smoked lamb chops, ribs, Reubens, French dips . . . and the list goes on. To find the smokehouse, follow your nose, or if your sniffer isn't highly trained, follow US 40 to the Airport Road exit and double back; it's about 30 miles west of St. Louis. Put your name on the restaurant waiting list before you shop at the smokehouse. Annie Gunn's is a popular place for locals and visitors alike.

Highway 100 along the Missouri River is a beautiful drive any time of year because of the white sycamores marking the river's course; in autumn it's spectacular. The Missouri River valley deserves plenty of time; there's a lot to see and experience.

St. Albans is an anachronism, a tiny planned community founded in the 1930s by the Johnson Shoe Company family. Five thousand acres of

Just a-Pickin' and a-Grinnin'

I once knew a man who played a 1932 gold-plated five-string Gibson Mastertone banjo. I took some acoustic guitar lessons at one point in my life, but . . . bluegrass music? I knew nothing about it. I was more into classical guitar and '60s folk music. That is, until he took me to a bluegrass festival near Dixon.

The festival usually begins on a Thursday, but people start showing up a week and a half before that. Usually as soon as there are three people at the site, the music begins. People show up in campers, RVs, and pickup trucks. Tents go up, instruments come out, and the music is nonstop until the last three people leave on Sunday or Monday night.

The actual festival consists of about 17 well-known musicians and groups that perform on a stage throughout the day and evening, but most of the really good music can be heard at the campsites in the woods—and goes on 24 hours a day. Don't plan to sleep much.

Although you do not have to play to enjoy the music, about 70 percent of the people attending do play. That's what makes it so much fun. All instruments are acoustic. People play banjos, steel guitars, and mandolins. People more oriented toward folk music play dobros, hammer dulcimers, and dulcimers and sing the lilting melodies of bygone days. Fiddle players compete with one another. Music is accompanied by both stand-up bass and washtub bass, and even spoons—all instruments early settlers might have made and played.

gorgeous rolling hills and meadows reminded Mr. Johnson of an area in England known as St. Albans, and he made it into a working farm. It is some 30 miles west of the city limits of St. Louis on Highway 100, an easy day trip and a destination not to be missed.

Aficionados of French cuisine may remember Le Bistro in the town of Chesterfield. Restaurateurs Gilbert and Simone Andujar closed that place when highway work made it difficult to reach, but take heart. Simone spotted the lovely gardens of St. Albans and chose the location for **Malmaison,** St. Albans (3519 St. Albans Rd.; 636-458-0131; gardensmalmaison.com). (Those whose French is a bit tenuous may wonder if the name means "bad house," and it would if it were two words. Native Frenchwoman Simone says that the lovely flowers reminded her of the garden where Josephine met Napoleon in her homeland, a garden named Malmaison.) Part of the experience is the scenic drive to St. Albans. The dining experience here is

While hundreds of festivals throughout the country celebrate bluegrass music, this arguably became the bluegrass capital of the Midwest when Dixon Park came to be. Some of the finest bluegrass bands play here. This place has a kitchen, guarded toilets and showers, parking for 1,000 cars, electricity for 400 RVs, and music, music, music.

A bluegrass festival is a family affair; there's "no alcohol, no drugs, no way!" allowed in the parks. You can literally bring your children to these festivals, have a check-in spot where you meet several times a day, and let them follow their own musical wanderings. It is always a pleasure to see a youngster working with his dad or grandpa. I saw a family with a 9-year-old girl who played the stand-up bass. They dug a hole in the ground for the bass and she stood on two wooden Coke cases to play, but play she did. In that same family, three daughters sang everything the Andrews Sisters ever knew. There were 8 people in this family, including Grandma and Grandpa and a boyfriend, and they all slept in one tent and cooked meals over a fire.

An amateur can join with a group a little above his or her ability at a campsite when they play a familiar melody. You simply turn your back to the group and play softly until you can keep up. When you get the courage to turn around and play with the group, they welcome you and you have moved up a step in your skill level.

There is an admission charge, but it's the best money you will ever spend. Maybe next year I'll take my guitar. The festivals are held annually over Memorial Day and Labor Day weekends. Visit bluegrasspickintime.com.

superb, as is the food; it's a favorite retreat for St. Louisians who want to linger over a meal. Hours are Thurs through Sun, 6 to 10 p.m., and reservations are definitely required.

Hard-core bicyclists love the St. Albans region. It is full of challenging hills near the Missouri River and great views. This is Missouri's Rhineland, the wine-growing region. Both oenophiles (wine connoisseurs) and devotees of wine coolers will enjoy tasting what the state has to offer. There are two schools of thought about Missouri wines: Some say that because a majority of the grapes grown here are European vines on wild grape or Concord root stock (and some self-rooted French hybrids), the wines will be different from California or French wines. Others, purists to be sure (and the Mt. Pleasant Winery falls into this category), say that they will hold Missouri's best wines against California wines in a blind tasting any day and challenge connoisseurs to single them out. They have done so for Les Amis du Vin, or Friends of Wine, a wine-tasting club. Whether you are a member of Les Amis du Vin or just a wine lover, you will notice that the wines of Missouri are as varied as the vintners who make them, so don't judge Missouri wines by the first place you stop.

The Frene Creek white wines rival those of the Rhine River Valley. Pop wine drinkers will love Missouri's blends of fruit wines. The peach wine made by Stone Hill and the cherry wine by Hermannhoff are a treat over ice in the hot summer months.

Washington Landing was first settled in the early 1800s. Lewis and Clark passed through the site of the future town of **Washington** (888-7-WASHMO; washmo.org) in search of the Northwest Passage and pronounced it promising because of its excellent boat-landing site. Located in the curve where the great river reaches the most southern point in its course, Washington is still a good place to stop when headed west.

Don't miss the Gary R. Lucy Gallery (231 W. Main St.; 636-239-6337; garylucy.com). You may recognize Gary's work if you've picked up a Southwestern Bell telephone book from recent years; his work has graced the cover.

Gary is an extremely thorough young man. To get just the right feeling in his series of Missouri River paintings, the artist took his boat as far upriver as was navigable, to Fort Benton, Montana, and explored interesting areas from there back to Washington. No wonder his paintings ring true. Gary's paintings are like those of other famous Missouri artists, such as George Caleb Bingham and Thomas Hart Benton. He paints river scenes seen only in his mind's eye. Gary mixes research and what he sees from the window of his studio to obtain historical realism. River scenes might include sidewheelers and keelboats, ironclads running Confederate guns, or a card game on a flatboat. The price of an original is approximately $34,000, and his early works have quadrupled in value. Prints of his oils are for sale in his studio, which is open 7 days a week. Hours are Mon through Fri from 9 a.m. until 5:30 p.m., Sat until 5 p.m.

Carolyn McGettigan offers a wonderful selection of coffees, herbs, teas, and dried bouquets at **Not Just Cut and Dried** (636-239-9084), which has moved to 301 Elm St. in Washington, and is twice the size it was before. Sit down and have a steaming cup of cinnamon coffee with Carolyn (she actually roasts the beans here), and she will make scouting Washington easier.

Go ahead and have a tasty dessert, too. Hours are 10 a.m. to 5:30 p.m. weekdays, 10 a.m. to 5 p.m. Sat, and noon to 4 p.m. Sun.

Only 50 years or so after Meriwether Lewis, his dog Scannon, and his partner William Clark passed by this likely town site, Bernard Weise built his home and tobacco store here on Front Street. Now that location holds the *American Bounty Restaurant* (430 W. Front St., Washington; 636-390-2150; bountyrestaurantandwinebar.com), where although the magnificent view is still one of soft moonlight reflecting on the river flowing outside, inside white tablecloths await lovers of fine food and wine. Owner Dan Hacker and chef Brian Manhardt have restored this more-than-100-year-old building to its original splendor. The food is what they call "New Age American," or American food with a flair. Examples include encrusted chicken rolled in hash-browned potatoes, nine-way pasta, and red baby-clam sauce. The green-apple cobbler is a specialty, but it takes a half hour to prepare, so order it with dinner to ensure it arrives hot when you are ready for it. Open Tues from 4 to 7 p.m., Wed through Sat 5 to 9 p.m., Sun 11 a.m. to 7 p.m. Lunch Thurs through Sat 11 a.m. to 1 p.m. Seating outside in the wine garden creates a romantic mood, and the wine list features both California and Missouri wines.

You are deep into wine country here, and there is no shortage of wineries along the valley. Most offer tastings; you can choose the ones most convenient for your schedule and location. Some offer unusual wines and are well worth the effort to search them out.

Bias Vineyards & Winery (3166 Hwy. B; 573-834-5475 or 800-905-2427) is in picture-postcard *Berger* (pronounced BER-jer, population 214) just off Highway 100. The setting sun at Berger reflects on the river and rugged limestone bluffs; it throws long shadows across the tilled bottom and along the river. Follow the signs to a wooded hillside. As you start up the hill, there is a railroad crossing at the foot of the rise to the vineyards.

Owner Jim Bias is a retired TWA captain. He and his late wife, Norma, bought the land more than 25 years ago when they were looking for a country spot within commuting distance to St. Louis's Lambert Field. It came with 7 acres of vines. They invested in a roomful of stainless-steel tanks and went into the wine business. One thing led to another, and soon a banquet business followed.

Saturday night buffet dinners are scheduled on the vineyard grounds from Mar to Dec; reservations are a must. Gourmet meals are served along with Bias's wines. Winter is less hectic and cross-country skiing is allowed on the property when the snow comes. Bias offers vine cuttings during the January pruning season for creating wreaths or smoking meats. Winery hours are 10 a.m. to 5 p.m. Mon through Sat and 11 a.m. to 5 p.m. Sun.

Bias now has a microbrewery at the vineyard. *Grublkes,* the brewery, makes many types of beer—wheat beer, porter, stout, amber, and pale ale. It is one of the only wineries to have a microbrewery. Visit the website at biaswinery.com for more information about Bias.

Country Cottage 1840 (301 Walnut St.; 573-834-7602; countrycottagebb.com) is open year-round. Innkeepers Susan and Terry Black offer you your own private cottage with the feel of old-world charm. Sit on the back porch overlooking the old Victorian gardens and relax. It's a great spot to stay for Oktoberfest (the first four weekends of October) or the Holiday Wine Trail in November. Susan will start your day with a fine breakfast and give you directions to everywhere you want to go. Rooms are $110 to $200.

Next on the road is *Hermann.* To orient yourself, begin at the *Hermann Visitors' Information Center* (312 Market St.; 800-932-8687; hermannmo.com). Founded in 1836 by members of the German Settlement Society of Philadelphia, Hermann was intended as a self-supporting refuge for German heritage and traditions, a sort of "second fatherland."

George Bayer, who had immigrated in 1830, selected a site in Missouri that resembled his home in the Rhine Valley in terms of climate, soil, and richness of wild grapevines. Bayer and the other German immigrants dreamed of building one of the largest cities in the US in the Frene Creek valley.

The dream quickly attracted a variety of professionals, artisans, and laborers who began the task of building the city of their dreams. It never did become that giant metropolis of the immigrants' dreams; now it is a city of festivals. There is Wurstfest in March, Maifest in May, and Oktoberfest in the fall, each drawing thousands of folks from all over the state. Hermann also boasts 7 area wineries. Amtrak helps to alleviate traffic on festival weekends.

In winter and on non-festival weekends, Hermann is just what it looks like—a quaint German town, quiet, and filled with B&Bs, the largest being the huge White House Hotel. You'll find galleries, shops, and brick homes snuggled right up to the street, European-style. During the festivals, though, it becomes crowded and noisy, as busy as Bayer's dream city. Portable toilets appear on street corners, and the revelry spills from wineries downtown. If you want to be off the beaten path around here, you should aim for a weekday in the off-season. Then a traveler has this sleepy hamlet all to himself.

If antiques are your thing, go to hermannhill.com for a listing of all the shops in town. It will show you places like **Red Barn Antiques** (at the end of W. 9th Street; 573-486-5544), where you can find a pig snooter (what? you don't know what that is?), a calf weaner (hey, what kind of antiques person are you anyway?), and all manner of authentic stuff. They are hanging from the ceiling and piled on tables, and believe it or not, owner John Wilding knows where everything is. The building is worth the trip. They bought a

lookingforsilver, theyfoundlead

The early French miners came looking for silver that was rumored to lie along the Meramec River but found instead one of the greatest lead fields in the world. The viburnum trend in the St. Francois Mountains now supplies more than 90 percent of the lead produced in this country, and high-grade zinc is smelted from the slag left from the lead-refining process.

100-year-old barn, marked all the pieces, toted it to Hermann, and rebuilt it. They filled it with hay knives, and ice-maker's tools. This shop is a history book. The barn is open year-round Mon through Sat 10 a.m. to 5:30 p.m.

Swiss Meats and Sausage (2056 S. Hwy. 19; 573-486-2086 or 800-793-SWISS; swissmeats.com) is owned by Mike Sloan and father Bill Sloan. If you didn't even know that there were 40 different kinds of bratwurst, then you are in for a treat. There is also andouille sausage, hams, bacon, bologna, link sausages, and even hickory-smoked turkeys. And to really get exotic: buffalo and elk jerky. Gift baskets can be made up for that guy-who-has-everything boss of yours with the addition of a choice of cheeses as well.

The **Stone Hill Winery** on Stone Hill Highway just off 12th Street, Hermann (800-909-WINE; stonehillwinery.com), was established in 1847 and until Prohibition (when it became a mushroom-growing facility), it was the nation's second-largest winery. Now it is owned by Jim and Betty Held. The world- renowned cellars are carved into the hillside and are reputed to be the country's largest underground vaulted cellars, and there's a breathtaking view of the town. **Vintage 1847 Restaurant** shares the picturesque hilltop location; a huge window at one end of the restored carriage house looks out on Missouri's blue hills. Visit the restaurant's wine cellar to choose the evening's libation, and do scrutinize the menu carefully—there's a cheesecake to die for.

Once in town, be sure to see the ***Hermannhof Winery Festhalle*** (330 E. 1st St.; 800-393-0100; hermannhof.com), the world's largest wine hall, where you can dance to live German bands every Sat and Sun, starting at noon. There is no entrance fee. Enjoy a festival German dinner or a *brat mit krauts* on a bun. Hours are Mon through Sat from 10 a.m. to 5 p.m. and Sun from 11 a.m. to 5 p.m.

There are so many great little antiques and craft shops that it would be impossible to list them all and, of course, there are many bed-and-breakfasts in Hermann. Among them is ***Birk's Gasthaus*** (700 Goethe St.; 573-486-2911; birksgasthaus.com). This Victorian mansion was built by the owner of the third-largest winery in the world and is furnished in period antiques, including some 6-foot-long tubs with gold eagle-claw feet, brass beds, and 10-foot-tall doors with transoms. Rooms are $95 to $175. Another B&B, ***Montagues*** (301 Schiler St.; 573-486-2035; montaguesbedandbreakfast.com), located in the heart of Hermann's Hispanic District, also serves fine smoked meat in Montagues BBQ. This three-story brick building (circa 1869) is walking distance to Amtrak, wineries, shops, and restaurants. Breakfast is served from 6:30 to 10 a.m. Bedrooms are $95 but you can reserve the entire floor—2 bedrooms, 2 baths, sitting room, and balcony for $190. The barbecue is Texas style, slow (16 hours!) mesquite-smoked brisket, sausage, chicken, and pork. Mon and Tues, breakfast and lunch 6:30 a.m. to 2 p.m.; Wed through Sat, breakfast, lunch, and dinner, 6:30 a.m. to 7 p.m.; closed Sun.

River's Edge Restaurant is right there, too, at 1720 Ferry Rd., Morrison (573-294-7207). Cajun food is the specialty here at the Gasconade riverbank location Fri from 5 to 10 p.m., Sat from noon to 10 p.m., and Sun from noon to 8 p.m. (Note: You can take the road or the ferry—off Highway J—to get to River's Edge.)

Captain Wohlt Inn (123 E. 3rd St.; 573-486-3357; captainwohltinn.com) is a beautiful old brick home (circa 1840) built by original settlers of Hermann. If you are traveling with a group or planning a family get-together, you can have the entire house. Some rooms have a deck or private garden area. Rooms are from $62.50 to $75.

Take US 50 to Loose Creek. Turn onto Highway A and go north 6 miles to **Bonnots Mill** (877-901-4144; dauphinehotel.com). This tiny town is so picturesque that the Jefferson City Active Sketch Club has come here to work many times. The views of the autumn foliage and the silvery river are glorious. On Iris Avenue, nestled in a valley between two bluffs, the **Dauphine Hotel** has found a new life. Part of Bonnots Mill since 1875, the hotel is one of the oldest lodgings in the state (circa 1840s) but until just a few years ago, it was just another old, two-story hotel with a for-sale sign hanging on it. Now it's a bed-and-breakfast inn with 7 guest rooms, each with a private bath. In the old days the hotel had one (yes, one) bathroom for all of its guests. A big breakfast is served in the eat-in kitchen or the dining room from 7:30 until 9:30 a.m. every day. The rooms have the original bead-board ceilings and wood floors and are filled with charming antiques—many of them dating from the original hotel—and handmade quilts. After breakfast guests can lounge on the double-decker front porch. Rooms range from $80 to $125.

Johnny Mack's Bar & Grill (106 Riverview Dr., Bonnots Mill; 573-897-2761) features smoked ribs and smoked tenderloin. Open Thurs through Sat 3 to 11 p.m.

The small village of **Westphalia,** south on US 63, perches like a lighthouse on the hill. There is only one street, with homes built right up to the sidewalk, as they are in Hermann. Everything is spic-and-span and a pleasure to the eye—*das ist gut.*

Huber's Ferry Bed & Breakfast, 4 miles north of Westphalia on US 63, at CR 501 (573-455-2979; hubersferrybedandbreakfast.com), has a magnificent view of two rivers. It sits high on a bluff overlooking both the Osage River and the Maries River. David and Barbara Plummer are the hosts in this 1881 Missouri German-style three-story, redbrick home. The house is near the intersection of US 50 and US 63, is surrounded by 4 acres, and boasts the original barn, built in 1894, the oldest in the county. There are 4 rooms, each with a private bath. Barbara's breakfasts begin with the aroma of homemade bread baking, and then there is fresh fruit, eggs—the whole nine yards. Rooms are $80 to $195.

On the east side of US 63 at **Vienna,** the **Americana Antique, Art, and Curio Shop** is a house, garage, and several outbuildings at 1114 Hwy. 63 North (573-422-3505), filled to the ceiling with what owner John Viessman calls "stuff": everything you can imagine, from old army uniforms to a reassembled log house that measures almost 6 feet wide by 9 feet tall. But his real passion is books, especially books about Missouri history. There are more than 30,000 books in the house, stacked two deep on floor-to-ceiling shelves running through what was once the home's living room. Volumes on the Civil War, Jewish folklore, and the black experience in America are crammed together in some kind of order. "It's a constant struggle," Viessman says.

Books are everywhere among the other stuff. There is a whole wall of *Life* magazines in the barn, set up by year so people can find their birthday issue. Viessman still carts stuff home from auctions and yard sales, as he has since 1969.

Viessman is at home most Fridays and weekends when he isn't at an auction. Until he quits his day job, the shop is open by chance or appointment. A large yellow billboard with an eagle on it stands by the driveway. An "open" sign is posted when he's there. He advises calling first if you're making a special trip.

Antiques lovers heading south on US 63 from Americana Antiques will want to keep a sharp eye out at the first right, Ball Park Road. If the ***Maries Hollow Antiques and Herb Farm*** sign is up, be sure to turn. Follow Ball Park Road (which becomes CR 213) across two bridges, one over a small creek and a concrete bridge over the Maries River, and take the first right. Follow the winding country road past an old farmhouse off to the right and through what looks like a private driveway but isn't, down another hill and to the left. What you will find for your 2-mile effort is the wonderful garden-theme shop run by Sandy Shelton that has been featured in *Country Gardens, Country Home, Decorating Garden Style,* and *Romantic Homes* magazines. The shop is usually open Fri, Sat, and Sun during Apr and May, and Sept through Nov. Call (573) 422-3906 or stop by and Sandra will show you everything.

You could also take a quick left on Highway 42 and stop by the ***Old Jail Museum Complex,*** which got its start during the town's centennial celebration in 1955, when some concerned citizens purchased the old stone jail building to prevent it from being destroyed. The jail became a museum; over time two local log cabins have been moved to the grounds and a large weatherproof shed has been built to house items donated by county residents. The Old Jail Complex, staffed by volunteers from the Maries County Historical Society, is open Sun from 2 to 4 p.m., Memorial Day weekend through June and from Labor Day weekend through Oct. Admission is $3. While you're in the courthouse, check out the paintings of historic buildings by John Viessman and other local artists.

Kathy and Tom Corey returned home to Maries (pronounced Marys) County after 30 years and built their dream home in the rock-strewn hills above the Gasconade River near Dixon. They decided to share it and a country inn was born. The name, ***Rock Eddy Bluff Farm*** (573-759-6081 or 800-335-5921; rockeddy.com)., comes from the location of the inn. It sits atop a rugged limestone bluff overlooking the river. Here the water curves and quickens over a shoal, then calms into a deeper pool set against the bluffs. A series of large boulders rises above the water (Thox Rock is the largest), which gave this section of the river the name Rock Eddy. The inn offers private access to the Gasconade River, and canoes are available. You can see 10 miles across the river valley between Vienna and Dixon from here. It is more a country retreat than a bed-and-breakfast, with hiking and a horse-drawn Amish spring wagon. Scenic Clifty Creek has worn a natural arch through the bluff. The inn's upper story boasts a pretty view of the river; it offers an upstairs suite that gives the sensation of being snuggled into the treetops, hence the name the Treehouse Suite. The cost per night for 1 or 2 people is $140. The handmade quilts and ceiling fans in this suite create a restful atmosphere. You can relax on the deck and eat breakfast or watch the sun set while soaking in the hot tub dubbed the Think Tank.

Turkey Ridge Cottage is away from the Bluff House and has 3 bedrooms and a fireplace. It is romantic and quiet. The breakfast room has a stocked fridge or you can dine nearby. One guest left a note saying, "I am convinced that time spent at Turkey Ridge does not count against life's allotted length." The cottages are $155 to nightly for 2 adults, or $900 per week.

The Line Camp Cabin is a new addition to the place. It was inspired by a herding cabin in Wyoming. Everything here is just like it was in the 1880s: heat from a wood stove, ice box (with ice), water from a pitcher pump, and light from kerosene lamps. Here you cook, sit in the porch swing, walk to the river, and relive the past. There's even a corral for your horse if you want to bring one along. The cabin is $100 a night ($10 for additional guests) or $600 per week. This is not for everyone, but if you like roughing it a bit, you will love it. It's worth every penny. You will see bald eagles that have been nesting there for years and a great blue heron rookery with about 50 nests in the clutch of trees.

Visit the website to see photos of the area. To find Rock Eddy Bluff Farm on the map, look for a small (nonexistent) town called Hayden off US 63, between Rolla and Jefferson City.

twenty-four andtwo

Missouri was the 24th state admitted into the Union, and the second state (after Louisiana) west of the Mississippi. The Missouri Compromise of 1820 allowed this state to enter the Union on August 10, 1821, as a slave state, but no other concessions were made in states formed from the Louisiana Territory. Missouri was a Confederate state that was held under martial law by the Union army from the very beginning of the war and where families were divided and brother literally fought brother.

Rolla is on US 63. Here the famous Rolla School of Mines is situated. If you are interested in mines or minerals, it's worth your while to see the museum. Be sure to take the time to see **Missouri's Stonehenge,** a half-scale version of the English one built 4,000 years ago. Missouri's version was built by the school's specialists in the fields of mining engineering, rock mechanics, explosives research, civil engineering, and computer science. It was built to honor the techno-nerds of long ago who built their version to pinpoint the solstices and changing seasons with moonlight and sunlight falling through precisely positioned stones. The new Stonehenge, however, was built of 160 tons of granite, shaped by cutting torches and high-pressure water jets, and aligned by computer. It also includes an "ana-lemma" solar calendar used by the Anasazi Indians in the American Southwest more than 1,000 years ago and a Polaris window for sighting the North Star. It was dedicated in 1984 on the summer solstice. A member of the Society of Druids offered ancient incantations over this blend of the ancient and ultramodern.

If you are an alumnus of the University of Missouri, Rolla, then the name of this B&B makes perfectly good sense to you. At least that's what Ron Kohsers thought when his wife, Barbara, voiced some doubts about it. **Miner Indulgence Bed and Breakfast** (13750 Martin Spring Dr., Rolla;

573-364-0680; bbonline.com/mo/miner) celebrates the Miners—Ron is on the faculty—and has plenty of alumni and parents as guests as well. It could be the peach French toast that is often part of the full country breakfast, or the hot cup of coffee on the porch before breakfast, or the swimming pool and hot tub outside the two-story redbrick colonial home that brings people back. Whatever it is you can surf on over on the web and make up your own mind or see it in person: Take exit 184 from I-44 and turn onto the south outer road (which is Martin Spring) and go 1.5 miles west. Rates are $85 a night.

After that have a major indulgence at a **Slice of Pie** (601 Kingshighway, Rolla; 573-364-6203), which was begun by a teacher and now serves the best pie you could ever want. Or, if you've eaten enough, you can visit the **Museum at the Old Courthouse** (305 W. 3rd St., Rolla; 573-364-5977), which dates from the Civil War. It has an art museum and a batch of little shops inside. Learn more about the city of Rolla at its website, rollacity.org.

Because Missouri is world-famous for its barbecue, it is important to point out the best of the best all over this state. Missouri has been the center of the meat industry since its beginnings and seeing the stands of hickory and oak everywhere, well, you know, the Show-Me State was just made for barbecue. Here in Rolla **Johnny's Smoke Stak** (201 W. Hwy. 72; 573-364-4838) is the only barbecue in town at this writing that cooks ribs the way they were meant to be cooked, far from flames and in the low and slow, lazy heat of smoke. As tradition demands, the meat is unsauced and fall-off-the-bone tender right from the pit. Sauce is made here, too, to add to the meat when it is served.

There's a lot happening in **St. James** on Highway 68 east of Rolla, if you are an oenophile (that's a wine lover, remember?). First, stop by **St. James Winery** (540 Sidney St.; 800-280-WINE; stjameswinery.com). Jim and Pat Hofherr came here in 1970 with their three children and invested everything they had to begin the winery. After Jim's death in 1994, Pat and her three sons, Andrew, John, and Peter, ran the winery, which won more than 75 awards in local, national, and international wine competitions in 1995. In fact, *Bon Appetit* magazine named St. James's 1993 Seyval one of the top 50 wines in the world. Hours are Mon through Sat from 8 a.m. to 7 p.m., Sun from 11 a.m. to 7 p.m. Winter closing is at 6 p.m.

Heinrichshaus Vineyards and Winery (18500 Hwy. U, St. James; 573-265-5000; heinrichshaus.com) is a family-owned winery specializing in dry wines, including Vidal Blanc and Chambourcin. Heinrich and Lois Grohe are the owners and wine masters. Heinrich is from southern Germany, and their daughter, Peggy, went to school in Switzerland, where she studied winemaking. The winery offers fresh grapes in season, Missouri cheeses and sausages, hand-thrown pottery, and original watercolors and prints by Missouri artists. Now this is a full-service winery—wine and cheese, a clay carafe, and original art to enjoy while you picnic on the winery grounds. Spring and fall bring festivals and bike tours. A loaf of bread, a jug of wine, and a picnic! Hours are 10 a.m. to 6 p.m. Mon, Tues, and Thurs through Sat; noon to 6 p.m. Sun. Closed Wed and holidays except the Wed before Thanksgiving.

Ferrigno's Winery and B&B (17301 Hwy. B, St. James; 573-265-7742; missouriwinecountry.com) is an interesting place to spend some time in the St. James area. Winemakers Dick and Susan Ferrigno grow 7 varieties of French hybrid grapes, such as the Chambourcin, a red grape, and the Seyval white grape. They now have 14 acres in vines and make 9 wines ranging from very dry to semisweet. Dick's favorite wines are made from the Cynthiana, which is a red grape, and Seyval grapes. Recent DNA testing proved what many winemakers had suspected for some years: that the Cynthiana and the Norton are the same grape. These wines are dry with a definite oak flavor. You may peer through glass to watch the winemaking process or wander in the surrounding vineyards. Susan serves dinner in the wine pavilion to private groups, and wine, sausage, and other items are always available for picnics on the grounds. Winery hours are Mon through Sat from 10 a.m. to 6 p.m. and Sun from noon to 6 p.m. The winery is open Apr through Dec, and weekends only Jan and Feb.

Deep underground in the unchanging atmosphere beloved by spelunkers, a long underground river flows silently through **Onondaga Cave** in **Daniel Boone State Park,** near **Leasburg** on I-44 east of St. James. This is a place of superlatives: Massive stalagmites rise like peaks from the floor of the Big Room, said to be the largest cave living room in the world. In Daniel Boone's Room the abundance of cave formations is enough to make you shake your head in amazement. Old Dan himself discovered the place in 1798—or rather, he was the first white man to do so. Native Americans had used the area as a hunting sanctuary in earlier times.

Organizers of the St. Louis World's Fair in 1904 encouraged the cave's owners to open it to the public—it was a great hit, as visitors came first by railroad and then by surrey and wagon to explore the wonders.

Bourbon, off I-44, was once a whiskey stop on the railroad—could you tell from the name? Now it's the home of **Meramec Farm Cabins and Trail Riding Vacations** (208 Thickety Ford Rd.; 573-732-4765; meramec farm.com). In the same family since 1811, and now into its seventh generation, this family farm has earned the Missouri Century Farm sign awarded by the University of Missouri to farms that have been in the same family for at least 100 years.

This is a real working cattle ranch, with critters and all—kids who don't have a grandma in the country will enjoy petting the horses, feeding the ducks, or playing in a real old-fashioned hayloft.

It's great for adults, too. Just enjoy the trail (1.5 miles follow the river's edge) that adjoins the highest bluffs on the Meramec River. Take a dip in a swimming hole, picnic on a gravel bar, or enjoy canoeing on a section of the Meramec that doesn't require a Class V rapids expert.

Price for the large cedar cabin is $100 a night for 4 people ($10 for each additional person); the log cabin is $80 a night for 2 people. The farm is just an hour's drive from St. Louis. It lies on a bend in the Meramec River near the Vilander Bluffs. A conveniently located 5-acre gravel bar is there for people who want to fish and swim. Tubing and canoeing are some of the favorite activities, along with hiking and horseback riding. Ask about the many special packages that let you ride the horse that is native to the area, the Missouri Fox Trotter. According to Carol Springer, owner of the spread, these horses really "smooth out the rugged hills." Pervian Paso and Tennessee Walking Horses have joined the scene, too. Horseback riding is $25 an hour; 4-hour trips are $75. The 3-day package includes 2 nights' lodging and 8 hours of riding for 2 people for $500.

You also can bring your horse with you and Meramec Farms will provide a corral for that member of your family. Carol asks that you call ahead for reservations and directions. This is a working farm, and drop-ins tend to arrive at just the wrong time, but Carol has been juggling it all since 1974, so she must be doing something right. For reservations visit the website or call.

Meramec State Park at Sullivan (mostateparks.com/park/mera mec-state-park), east on I-44, is an excellent spot for canoeing and exploring, though it is often crowded on summer weekends. Meramec State Park on the scenic Meramec River winds through the rough, timbered hills just east of Little Bourbon.

Missouri is known as the cave state, with more known caves than any other state—5,200 counted so far. There are some 22 within the park. One, Fisher Cave, is open for guided tours; others are protected as habitat for an endangered bat species. (You didn't really want to go in that badly, did you?)

The folks at **Stanton,** farther east on I-44, argue with the people of St. Joseph, who say Jesse James died there. Stanton proponents believe that the murder of Thomas Howard on April 3, 1882, was a clever plot to deceive investigators and authorities—with the backing of then governor of Missouri Thomas T. Crittendon!

Skeptical? Well, that's the true Show-Me attitude. Take your pick. Believe that Jesse died in 1951, just three weeks shy of his 104th birthday, or that he was gunned down by his cousin more than 100 years ago. Of course, DNA testing on the body buried in Kearney proves them wrong, but old legends die hard.

Jesse was a member of Quantrill's Raiders, who captured a gunpowder mill and used the caverns as hideouts; beneath Stanton's rolling hills lies a complex of caves and finely colored mineral formations, as rare as they are beautiful. The nearby Meramec Caverns has guided tours, restaurants, and lodging.

Wild Lands

South from St. Louis you have the choice of I-55 or old US 61. (You can also take I-270 if you want to bypass the city entirely.) However you get there, don't miss the museum and displays at **Mastodon State Park** (636-464-2976; mostateparks.com/Mastodon.htm) near Imperial; the kids will love it and so will you.

The museum features life-size dioramas, reconstructed mastodon skeletons, Ice Age fossils, and artifacts more than 10,000 years old. Ancient Indians hunted mastodons with stone-tipped spears. This was the first place that archaeologists found definite evidence of them, and it was an important discovery, to say the least. And here is an interesting tidbit: Four women fought back when developers tried to buy the important archaeological site.

Marilyn King, Dorothy Heinze, Hazel Lee, and Rita Naes organized fund-raising to match the bid. They kept pestering state officials until the land was made into a state park. "They'd say, 'Here comes those crazy housewives again,'" said Marilyn King (the last of the four women living) in an interview. We in the Show-Me State thank them for their persistence. There is a small admission charge for adults. Museum hours are 9 a.m. to 4:30 p.m. Mon through Sat and noon to 4:30 p.m. Sun. (Winter hours are in effect during Jan and Feb: 11 a.m. to 4 p.m. Mon and Thurs through Sat, and noon to 4 p.m. Sun. The museum is closed Tues and Wed.)

This area contained mineral springs, which made for swampy condi-tions perfect for preservation. Large mammals became trapped in the min-eral-rich mud, which preserved their remains perfectly as the mud hardened to stone. You can still see the ***Kimmswick Bone Bed,*** which is one of the most extensive Pleistocene beds in the country and of worldwide interest to archaeologists and paleontologists. Explore the visitor center, too. It offers a life-size replica of a mastodon skeleton, Clovis points, and other remnants of early human occupation. Access to the Bone Bed begins at 1050 Charles J. Becker Dr., Imperial.

Now aim just south for the town of ***Kimmswick,*** laid out in 1859 by a German named Theodore Kimm. In the early 1880s, Kimmswick's beautiful Montesano Park attracted people from St. Louis by excursion boat. River-boats and railroads stopped here. But the horseless carriage changed the destiny of Kimmswick; the new highway system bypassed the town and left it to become a sleepy little backwater. Even the trains and boats no longer stopped to trade. Contact the visitor center in Kimmswick at (636) 464-6464 or visit them on the Web at visitkimmswick.com. Kimmswick's shops and restaurants are some of the best along the riverfront, BUT ALL SHOPS AND RESTAURANTS ARE CLOSED ON MONDAY. Did I make myself clear? Don't want you to find out the hard way.

You can still get to Kimmswick by riverboat, yes you can. The ***Tom Sawyer Riverboat*** goes to and from the town to the Gateway Arch River-front in St. Louis. There is the 2-hour Express Cruise or the 4-hour Leisure Cruise. Both let you go on shore and explore the town by foot and include lunch at the Blue Owl. Book reservations at (877) 982-1410. The price is $62 per person, all inclusive. Low river levels will cause cancellations, so check dates ahead.

Mary Hostetter, owner of the **Blue Owl Restaurant and Bakery** at 2nd and Mill Streets (636-464-3128; theblueowl.com), says that Kimmswick refuses to be "gobbled up by St. Louis" and works to maintain its individuality as the "town that time forgot." Mary invites you to sit in front of a cheery fireplace and try a few of her specialties.

The building was erected in 1900 and was called Ma Green's Tavern until the 1950s. It was restored in the 1970s and now has warm wood floors that are charmingly out of level, and lace curtains in the windows. Railroad-car siding covers the walls, and waitresses dressed in long pinafores serve lunch on delicate blue-and-white china. Mary added Miss Mary's Veranda, a Victorian veranda, for outdoor dining. A new dining room has opened, too, so now there are 5 dining options. There is live German music with Austrian Paul Knopf on the accordion. Parking is available in the restaurant's lot.

The Blue Owl is open year-round Tues through Fri from 10 a.m. to 3 p.m. and Sat and Sun from 10 a.m. to 5 p.m. From country breakfasts and homemade soups (the Canadian cheese soup is marvelous) on weekdays to the wonderful Sunday special of homemade chicken and dumplings, Mary will try to fill you up. If you happen to see the pastry case as you come in the door, you won't allow that to happen until coffee and dessert. Take a good look at the temple of temptation: Lemon dobosh has 8 layers of lemon cake with filling between each and whipped cream on top. There's an Italian cream cake, Irish apple cake, red velvet cake, and the favorite, Death by Chocolate. The Levee High Apple Pie was created to celebrate the Great Flood of 1993, when the river crested at 39.9 feet against the 40-foot levee. (Have you ever seen a 16-pound apple pie with 18 apples in it? It's the size of your head.) There is outdoor dining May through Oct.

Walk around Kimmswick (visitkimmswick.com); there is a lot to see here, from historic homes and businesses to some fine little restaurants and shops. But keep in mind that everything is closed on Monday.

Swing southwest on US 67 at Crystal City to the city of **Bonne Terre,** a year-round resort, as interesting in December in the middle of a blizzard as it is in the heat of a 100-degree summer day. There isn't all that much to see—aboveground, that is. But if you choose **Mansion Hill** as your first stop and meet owners Doug and Cathy Georgan, the town will come alive for you. In this setting it would have to; the mansion occupies the highest point in Bonne Terre, on 132 acres of timber in the Ozark foothills. Each room has its own view of the estate (which has a 45-mile view of the surrounding area). Four huge fireplaces warm the great rooms.

The 1909 mansion was built by the lead-mining baron responsible for **Bonne Terre Mines** (the world's largest man-made caverns), which honeycomb the earth under the city. Hand-dug with pick and shovel, the mines are now flooded. They are the pride of the Georgans, who also own West End Diving in St. Louis. The mines can be explored two ways in any weather: by scuba diving, as do hundreds of divers who make the trek to Bonne Terre winter and summer, or by walking along the above-water trails. The dive experience in the mine has been named one of America's Top Ten Adventures by *National Geographic* magazine. For information about this unique experience, call (314) 209-7200 or visit 2dive.com.

Your first view of the mine is breathtaking; under the crystal-clear water, illuminated from above by electric lights, divers can see all the remnants of the mining days, including ore carts, elevator shafts, buildings—even tools and drills left when the mine was abandoned in 1961. No less a personage than Jacques Cousteau was a guest at the mansion and filmed a dive here. Rooms at the mansion are worth every penny—$275 a night. The place is gorgeous.

From the entrance to the mines, turn right onto Park Street and go to Allen Street. Follow it until you see the old St. Joe Lead Company Headquarters on the right and the 1909 depot on the left. **The Depot** (573-358-5311) is built in the Queen Anne and Stick architectural styles and is on the National Historic Register. The English-style phone booth outside, a caboose, boxcars, and rail lamps and posts give it a 19th-century flair. Inside the depot, the Whistle Stop Saloon is filled with train memorabilia and open for banquets only. The second and third floors are part of a turn-of-the-20th-century bed-and-breakfast. Rooms are $100 to $120 a night. The mansion and depot are filled almost every weekend, year-round, by clubs who travel here to scuba dive. All rooms have twin beds to accommodate the divers. Call (888) 843-3483, which is the main office and reservations center for everything at the Bonne Terre Mines.

Located in an area of the Eastern Ozarks known as the Old Lead Belt, **Missouri Mines State Historic Site** (4000 Hwy. 32; 573-431-6226) showcases the mining industry in a 19,000-square-foot former mine-mill powerhouse. In 1975 the St. Joseph Lead Company donated 25 buildings and the surrounding land to the Missouri Department of Natural Resources. There is also an excellent mineral collection at the museum, as well as a gift shop that sells very reasonably priced specimens. The Missouri Mines State Historic Site is open Mon through Sat 10 a.m. until 4 p.m. and Sun noon until 5 p.m. Sun hours are extended in summer until 6 p.m. The museum is located on Highway 32 just outside Park Hills.

History buffs shouldn't miss the Civil War battlefield at **Fort Davidson State Historic Site at Pilot Knob** (118 E. Maple; 573-546-3454). You can still see the outlines of the hexagonal fort built in 1863 by Union forces. Flanked on three sides by high hills, the fort was vulnerable to attack from above, which must have been apparent to General Thomas Ewing. After losing 75 men in the Battle of Pilot Knob, he had his soldiers muffle their horses' hooves with burlap and evacuate during the night. At the park you can get dates and times of battle re-enactments.

If you happen to be on Highway 32 headed westbound for Dillard Mill, canoeing in Salem, or hiking in the Indian Trail State Forest, you might enjoy shopping in **Bixby** at the **Good Ole Days Country Store** (573-626-4868) on Highway 32. You will notice the bright red 1946 Missouri Pacific caboose tucked against one side of the store. Owners Tony and Bridget Bohac have modern gas pumps and Model-A vintage pumps (also painted bright red) out front, and inside is the same blend of old and new. Twenty-five cents buys a cup of coffee (on the honor system), while above your head an O-scale model train runs on a track suspended from the ceiling, complete with flashing lights and whistles. There's more to see. Antiques fill almost every available inch of space on the hardwood floors. Out back is an old log cabin–turned–antiques store, which also houses a collection of minerals from surrounding hills.

Bixby's General Store has never closed since it was first opened in 1906 when the railroad put a railroad siding right next to the store. The store sold everything from casket materials to plows to groceries; locals didn't have to go anywhere else (not that there was anyplace else to go anyway). Now the store has passed the 100-year milestone. The store still has a lot of convenience items and a good deli for lunch and ice cream (get a real malt to eat in the caboose). Hours are 4 a.m. to 6:30 p.m. Mon through Sat and 10 a.m. to 6 p.m. Sun.

One of Missouri's best-kept secrets is the **Arcadia Valley**—and its villages of Arcadia, Pilot Knob, and Ironton—where there are quite a few antiques shops.

Just up the road from the forge is **Wilderness Lodge** (573-637-2295; wildernesslodgeresortltd.com), also on Peola Road in Lesterville; this great old-fashioned Ozarks experience includes Black River canoe and inner-tube floats in its package. The lodge is made of logs, and the cottages are quintessential rounded Ozark-river stone, each with a fireplace. Note: The lodge is closed during the winter after Dec 1. The lodge is open the first weekend in Apr through Thanksgiving weekend. Rates are $89 for adults, $39 for children ages 1 through 12, and free for children younger than age 1. The Riverside Suite is a bit more at $99/night per adult, and $49/night per child. Rates include dinner and breakfast. Float trips are an additional charge.

Highway 49 leads to the town of **Annapolis** and a turn-of-the-20th-century home near several rivers and lakes. Innkeepers Sharon, Joe, and Rachel Cluck invite guests of **Rachel's Bed and Breakfast** (202 2nd St.; 573-275-6000; rachelsbb.com), in the historic Bolch Mansion, to share the large common room and the deck or veranda overlooking the attractively landscaped grounds. The secluded location of one suite makes it a favorite for honeymooners, but the Waterfall suite and the Promise suite are beauti-ful, too. The Mathima suite has French doors to a private veranda and a fireplace. The Upper Room is less expensive and has a separate lounge area with an easy chair, fireplace, refrigerator, and private bath with a Jacuzzi tub. Rooms are $110 to $145. Dining at the inn provides a quiet ambience and good food.

Rachel has opened **Black River Cottage** (573-598-4656 or 888-245-7771; blackrivercottage.com), a cozy three-bedroom bungalow (surrounded by rose gardens) with a fully equipped kitchen that at $150 (2-night mini-mum) a night is great for traveling families or friends (who are close enough to share a bathroom). There is a TV and laundry equipment. The cottage sleeps 8 people, has a grill and fire pit, is walking distance to fishing, and is only 5 minutes from the float area on the Black River. It's right next door to the B&B.

Nearby **Ironton** is the home of **Bobby Powell's Jamboree** (135 S. Main St.; 573-546-1441; avjamboree.com), where bluegrass music is played, featur-ing not just bluegrass, but country, folk music, and oldies in a Branson-style show. The jam sessions begin at 6 p.m. and the show is from 7 to 9 p.m. Mar through Dec. Tickets are $10 adults, $5 ages 12 and under.

Ready for some action? ***Bluff View Marina*** (bluffviewmarina.com) in nearby ***Piedmont*** has boats and pontoons for rent. In the summertime (May 15 to September 30) they are open 7 days a week from 9 a.m. until 6 p.m. Even off-season you can stop by the trailer and talk to someone about renting.

The nearby ***Johnson's Shut-ins*** (north of Lesterville on Highway N) will surprise you with their rugged beauty, which is like terrain you'd expect to find in Maine or Colorado. These worn and convoluted forms have a story behind them; would you believe Missouri once had its own Mount St. Helens? Prehistoric volcanic eruptions spewed tons of magma, towering clouds of ash, and acid debris, flattening vegetation and covering whole areas with newly formed igneous rock. Some 250 million years passed, and shallow inland seas encroached, covering the already ancient volcanic mountains with layers of sedimentary rock. Over the course of many millions of years, these layers built up until they were hundreds of feet thick. There were more violent uplifts across the Ozarks; the seas retreated; rain, wind, and moving water eroded the softer sedimentary rock layers, cutting the river valley ever deeper. Swirling over and between the buried igneous hills, the river scoured and carved potholes, chutes, and spectacular gorges. It is amazing that something as penetrable as water can cut the hardest stone—here's proof.

The Johnson's Shut-ins are pocketed away in the scenic St. Francois Mountains; when you see them, you will understand the name. You feel isolated, hidden, shut in—but without a trace of claustrophobia. The Black River flows through the park and winds past some of the oldest exposed rock in the country. There are little waterfalls and swirling water everywhere. Adding to the unique nature of the area are the drought-adapted plants commonly found in the deserts of the Southwest. Scorpions and the rare eastern collared lizard (which rises to an upright position to run on its hind legs and is a treat to see) also find a home in the glades. (Never put on your boots in the morning without first shaking them out—scorpions love hiding places.) Call (573) 546-2450. The website mostateparks.com can give you more information about the park and other parks in the state.

East of the park, the Taum Sauk section of the Ozark Trail leads to ***Mina Sauk Falls*** (the highest falls in Missouri) and ***Taum Sauk Mountain,*** the highest point in the state at 1,772 feet above sea level. (Okay, no snickering—this is not Colorado.)

According to Indian legend, the mountain's rugged face shows the grief of Mina Sauk, daughter of Taum Sauk, chief of the Piankishaws. Because of her improper marriage, her new husband (of the Osage tribe) was thrown off the mountain. In her despair, she leapt from the peak. The spot where she landed is considered the origin of Mina Sauk Falls, which cascade 200 feet over the granite ledges.

The *Ozark Trail* winds through the heart of Missouri. Miles and miles of rocky terrain ramble from Steelville and West Plains along glades, forests, and prairies. Here you can hear the wind and feel a snowflake on your face. The more than 300 miles of pathways are serene and quiet, with scarcely another person along the trail. The solitude can be overwhelming and the views breathtaking. Some of the best views in the Ozarks can be found at Onondaga, Taum Sauk, and Johnson's Shut-ins. (Construction has begun to expand the trail to 500 miles of Missouri wilderness and continue it into Arkansas for an additional 500 miles on the Ozark Highlands Trail.) The northernmost part of the trail—the Courtois Creek Section near Steelville—offers a blend of bottomland and hardwood trees. The area of the *Mark Twain National Forest* boasts some of the Ozarks' tallest standing pines, and of course there are creeks, bluffs, and small waterfalls. The Berryman Trail for mountain bikers has a trailhead 17 miles east of Steelville and intersects the Ozark Trail at Harmon Springs. A fine spot to camp waits here with a spring and small pond. Many of these trails teemed with deer, elk, and herds of bison when they were traveled by Native Americans in the 1800s. The red wolf lived here, although none has been seen in years. Guides say black bears and wild horses may be seen. The trail offers views of the current river valley, old graveyards, caves, and bluffs. Rigorous hiking as well as more moderate hiking spots near the state parks are here as well. Primitive camping (at least 100 feet from the trail, water, and scenic areas) is allowed along most sections of

highestwaterfall **in**missouri

Mina Sauk Falls is the highest waterfall in the state. During the wet season the waterfall cascades 132 feet down a series of volcanic ledges into a sparkling clear pool with a rock bottom.

the trail. Some areas are open to horses and mountain bikes. Although the trail is open year-round, the best times to visit are in the spring when the dogwoods bloom or in the fall under a canopy of russet leaves. The winters are mild in the Ozarks, though, and winter hiking can be fun. Summers in Missouri are not the best for hiking—they tend to be humid and buggy. But whatever the season, be prepared. Have a map, appropriate rainwear gear, and water—and let somebody know where you are going. For Ozark Trail Section Maps and other information, contact the Ozark Trail Coordinator, Missouri Department of Natural Resources, PO Box 176, Jefferson City 65102; (573) 751-5359 or (800) 334-6946; fs.usda.gov/main/mtnf/maps-pubs.

North of the Shut-ins, through some of the prettiest hills this side of the Great Smoky Mountains, are **Dillard** and the **Dillard Mill State Historic Site.** Like a Currier & Ives scene beside its mill run, it is one of the state's best-preserved water-powered gristmills. This picturesque red building sits squarely at the juncture of two of the clearest-flowing Ozark streams, Huzzah and Indian Creeks. The original mill machinery is still in operation, grinding away.

strangeasit sounds

In the Mark Twain National Forest you will see what are called "blossom rocks," moss- and lichen-speckled sandstone rocks that appear to have just "blossomed" from the ground. The massive rocks project from the gentle slope of a wooded hillside and appear where other rocks are present. One blossom rock—125 feet in diameter and 50 feet high—is covered with flowers in early spring.

When you've finished with industrial history, check out the natural history. Dillard has a 1.5-mile hiking trail through oak and hickory forests that ends at a pine-topped plateau.

Backtrack a bit on Highway 49 and turn east onto Highway 32 to **Elephant Rocks State Park** (573-546-3454) near **Graniteville.** It is the first park in the state to have a trail designed especially for the visually and physically impaired. Signs along the trail, written in braille and in regular text, describe the origin of the elephant rocks and guide visitors along a paved 1-mile path.

Elephant Rocks is one of the oddest geological formations—more than a billion years old—you're likely to find in Missouri. Here monolithic boulders stand end-to-end like a train of circus elephants, dwarfing mere mortals who stand beside them. Made of billion-year-old granite, the rocks were formed during the Precambrian era when molten rock forced its way to the surface, pushing the earth's crust aside. The magma cooled and hardened slowly as this area became less volcanically active; it broke in vertical cracks, which weathered and rounded to form the huge "elephants." This weathering eventually breaks even the largest rocks down into pebbles and gravel, but not to worry: More stone elephants are in the making all the time. The pink patriarch of the pachyderm herd is Dumbo, at 27 feet tall and 35 feet long and weighing in at a sylphlike 680 tons. Winding trails, colorful lichen and wildflowers, cool, oak-shaded grottoes, and a picnic area in the shadow of the rocks add to the attractions here.

River Heritage Area

If you didn't head off into the wilderness back on US 67 at Crystal City but stayed on I-55 or US 61, you will now enter the River Heritage area. From river bluffs and hills to lowlands, from historic towns to waterways, the River Heritage region boasts enough destinations for several vacations. The French influence is visible everywhere you look in **Ste. Genevieve,** from the name itself to the many buildings à la française. The earliest records of the Missouri Territory invariably mention Ste. Genevieve and its ball-loving inhabitants! French colonial-era homes are tucked in all along the Great River Road from St. Louis south to Cape Girardeau on the Mississippi River's banks. Wide porches and steep roofs have cooled these homes for more than 200 years. The homes predate the Louisiana Purchase, dating from when the French were coming up the Mississippi River from New Orleans and bringing style, food, and traditions with them.

Ste. Genevieve has been clinging to the riverbank here since the 1730s, when French trappers sought valuable beaver pelts. The 5,000 people who call Sainte Gen home still celebrate Bastille Day and are justifiably proud of their French Creole–style buildings. The Great Flood of 1993 threatened the town, but it managed to stay dry with a lot of sandbagging by citizens and history-minded volunteers from across the nation.

Many visitors to Ste. Genevieve are research scholars and genealogists from around the world. The records at the library, courthouse, and churches are the oldest in the West. St. Genevieve calls itself the oldest town west of the Mississippi (more than one Missouri town makes this claim, though) and says "all history of the West begins here."

vivebastilleday!

In Ste. Genevieve the annual Bastille Day celebration on July 14, which celebrates the town's proud French heritage, rivals our own Independence Day.

Stop by the information center on 3rd Street. Many of the town's homes date from the 1700s and are preserved as historic sites and open for tours. Start with the *Ste. Genevieve Museum,* which houses one of the first bird mounts by John James Audubon himself, who did business—albeit briefly—here in the early 1800s. You'll see French-style sabots (wooden shoes), early songbooks, a flute belonging to Audubon's partner Rozier, and much more.

The *Bolduc House Museum* (125 S. Main St.) was built circa 1770 and moved to its current site in 1785. The two-room French colonial is one of the best examples of its type of architecture along the Mississippi. Tour guides in period costume lead visitors through the building, where the yellow glow of tallow lamps dimly light the flintlock rifles above the mantel and the bison rug on the floor. Outside an herb garden, a well, and an orchard are inside a typical French-style palisade enclosure.

Then choose among the homes, churches, shops, and country inns dotting the town. Search out places for little treats, such as Sara Menard's *Sara's Ice Cream and Antiques* (124 Merchant St.; 573-883-5890). More than just hand-dipped ice cream and fountain sodas, Sara's has antiques and collectibles and hand-crafted toys. Sara's is closed from Oktoberfest through Mar. Hours are 10 a.m. to 6 p.m. and until 9 p.m. when school is out.

You can't help but notice the *Old Brick House,* built in 1780, which faces the courthouse square, at 3rd and Market Streets in Ste. Genevieve (90 S. 3rd St. for your GPS; 573-883-2724; theoldbrickhouse.com). It's owned by Rosie Schwartz. The favorite entree is liver knaefly, a liver dumpling. Before you liver-haters turn up your noses, this German cook urges you to try the dish. It wouldn't be a regularly scheduled favorite if it weren't great, right? Okay, you want something you know—how about a sizzling steak or secret-recipe fried chicken? Whatever you eat, enjoy the surroundings while waiting. They say that the bricks that built this wealthy merchant's home in 1785 arrived as ballast on French ships, and it is thought to be the first brick building west of the Mississippi. The building spent years as a courthouse, a school, and a tavern. In 1816 a duel was fought on its steps and a man was killed. Today the polished wood floors and lace curtains offer a more peaceful environment and the most dangerous thing here is the coconut cream pie. Hours are 8 a.m. until 9 p.m. weekdays, 11 a.m. until 10 p.m. Sat, and 11 a.m. until 7 p.m. Sun.

Just a couple of doors down the street from the Old Brick House is **The Anvil** (46 S. 3rd St.; 573-883-7323), a bar and restaurant that serves great fried chicken and other real down-home food. It is in a building built to house a hardware store in 1850. Then it became the Anvil Saloon in 1855 (a gentlemen's saloon and barbershop, actually). Interesting story: The bar and back bar were moved to the saloon in 1855 by oxcart from a steamboat that had run aground on a sandbar and needed to lighten up. Weekday hours are 11 a.m. to 8 p.m. and until 9 p.m. on weekends.

Down the block at 146 S. 3rd St. is the circa 1790 **Southern Hotel** (573-883-3493 or 800-275-1412; southernhotelbb.com). Mike Hankins saw the old wreck, which had been abandoned since 1980, and fell in love with the redbrick, federal-style three-story hotel. It is believed to be the oldest operating hotel west of the Mississippi River. The hotel is full of antiques and claw-foot tubs. Meals feature fresh herbs from the garden

trivia

The Mississippi River is the reason St. Louis exists. It was the original highway for every civilization that thrived in the middle of the country. But it is also the most diverse inland river in the world. More than 500 species of wildlife use the river and its flood plains.

behind the hotel, and flowers from the garden fill the rooms. The garden itself is magical. An arbor leads to a wide cedar swing at the center; Mike has wired the whole area with thousands of tiny white lights. When he hits the switch at dusk the garden is a romantic fairyland. Tucked away in a corner of the garden is a great little shop with dried flowers, herbal soaps, and hand-painted goodies—don't miss it! You can buy the Pepper and Rose Cookbook or enroll in the "Cooking Experience" class.

It has been open since 1987 with 8 guest rooms, each with its own bath. Rooms cost from $93 to $160 and include such wondrous French breakfast items as strawberry soup, artichoke-heart strata (a layered egg-and-bread dish), croissants, homemade lemon bread, juice, and coffee. Mike and Cathy will make you feel at home.

Inn St. Gemme Beauvais (573-883-5744 or 800-818-5744; innstgemme-beauvais.homestead.com) and *Dr. Hertich's House* are respectively at 78 and 99 N. Main St., Ste. Genevieve. Both are on the National Register. Built in 1848 and 1850, the inn is the state's oldest continually operated bed-and-breakfast. This lovely old Victorian will spoil you. All the rooms are suites, with big easy chairs in the sitting room and canopy beds and rockers in the bedrooms. Tea time is every day at 2 p.m., and wine and hors d'oeuvres are offered every day at 4 p.m. A full gourmet breakfast, of course, is served in the morning at 8 and coffee is ready even earlier in the second-floor lounge for you early birds.

There is also a restaurant that can seat up to 26 people. The cuisine is French. Dinner banquets can also be arranged anytime. Outside is a lovely herb and flower garden to enjoy. The hotel is on Main Street, and so it is within walking distance to everything. Suites range from $99 to $189. Dr. Hertich's House was the residence and clinic of the first town doctor. It has 4 suites all with gas fireplaces and whirlpool baths.

The information presented here only begins to touch on what is available in Ste. Genevieve. Looking for wine? There's the *Sainte Genevieve Winery* at 245 Merchant St. (open 11 a.m. to 5 p.m. daily; 573-883-2800). How about candy? The *Sweet Things* confection shop at 242 Market St. (573-883-7990) features fine chocolates (try their famous fudge Creole). There's also all manner of antiques shops and restaurants, and a whole list of bed-and-breakfasts. The town's website is ste-genevieve.com.

At *Perryville,* off US 61, is the *St. Mary of the Barrens Church,* dating from 1827. The grounds are open to walk through; be sure to visit the church's museums. This is also the National Shrine of Our Lady of the Miraculous Medal. Regular guided tours are offered Mon through Fri 10 a.m. and 1 p.m., Sat and Sun 1 and 3 p.m. There is no charge to visit St. Mary's Barrens.

For more history (and fun), detour east a bit on the Great River Road and watch for *Tower Rock* jutting up 85 feet out of the Mississippi. Don't miss the little German towns of Altenberg, Whittenberg, and Frohna.

Stay on US 61, and the next stop is *Jackson;* all aboard the old Iron Mountain Railroad. The oldest Protestant church west of the Mississippi, the Old McKendree Chapel (circa 1819), a national Methodist shrine, is here.

The best attraction for you railroad fans is the ***Iron Mountain Railway*** (505 Benton Rd., Jackson; 573-243-1688 or 800-455-RAIL for schedule and prices; slimrr.com/sitemap.html). Ride a piece of history. Sights and sounds will carry you back to the late 1800s and early 1900s, when this was the preferred method of travel.

The "mother line" of nearly all the smaller rail lines that eventually became the historic Missouri Pacific, the Iron Mountain Railway is part of the St. Louis, Iron Mountain, and Southern Railway Company. Darren the Magician roams the train to entertain the child in you. There's the Dinner Train, or you might relive the 1880s train robbery by the James Gang, or experience the intrigue of murder on a Murder Mystery Train. Take I-55 to exit 99 and go 4 miles west on US 61 to the intersection of US 61 and Highway 25.

If you want to experience the elegance of the 1800s, stop by the ***Oliver House*** (224 E. Adams St., Jackson; 573-243-0533). The lady of the house is known as Missouri's Betsy Ross. Marie Oliver and a friend designed and made the first and only official state flag. The house is decorated with authentic furniture of the period, and music plays on the Edison Victrola. Visiting hours are on the first Sun of the month from 1 to 4:30 p.m. May, July, and Oct, and the three Sun before Christmas for the candlelight tour.

While you're near Jackson, take a side trip to ***Burfordville*** on Highway 34 East. The ***Bollinger Mill*** has been in continuous operation for more than 180 years—these people really kept their noses to the grindstone, didn't they? Located on the Whitewater River, the four-story, stone-and-brick structure shares the setting with the ***Burfordville Covered Bridge,*** one of five covered bridges remaining in the state.

The building of the bridge began in 1858 and, like much of Missouri's everyday life, was put on hold by the Civil War. The Burfordville Bridge was completed in 1868. It is a 140-foot span of incredibly long yellow poplar timbers, which grow near the river. It's another excellent setting for artists and photographers, not to mention history and nostalgia buffs.

You're deep in southern Missouri now, and headed for "Cape." On I-55, ***Cape Girardeau*** (cityofcapegirardeau.org) is the biggest city in the area, with a population of almost 35,000. But Cape Girardeau has also preserved its heritage carefully, and it's a beautiful city in spite of—and in the midst of—phenomenal growth.

Gothic Splendor

An outstanding example of Renaissance architecture in the gothic style is the Old St. Vincent's Church in Cape Girardeau. It was built in 1853 and contains more than 100 medieval-design plaster masks and intricate interior work. It is listed on the National Register of Historic Places.

Cape Girardeau is radio- and- television talk-show host Rush Limbaugh's hometown, and the city offers a self-directed (very conservative) tour (with nothing but right turns?) past the hospital where he was born, his boyhood home, his high school, and the barbershop where he got his first job. Then you can have lunch at his favorite hamburger joint, Wimpy's. Pick up a brochure at the visitor bureau at 1707 Mount Auburn Rd. (800-777-0068; rosecity.net/rush/rushtour.html).

Drive through the city and note the many 19th-century buildings. The beautiful Glenn House, circa 1880, is a good example. The old Court of Common Pleas has a lovely hilltop setting, and Cape Rock Park is a reminder of the early trading post that predated the city itself. Civil War fortifications still remain in the area. The convention and tourism bureau is at 100 Broadway; if you plan to spend some time here, it may pay to stop. You can also visit on the web at capegirardeaucvb.org.

Although Cape is modern and expanding too fast, all is not lost. Proceed directly down to Water Street, which, as you may have guessed by the name, is along the mighty Mississippi. Unfortunately, a rather tall, ugly wall has been built to protect the area from flood, so the view lacks something—water, to be exact. There is an opening and a deck you can drive onto to enjoy the sights, though, if you are fond of rivers—and who isn't? There's just something about the power of that big river.

Get a feel for the history of the area with Cape's unique Great Murals Tour. It all began at the *Southeast Missourian* newspaper building where "The Art of Printing" and "The Art of Making a Newspaper" were done in 1947. Tourists enjoyed finding famous faces in the ceramic murals, which were the first of their kind in the country. They were joined by the "Jake Wells Mural," representing the people whose dreams carved the region's progress. This is one of the largest murals in the state. In the city's downtown area five more murals celebrate the Mississippi River (in Waterfront Park), the Riverfest, the Riverfront, the Bicentennial, and the Silver Coronet Band Mural about Cape's musical legacy. The Missouri Wall of Fame has 45 panels featuring famous Missourians. Those depicted on the wall include Burt Bacharach, Josephine Baker, Thomas Hart Benton (painter), Thomas Hart Benton (senator), Yogi Berra, George Caleb Bingham, Susan Elizabeth Blow, Omar Bradley, George Brett, Lou Brock, Jack Buck, August Busch, Jr., Calamity Jane, Dale Carnegie, George Washington Carver, Kate Chopin, Walter Cronkite, T. S. Eliot, Don Faurot, Eugene Field, Redd Foxx, Joe Garagiola, Linda M. Godwin, Betty Grable, Jean Harlow, Langston Hughes, John Huston, Jesse James and Frank James, Scott Joplin, Rush Limbaugh, Stan Musial, Marie Elizabeth Oliver, Rose O'Neill, James Cash Penney, Marlin Perkins, John J. Pershing, Vincent Price, Joseph Pulitzer, Ginger Rogers, Tom Sawyer, Dred Scott, Jess Stacy, Harry S Truman, Porter Wagoner, Laura Ingalls Wilder, and Tennessee Williams.

If you love trains, especially Lionel electric trains, hunt up **Sneathen Enterprises** (2526 Boutin Dr., Cape Girardeau; 573-335-8091), where Bill Sneathen will sell, buy, or trade with you. Hours vary.

The **Glenn House** (325 S. Spanish St., Cape Girardeau; 573-334-1177; rosecity.net/glenn.html) is a circa 1883 two-story Victorian that is open for tours and contains period furnishings, 12-foot stenciled ceilings, and some good displays devoted to the steamboat era on the Mississippi. It is open from May through Oct and Dec on Sat and Sun from 1 to 4 p.m. or by appointment.

About a block away is what will probably be your favorite place if you have any Cajun instincts at all. **Broussard's Cajun Restaurant** (120 N. Main St.; 573-334-7235; broussardscajuncuisine.com) even has a test on the back of the menu to see if there is a trace of Cajun blood in your veins. The "How to tell a full-blooded, dipped-in-the-bayou Cajun from someone who just wishes he was" test begins with the question "Did your grandmother regularly eat *couche* for breakfast?" and ends with "If someone stepped on your toe would you yell *'ho yii'* instead of 'ouch'?" If any of you good ol' boys are missing home, this is the place for you.

The food here is authentic, fire-breathing Cajun. The menu has a glossary of terms and a key to spicy foods for those of you who don't like surprises. It is an inexpensive, casual place, but bring enough money to try a Cajun Combo, which includes a little bit of everything. Also, if you have room, the special includes a salad and french bread. Other entrees are the traditional red beans and rice with sausage and fried crawfish tails. Polish it off with a draft.

It features a live band playing blues and dance music Fri and Sat from 8 p.m. until closing time. Broussard's motto is *"Laissez les bons temps rouler!"*—Let the good times roll.

trivia

Cape Girardeau was named after Jean Baptiste Girardot, who established a trading post here in 1733. When Spain offered inexpensive, tax-exempt land, Spanish immigrants were drawn to the area. Cape Rock (2 miles northeast via Highway 177 and E. Rock Drive) is the site of Girardot's trading post. Although nothing remains of the original settlement, views of the Mississippi River are wonderful from the bluff. Good spot for a picnic.

For a lovely bed-and-breakfast, try the **Bellevue Bed and Breakfast** (312 Bellevue, Cape Girardeau; 573-335-3302 or 800-768-6822; bellevuebandb.net). This 1892 Queen Anne Victorian is listed on the Historical Register and has been faithfully restored—right up to the stenciled ceilings—and filled with period furniture. The parlor has a coal-burning fireplace, but queen-size beds and private baths make this a very comfortable place to stay. Innkeepers Brian Langlois and his wife, Linda Delan, draw guests into the dining room for breakfast with the aroma of baking bread. The home is within walking distance of the riverfront and the many nearby shops. Rooms are from $115 to $185 and all have private baths.

River Ridge Winery (CR 321, Commerce; 573-264-3712; riverridgewinery.com) is in a century-old farmhouse nestled in the hills where Crowley's Ridge meets the Mississippi River, 2 miles north of **Commerce,** south of Cape on Highway N. The hand-tended French hybrid grapes are grown on the hills behind the winery. You may sample the fine dry and semi-dry table wines crafted by winemaker Jerry Smith. He and his wife, Joannie, also have a showroom of unique wine-related items. You can picnic by the river or in the vineyards, or relax by a warm fire at the house and enjoy some wurst and bread. Open 11 a.m. to 6 p.m. daily.

Near Cape Girardeau grits begin to sneak onto the breakfast menu, and the accent begins to sound slightly more Southern than Midwestern.

The Evil that Men Do

During the forced removal in 1838, 12 detachments of Cherokee were ordered by General Winfield Scott to move to Oklahoma. All entered Missouri in Cape Girardeau County. Rain, snow, freezing cold, hunger, and disease took their toll on the emigrants as the ice prevented both boat and horse from moving. More than 4,000 Cherokee—nearly one-fifth of the Cherokee population—died in camps by the river waiting for the journey to resume. To learn more about this march, you can visit the office of the Northern Cherokee Nation of the Old Louisiana Territory on Independence Street (Tues through Sat). You can also visit Trail of Tears State Park, located approximately 10 miles north of Cape Girardeau on Highway 177.

On US 61 South watch the signs for **Lambert's Cafe** (2305 E. Malone, Sikeston; 573-471-4261; throwedrolls.com), home of "throwed rolls." Lambert's is a most unusual place. Yes, they do throw rolls there.

It all began on a busy day in May 1976 when passing rolls real nicelike got too slow and a customer hollered, "Just throw me the *x*#_ thing!" Before you could say "thank you kindly," others cried out for service, and they have been throwing rolls at Lambert's ever since.

The folks here take control of your dinner needs—and control is the right word (got to have it when you're lobbing a long one). Want another roll? Sing out and look alive, because one will come whizzing by. To complement the rolls thrown your way, another ladleful of sorghum (Missouri's answer to Vermont maple syrup) will be slopped onto your roll, which is already dripping butter. This will require a trip to the restroom to unstick your fingers. Lambert's is fun—if you like noise, confusion, and a lot of food and attention from the waiters. If your plate begins to look empty, someone comes by with a ladle of beans, fried okra, or applesauce and plops it in the middle of your plate; when you finish dinner, you will be full. Very, very full. Then you will discover that Lambert's is famous for the size of their slices of homemade pie and cobbler. The drinks are served in gallon mason jars, and the atmosphere is a madhouse on a good day, but it's a spot you can talk about for years. Hours are 10:30 a.m. until 9 p.m. or so 7 days a week.

Old Mountain Region

Now you have a choice—go south to the Bootheel region or loop back up toward St. Louie. West on US 60 toward Dexter, the flat, Kansas-like real estate will begin to curve again in the distance.

Maybe you saw geese in the air and heard their wild cries as you ate your frog's legs. A short trip will take you through **Paxico** to **Mingo National Wildlife Refuge,** a vital 21,676-acre link in the chain of refuges along the Mississippi flyway.

The hills flatten into wetlands and plant varieties change visibly. Mingo Swamp was formed some 18,000 years ago when the Mississippi abandoned its bed, leaving an oxbow that filled in with dense swamp species. Abundant artifacts point to the area's use by Native Americans, drawn here by swamp-loving wildlife. (No artifacts can be removed from Mingo, however, so arrowhead hunters, take note.)

The area offers a brand-new boardwalk nature trail with 7 interpretive stations and a chance to see wildlife in its natural habitat. There is a resident waterfowl flock as well as thousands of seasonal migrants, and 2 active bald eagle nests are located on the refuge. Be sure to stop by the refuge visitor center before heading into the swamp (especially during the winter months), not only to let someone know where you are going, but also to enjoy the interpretive displays. The trails are accessible for all, including those with disabilities. It's pretty impressive.

Together with the adjacent Duck Creek Wildlife Area, a state wildlife management area, this is the largest hardwood swamp remaining in the state. Lake Wappapello is also nearby; watch for signs.

If you didn't expect to find a museum of fine art in the Ozarks, you're in for a surprise. The **Margaret Harwell Art Museum** (421 N. Main St.; 573-686-8002; mham.org) in **Poplar Bluff** boasts a growing collection of works by contemporary Missouri artists. Housed in a beautiful 1883 home, the museum has mounted one-man shows by important artists such as sculptor Ernest Trova, Swedish artist Anders Zorn, and Missourian Thomas Hart Benton. There is no charge to view the 2 exhibits. The museum focuses on themes ranging from contemporary photography to fiber art and recognizes the importance of the native arts of the Ozark region. It has held exhibits of folk art, including quilting and basket making. It is the only art center within a 90-mile radius and the only art museum within 150 miles of Poplar Bluff. Docents conduct regular tours of the exhibit. The museum is closed Mon. Hours are Tues through Fri noon to 4 p.m., Sat and Sun 1 to 4 p.m. Tours are by appointment only.

But that's not all this fun little city has to offer. **Fisherman's Net,** 8815 Hwy. T (573-222-8083; fishermansnet.net), 2 miles south of the dam in nearby Lake Wappapello, is a restaurant that can be recommended on a first-person basis. Not only that, but the person in question tasted each and every thing on the menu. Well, okay, it was a group of about 15 people who decided that they would just try it all. And they did. If you have never tried fried cabbage, fried corn on the cob, or fried green tomatoes,

trivia

The Margaret Harwell Art Museum is housed in a home built by James Dalton, who invented the 10-key calculator. The home was later purchased for Poplar Bluff with money donated by Harwell.

this is the place to do it. Just appetizers, of course, but wait! Here come the fried catfish fillets, country-fried steak, and frog legs. Hush puppies begin to appear by the basketful. Oh my, save room to try the seafood platter (crab cake, peel-and-eat shrimp, clam strips, and the above-mentioned frog legs and catfish). Too much fried food? Did I mention the baby back ribs? Shrimp scampi, prime rib, steak, or crab legs should do the trick. Seriously, the whole smoked pork loin with sweet potato smothered in brown sugar and butter will fill the bill nicely, too. There's still room for dessert, isn't there? The dessert du jour on our visit was old-fashioned strawberry shortcake with real whipped cream. Okay, it was a lie. We didn't taste everything; we didn't have room for dessert. There is lots more. The Net is open Wed through Sun from 6 a.m. for breakfast to 9 p.m. All the food is cooked to order, so don't be in a hurry.

The **Lake Wappapello Outdoor Theatre** next door to the Fisherman's Net comes alive on Fri and Sat nights at 6:30 from May through Oct with live bluegrass and gospel music. There is no admission fee but donations are appreciated. Bring your lawn chair and settle in to enjoy the music. When it rains, everyone moves to the music barn.

Stop by **Bullwinkles Lounge, Rustic Lodge, and RV Park** (399 Hwy. T, Poplar Bluff; 573-778-9278; bullwinklespub.com), where owner Mike

Bridges will let you park your rig in the RV park, fix you a drink, and let you play pool amid the amazing collection of "curious articles" suspended from the ceiling and walls. In good weather you can enjoy barbecue at the outside beer garden or screened gazebo. The lodge has 16 hotel rooms as well. Pub hours are 11:30 a.m. to 1:30 a.m.

For just a quick barbecue fix, **Myrtle's Place Backalley BBQ** (109 N. Broadway, Poplar Bluff; 573-785-9203) has carry-out as well as the restaurant there in town. Owners Debbie and Tommy Sliger have it all, including breakfast. If you call in advance they will cook you a ham, turkey, pork butt, ribs, or chicken for your next get-together. Hours are Mon through Fri from 5 a.m. (yes, that's a.m.!) to 3 p.m. and on Sat until 2 p.m. Poplar Bluff isn't all fried and barbecue, though. You can *mangiare benne* at Castello's Ristorante (2775 N. Westwood Blvd.; 573-776-1701; castellosonline.com), which serves old-country Italian food just like Nana Ginni Castello taught the family to make. Being Italian myself, I can recommend the sauce. You can do Castello's for breakfast Mon through Fri 6:30 to 9:30 a.m., Sat 7 to 11 a.m., and Sun 7 to 11:30 a.m. Or go for dinner Mon through Thurs 5 to 9 p.m., Fri and Sat 5 to 10 p.m. Closed Sun. **Tony's,** the bar at Castello's, is open Mon to Sat from 5 p.m. (happy hour 5 to 7 p.m.).

There's Mexican, too. **El Acapulco** (2260 N. Westwood Blvd.; 573-776-7000) has a huge menu (the sizzling fajitas come to the table on very hot skillets) and it is open 7 days a week from 11 a.m. until 10 p.m.

Bootheel Region

You are in Missouri's Bootheel now—not really the Midwest anymore, more like the South.

Southeast of Sikeston you'll find hills that really roll. **Big Oak Tree State Park** tells the story of the 1811 New Madrid earthquake, which altered the topography of the southeast lowlands. All the land from Cape Girardeau south to Helena, Arkansas, sank from 10 to 50 feet, flooding most of what is now New Madrid, Pemiscot, and Dunklin Counties. Rich Bootheel forests were converted to swampland, providing temporary protection for the giant oak that gave the park its name. You may see trees 120 to 130 feet tall. Enjoy a bayou setting for picnics or fishing. Big Oak Tree is east off Highway 102.

Nearby **Towosahgy State Historic Site** (off Highway 77) is 64 acres of prehistory. Archaeologists believe the site was inhabited between AD 1000 and AD 1400. Although other groups had lived in this area before that time, their societies did not reach such a highly organized level as that of the Indians at Towosahgy. Experts believe their use of the Mississippi for trade and transportation contributed to this advancement. The river was the link between Towosahgy and the ceremonial center near the present site of Cahokia, Illinois.

Cotton fields join wheat fields as you approach **New Madrid** (that's pronounced MAD-rid, much more Midwestern than Spanish) on I-55. The Mississippi River Observation Deck offers a panoramic view of the New Madrid oxbow; 8 miles of river are visible from the top of the most perfect oxbow on the Mississippi.

The oldest city west of the Mississippi (see, there's that claim again) has something for everyone. Begin at 1 Main St. This building, on the banks of the Mississippi near the observation deck, was once the First and Last Chance Saloon. There were no roads to New Madrid; all the traffic came off the mighty river. Here was the first—and last—chance to get a drink back in 1783. It is now the **New Madrid Historical Museum.**

New Madrid looks sleepy, dreaming away beside the river. It looks safe. It looks as if nothing much could happen here—indeed, as if nothing much ever has. If that's what you think when you see the place, you're wrong.

It balances precariously on one of the most active earthquake faults on the continent. In 1811 the balance shifted. The earth shrugged. The mighty Mississippi was suddenly dammed and ran backward, boats broke up and sank at their moorings, homes disintegrated before their owners' horrified eyes. John James Audubon recounted a hilarious—if

swampattacks nomore

In Missouri's early days, the lowlands around the Bootheel were known as the "Big Swamp" because they were covered with stagnant waters of marshes, swamps, and bayous. There were mosquitoes everywhere that were the deadly enemies of settlers. A series of earthquakes in 1811 and 1812 further discouraged settlers. Today "Swamp-east Missouri" has been changed—through drainage projects—to some of the most productive land in the state.

frightening—tale of a wedding party broken up by the quake, and the naturalist John Bradbury described it in harrowing scientific detail as he calmly watched the earth come apart. The quake was so violent that it rang church bells in Boston.

All is not peace and quiet, even now. There is a measurable tremor on the seismographs almost every day that can be felt by local folks. The Center for Earthquake Studies at Southeast Missouri State University informs us that a major quake is not just possible, but inevitable; stresses within the earth slowly mount until something has to give. When it does, the area of damage will be more than 20 times that affected by a California quake because of the underlying geologic conditions—the ground will literally liquefy.

trivia

The city of Kennett here in the Bootheel is proud of its daughter, singer Sheryl Crow, who attended Mizzou before launching her career.

Residents have developed a wonderful gallows humor—you'd have to! T-shirts read, with a certain quirky pride, "It's our fault" and "Visit New Madrid—while it's still here." So, you want real excitement? Head for New Madrid. (Of course, the author files a disclaimer here. If there's a quake while you're in town, it's "not my fault.")

While in New Madrid, visit the ***Hunter-Dawson Home and Historic Site.*** Built in 1859 by William Washington Hunter, this crisp white house with its ornate trim and contrasting shutters recalls a more genteel era. The costumed guides who answer all your questions treat you with that special Southern charm and add to the atmosphere. A small admission fee is charged.

As you continue south from Sikeston and New Madrid, the land becomes flat bottomland. Southern-style cotton, soybeans, and peaches are the important crops here. From Kennett and Malden on the west to Hayti and Caruthersville on the east, hospitality is just what you would expect in this area of Southern heritage, and Missouri begins to feel like Dixie. Welcome, y'all.

Places to Stay in Southeast Missouri

*has restaurant

ST. LOUIS

Hyatt Regency Downtown
1 St. Louis Station
(314) 231-1234
Moderate

Red Roof Inn
11837 Lackland Rd.,
Westport
(314) 991-4900 or
(800) 843-7663
Inexpensive

Ritz-Carlton, St. Louis (Clayton)
100 Carondelet Plaza
(314) 863-6300 or
(800) 241-3333
Expensive

St. Union Station Drury
201 S. 20th St. Inn
(314) 231-3900
Inexpensive

CUBA

Motel 6
97 Ozark Dr.
(573) 885-0100
Inexpensive

Super 8 Motel
I-44 & Hwy 19
(573) 885-2087
Inexpensive

PILOT KNOB

Ft. Davidson Motel
Highway 21 & V
(573) 546-7427
Inexpensive

EUREKA

Holiday Inn at Six Flags
I-44 and Allentown Road
(800) 782-8108
Inexpensive

SULLIVAN

***Econo Lodge**
307 N. Service Rd.
(573) 468-3136
Inexpensive

VIENNA

Scenic 63 RV Park and Motel
Highway 63 South
(573) 422-3907
Inexpensive

FARMINGTON

***Days Inn**
1400 Liberty St.
(314) 756-8951 or
(800) DAYS INN
Inexpensive

LESTERVILLE

Black River Family Restaurant & Motel
Highway 21
(573) 637-2600
Inexpensive

PERRYVILLE

Days Inn
1500 Liberty St.
(573) 547-1091
Inexpensive

CAPE GIRARDEAU

Drury Lodge
104 S. Vantage Dr.
(573) 334-7151
(free hot breakfast buffet)
Inexpensive

Holiday Inn
3253 William St.
(573) 334-4261
Inexpensive

STE. GENEVIEVE

Family Budget Inn
17030 New Berman Rd.
(573) 543-2272
Inexpensive

JACKSON

Drury Inn
225 Drury Ln.
(573) 243-9200
(quick-start breakfast, free evening cocktails, cable)
Inexpensive

POPLAR BLUFF

Super 8 Motel
2831 N. Westwood Blvd.
(573) 785-0176
Inexpensive

SIKESTON

Holiday Inn
120 S. Interstate Dr.
(573) 481-9500
Inexpensive

NEW MADRID

Super 8 Motel
I-55, exit 40, Marston
(573) 643-9888
Inexpensive

Places to Eat in Southeast Missouri

ST. LOUIS

LoRusso's Cucina
3121 Watson (on The Hill)
(314) 647-6222
lorussos.com
Moderate

WASHINGTON

Cowan's Restaurant
114 Elm St.
(636) 239-3213
Inexpensive

NEAR DIXON

The Point Steakhouse
Highway 28
(573) 759-6100
Inexpensive

SOUTH OF VIENNA

Maryland's Restaurant
Highway 63 at 13448
Maries Rd. 325
(573) 422-9918
Inexpensive

FARMINGTON

Spokes Pub & Grill
1627 W. Columbia St.
(573) 756-6220
Inexpensive

CAPE GIRARDEAU

Cedar Street Restaurant & Bar
104 Vantage Dr.
(573) 332-7427
Inexpensive

Port Cape
19 N. Water
(573) 334-0954
Inexpensive

NEW MADRID

Rosie's Colonial Restaurant & Tavern
Highway 61 North
(573) 748- 7783
Inexpensive

ROLLA

Alex's Pizza
122 W. 8th St.
(573) 364-2669
Inexpensive

Gordoz
1212 Hwy. 72
(573) 364-2780
gordozrestaurant.com
Inexpensive

Hickory Pit BBQ
201 W. Hwy. 72
(573) 364-4838
Inexpensive

FINDING HELPFUL VISITOR INFORMATION

Lebanon
lebanonmissouri.org
(417) 588-3256

New Madrid
mo-newmadrid.civicplus.com
(573) 748-2866

St. Louis
explorestlouis.com
(800) 325-7962

SOUTHWEST MISSOURI

Mark Twain National Forest covers thousands of acres of southwest Missouri. Hundreds of miles of hiking and horseback trails free you from even the small, state-maintained highways. If you wander too far off the beaten path here, you will find yourself lost in the woods (and Missouri's bright bluebirds and crimson cardinals will clean up your trail of bread crumbs).

Many of the lovely, quick-running streams are designated National Scenic Riverways, and the "Tri-Lakes" area has water, water everywhere. Resort towns are crowded in the summer and deserted in winter. Spring and fall (while school's in session) are just right for exploration. Campgrounds and canoe rentals are everywhere, and there are both gentle rivers for floating and whitewater for adventure.

If caves fascinate you, if you like spectacular rock formations, or if you collect rocks or minerals, southwest Missouri will keep you busy. Truitt's Cave at Lanagan, Ozark Wonder Cave at Noel, the Tiff Mines near Seneca, and the Carthage Marble Quarry at Carthage are a few spots you'll want to check out, along with Fantastic Caverns, at 4872 N. FR 125, Springfield.

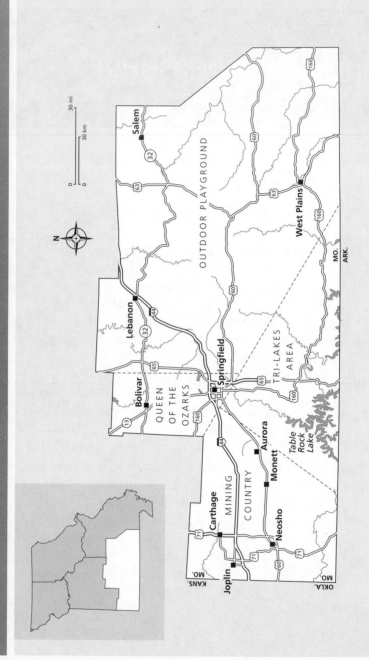

SOUTHWEST MISSOURI

Bed-and-breakfast fans can write Glen Cameron at Ozark Mountain Country Bed & Breakfast Service, Box 295, Branson, MO 65616. You can call him, too, at (417) 334-4720 or (800) 321-8594 for a list of B&Bs in the area. Reach him online at camerons-crag.com. More about Glen later.

Queen of the Ozarks

The hub of southwest Missouri is *Springfield,* the state's third-largest city, on I-44. Its location on the spacious, grassy uplands of Grand Prairie and Kickapoo Prairie, the rural landscape of the Springfield Plain, is one of the most beautiful in Missouri.

Here's a happy combination of forests, running water, and magnificent rock outcrops dotting a farmland that resembles the bluegrass area of Kentucky. Herefords, Black Angus, Charolais, and Simmental graze in the cleared uplands. Lespedezas, orchard grass, and fescue glaze the gently rolling pastures with green. The city website is springfieldmissouri.org.

If you are an antiques hunter, Springfield's Commercial Street Historic District is a good place to wander around. S. Campbell Street and Boonville Avenue shops just north of Park Central Square and the stores just below the square on South Street are all filled with antiques, too.

Okay, **Bass Pro Shops Outdoor World** at 1935 S. Campbell—a major intersection in Springfield—is rather on the track. It bills itself as the world's greatest sporting-goods store, then lives up to that boast. How many sports shops have a two-story log cabin right in the store? Or a sumptuous restaurant like Hemingway's, serving lobster dinner and a glass of fine wine in front of a room-size aquarium (with white-bellied sharks smiling through the glass and a 15-foot eel hiding in the filter system)? You just gotta love this place and you can spend hours here (all free!).

Across the aerial walkway from Hemingway's is the old-fashioned Tall Tales Barbershop. There is original wildlife art, a museum of the outdoors, trophy animals by the hundreds, and the biggest live bass in captivity. You can buy a hand-knit sweater, get wet beside an indoor waterfall, practice with your new shotgun in the shooting range downstairs, and buy a pair of gym shoes or a fishing rod. Just plan on spending a couple hours when you go in, and take a camera—there are photo opportunities indicated everywhere; you can pose with 10-foot black bears or tiny fawns. Call (417) 887-7334 or visit the website at basspro.com for hours.

From Bass Pro, go east on Sunshine until you come to Kentwood. Turn right onto Kentwood and you'll be at *Nearly Famous Deli & Pasta House* (1828 S. Kentwood; 417-883-3403; nearlyfamous.net). This family-owned restaurant turns out the most scrumptious of soups (try the chunky tomato, a daily house specialty), salads, sandwiches, dinner items, and heavenly desserts that will make you wonder why this restaurant is not called the Famous Deli. My favorite combo is tomato soup and an egg salad sandwich; both are memorable. Hours are 11 a.m. to 9 p.m. Mon through Sat.

battleplunges missouriintowar

Located 10 miles southwest of Springfield is the site of the Battle of Wilson's Creek, which occurred August 10, 1861, and marked the beginning of the Civil War in Missouri. The park has an interactive visitor center featuring a movie and a battle map. You can take a self-tour or a guided tour or bring your horse and ride the trails of Wilson's Creek.

You will notice a Chinese restaurant on almost every corner in Springfield. This town is known as "the home of cashew chicken." This specialty is on every menu, so just pick a restaurant and try this Ozarks invention (yes, seriously).

If you're in the mood for Italian, then you are in luck. Also just south of Bass Pro, *Digiacinto's Italian Restaurant* (2259 S. Campbell St.; 417-882-5166) has really good Sicilian food. On weekends, soft piano music accompanies dinner. Hours are 11 a.m. to 9 p.m. Tues through Thurs and Fri and Sat until 9:30 p.m.

Springfield is a major city, but as in most big cities, there are hidden treasures. Gary and Paula Blankenship's *Walnut Street Inn Bed and Breakfast* (900 E. Walnut; 417-864-6346 or 800-593-6346) has a quiet ambience to counter the big-city feel. Each of the 12 rooms includes a private bath, some with original porcelain antique fixtures, hardwood floors, and antique furnishings. Ozark specialties such as persimmon muffins and walnut bread are featured along with a full breakfast. The inn now offers something even more tempting: in-room massage from a certified masseuse! They also have a two-person steam bath. What a fine weekend retreat this has turned out to be. Rates are $99 to $179 per night for 2 people.

The inn caters to business travelers and an additional phone line is in each suite for computers. In the main house and in the carriage house, Wi-Fi is available. The new AA baseball stadium is located just 2 blocks north of the inn on John Q. Hammons Parkway, now the home park of the Springfield Cardinals, a minor league team affiliated with the St. Louis Cardinals. If you want a more complete view, call up the inn's website at walnutstreetinn.com.

The art of pastry making is alive and well in the Ozarks at ***Elle's Patisserie*** (1454 E. Cherry St., Springfield; 417-832-2171). This is the type of French bakery that specializes in pastries and sweets, such as chocolate truffles infused with Copper Run rum. Elle's also offers baked goods including croissants, cakes, cookies, French baguettes, and cream puffs. It is open Tues through Thurs from 7 a.m. (when is a pastry any better than early in the morning in a Paris cafe overlooking the Seine . . . ah, but I digress) to 2 p.m., Fri from 8 a.m. to 9 p.m., and Sat from 8 a.m. to 9 p.m. Elle's also serves French press coffee and ice cream, too.

The circa 1856 ***Gray/Campbell Farmstead*** in Nathanael Greene Park (2400 S. Scenic; 417-725-4921; graycampbellfarmstead.org) is the oldest house in Springfield. Guides present the history of the farmstead and conduct tours of the log kitchen, granary, two-crib barn, and family cemetery. It is open during Apr and Oct on Sun from 1:30 to 4:30 p.m.; May through Sept, Sat and Sun from 1:30 to 4:30 p.m.; or by appointment.

Also in this park is the ***Mizumoto Japanese Stroll Garden,*** a 7.5-acre stroll around 3 small lakes with extensive landscaping. There is a teahouse, a moon bridge, and other features unique to a Japanese garden. It is open from Apr through Oct, Fri through Mon from 11 a.m. to 7:30 p.m.

An outstanding nature center, designed by the Missouri Department of Conservation, is at 4600 S. Chrisman (417-888-4237). Want to know how to tell a hawk from a heron when they're far overhead? One of the volunteers

TOP RECOMMENDATIONS IN SOUTHWEST MISSOURI

will show you silhouettes suspended from the ceiling that correspond to identifying shapes on the floor. Another room invites you into the dark with displays that light up—or sing out—as you press a button or break a light beam. See a barred owl, hear a whip-poor-will, watch a flying squirrel—it's all here—3 miles of nature trails take you through Ozark woodlands—80 acres of hilly wilderness—and a small bog; cross genuine suspension bridges and learn while you take in the fresh air.

Springfield is a mecca for watercolorists. For more than 40 years, the **Springfield Art Museum** (417-837-5700) has been the locus for Water-color USA, one of the most prestigious shows in the nation. Every June and July the museum displays the best and the brightest; you may browse or buy at 1111 Brookside Dr. (You'll know you're close when you see the large yellow sculpture called *Sun Target*; local kids call it the *French Fries.*) The museum owns a fine permanent collection of original works. Visit at any time of the year. Museum hours are Sun from 1 to 5 p.m., Tues, Wed, Fri, and Sat from 9 a.m. to 5 p.m., and Thurs from 9 a.m. to 8 p.m. The **Landers,** at 311 E. Walnut, is the home of the Springfield Little Theatre, which features

civilwarstrife

Missouri gave 109,000 men to the Union cause and about 30,000 men to the Confederacy. Vicious guerrilla action terrorized the state, especially near the Kansas border. The Battle of Wilson's Creek near Springfield was one of the bloodiest of the Civil War.

talented actors from around the Ozarks. Kathleen Turner and Brad Pitt got their starts here. In 1909 theater architect Carl Boller designed the theater to look like a jewel box and a cartouche. It has a high, curved ceiling resembling a crown. The theater has been refurbished to its original splendor. There are the original wooden armrests and floral ironwork on the seats. The ribs going up the cartouche are like a crown inset with jewels, where the lights sparkle surrounded by 14-karat gold leaf and sterling painted moldings. The baroque decor and heavy draperies give it an elegantly royal feel. The $400,000 renovation of this magnificent theater alone is worth seeing, but the fact that it also offers a 6-show main season (each show running three weeks), the Springfield Opera, the Springfield Ballet, and the Mid-America Singers makes it all the more worthy of a visit. Call the box office at (417) 869-1334 for current productions, or visit springfieldlittletheatre.org.

You will want to call Kathy Adamson and visit her shop, **Woodland Carvings** (2269 N. FR 45, Bois D'Arc; 417-672-2278), while you are in the area. Kathy carves original and functional art—doors, screen doors, beds, fireplace mantels, lamps—as well as gift and art items. Her hours are irregular because of her show schedule, but it is worth the effort to contact her and see what she does. Her outdoor and western art has evolved from hand-carved deck plates and yokes that are used as braces on canoes, as well as intricately carved canoe paddles. She carves river gods with long flowing beards (that resemble her husband, Sonny) for the yokes of canoes. Kathy doesn't just carve canoes, however: She works "relief carving" on flat wood and creates three-dimensional scenes. Her river series showing life along the

"Whistle Stop" Trail

The **Frisco Highline Trail** is the KATY Trail of southwest Missouri. The 36-mile trail is now open from Springfield to Bolivar. The most beautiful part is the 18-mile stretch from Walnut Grove to Bolivar; it winds its way through pasture and forest, over 16 trestles, and right through La Petite Gemme Prairie Natural Area. This is the second-longest hiking, biking, and equestrian trail in the state. But here's a trivia note you might enjoy: It is the route once traveled by Harry S Truman as a precursor to his "Whistle Stop Campaign" in 1948. For more information about the trail, go to friscohighlinetrail.org.

river looks real enough to walk into. She carves mantels, clocks, and doors. She began by carving pieces for her own canoe, and the results were so beautiful that others asked her to personalize their crafts.

Kathy uses teak, butternut, mahogany, cedar, and walnut, relying solely on her own strength and sharp tools to create the delicate layers in the wood. She uses earth-toned artist oils and stains to add a bit of color to the carvings while allowing the grain to show through.

Outdoor Playground

Just outside Springfield on US 65 is another kind of mecca—tiny *Galloway* is wall-to-wall antiques. It's as if the town had been invaded by aliens selling oldies; nearly every building and home is now a shop. Find everything from a vine- and thorn-wrapped birdhouse (to discourage cats, of course) to European china, but don't stop before you get to the flea market a half-mile or so north of the other shops. Here are two floors of great bargain flea-market antiques.

West of Springfield in *Republic* you can tour *General Sweeny's Museum of Civil War History* (5228 S. Hwy. ZZ; 417-732-1224; civilwartraveler.bravepages.com/GenSweeney_2/GSMP1.htm) and see thousands of items from the bloody war fought in Missouri, Arkansas, Kansas, and Indian Territory. In this area families were split between blue and gray uniforms, and bands of killers disguised in those uniforms raided cities and farms. More than 50 exhibits will show you the progression of the war here from the 1850s in "Bleeding Kansas" to the surrender of the last regiments of Confederate Missouri troops at Fort Blakely, Alabama. There are rare photos, guns, swords, flags, uniforms, and more. The museum is open from Mar through Oct, Wed through Sun 10 a.m. to 5 p.m.; Nov through Feb, Sat and Sun 10 a.m. to 5 p.m.

Head north on I-44 to *Lebanon,* a town loaded with surprises. Flea markets and antiques shops are all over the place, more than 23 at last count. The *Heartland Antique Mall* (2500 Evergreen Pkwy.; 417-532-9350; heartlandantiquemalllebanon.com) is a 40,000-square-foot, 250-dealer antiques mall voted #2 in the state as "Best Antiques Mall." Open every day from 8 a.m. until 8 p.m. And here's a good deal: The Russell Stover Candy store is next door!

Nancy Ballhagen's Puzzles (25211 Garden Crest Rd., Lebanon; 417-286-3837; missouripuzzle.com) may not be for everyone, but if you are a jigsaw puzzle fan, this is a must. Nancy Ballhagen has the only such shop in the Ozarks. They have the world's largest puzzle (18,000 pieces, which measures 6 feet by 9 feet). There are double-sided puzzles, round puzzles, and puzzles within puzzles, not to mention movie poster puzzles, postage stamp puzzles, and puzzles covering any subject you can think of. Nancy says she and her family just always liked to do puzzles, especially when the children were young, and it sort of grew into a business. More than 3,400 puzzles are

TOP ANNUAL EVENTS IN SOUTHWEST MISSOURI

MAY

Plumb Nellie Days
(417) 334-1548
downtownbranson.org

AUGUST

Ozark Empire Fair
Springfield
With live music.
(417) 833-2660

Old Soldiers and Settlers Reunion
Cassville
(417) 847-2814

Marion Days
Annual religious events for Vietnamese Catholics.
Carthage
(417) 358-7787
carthage-mo.gov

SEPTEMBER

Laura Ingalls Wilder Festival
Mansfield
(417) 924-3626

Annual Autumn Daze Craft Festival
Branson
With more than 150 crafters.
explorebranson.com/calendar/event/1938
(888) 322-2786

DECEMBER

Old Time Country Christmas
Silver Dollar City
With lights, music, and special Christmas attractions for adults and children.
(800) 952-6626

Trail of Lights at Shepherd of the Hills
Branson
A spectacular drive-through display of lights.
(417) 334-4191 or (800) 296-0463
explorebranson.com

displayed in the shop and they now are carving their own wooden puzzles. To find puzzle paradise, take exit 135 (Sleeper exit) from I-44 and follow the east outer road ¾ mile to the first mailbox on your left—you can see it from the freeway. Hours are 11 a.m. to 5 p.m. daily. Call first on Sun.

Well, maybe they don't have the only jigsaw puzzle shop in the Ozarks. Their son, Richard Ballhagen, inherited the puzzle mania from Keith and Nancy and opened **Richard's Puzzles** (23480 Route 66; 417-532-5355; rbpuzzles.com), where he makes only hand-cut wooden puzzles. Although it's still all in the family, Richard's work is different. He creates heirloom puzzles or puzzles from your favorite photograph or print. Just about anything you can imagine, he can carve. The intricately cut puzzles are made of ¼-inch wood and include a variety of special effects such as silhouette pieces, sculpted borders, or a name cut right into the puzzle for a personal touch. A slide-top wooden box for storage is included with every puzzle. He keeps odd hours because he works a full-time job as well, so call ahead for an appointment.

While you are in the Lebanon area you might want to visit **Whirlwind Ranch,** where the alpaca are part of the family. The ranch's Whirlwind Ranch Store, at 24649 Snowberry Dr., has a beautiful selection of products made from 100 percent baby alpaca fiber and blends of 70 percent alpaca and 30 percent acrylic. There are ponchos, sweaters, and blankets along with alpaca toys and teddy bears. You can even buy a pet bed stuffed with alpaca fiber for your dog or cat. In winter, there is nothing warmer than hats, scarves, ear warmers, or hiking socks made of alpaca. If you enjoy knitting, crocheting, spinning, or weaving, there is a colorful assortment of sport-weight and fingering-weight yarns, hand-dyed and made right at the ranch. Liz, Linda, and Walter Mitchko will welcome you. The website whirl-windranch.com will tell you all about the ranch. From I-44 take exit 129 and turn right to the first traffic light. Turn left onto Highway 32 East. Go about 7 miles to Snowberry Drive (the second dirt road on the left after B Highway), turn left onto Snowberry Drive, and go 2 miles—the driveway entrance is on the left at the top of the long, steep hill. Stop at the first house. Please call ahead (417-533-5280) to schedule your visit.

If you are into horses and you have your horse along, a small side trip south of I-44 on Highway J will quickly take you to **Waynesville** and the **4J Big Piney Horse Camp** (573-774-6879; 4-j.net). This is a chance to get off the road and into the woods, so bring your horses and ride over mountains, through beautiful valleys, along the edge of bluffs, through quiet forests, and along the famous Big Piney River. There are all types of fun activities for when you are enjoying time off the horse as well. The campsites have water and electricity, and Betty Laughlin does the cooking in a dining hall that seats up to 300 people. Modern restrooms, showers, and electricity are available, too, and horses are comfortable in their box stalls. Brothers Jimmy, Jay, Jeff, and Joey are partners in the operation. Sunday church services are held in the dining hall and on the trail. Camping arrangements must be made in advance, so call for camping and riding dates from May through Oct. Enjoy the thrill of feeling the wind in your hair as you ride through this Missouri paradise.

On the square in Waynesville is the *Old Stagecoach Inn Museum,* which has been totally renovated and is exactly as it was when the stage stopped here at the courthouse. It is listed on the National Register of Historic Places and is open Apr through Sept on Sat from 10 a.m. to 4 p.m. Guided tours are available.

The Cave Restaurant and Resort might be Missouri's most unusual place to eat. Park in the gravel lot at 26880 Rochester Rd. (573-765-4554; thecaverestaurantandresort.com) just a few miles from Richland, then board the van to where an elevator takes you up to the restaurant, located inside a cave. It took five years of incredible labor and five years of jackhammer and shovel to remove 160 tons of rock to make enough room to seat 200 people in this former resort dance hall. Renovators tried not to change the cave's appearance too much and were quite successful. A dehumidifier keeps the restaurant dry, and small waterfalls into a goldfish pond allow natural water to drip from the ceiling. The restaurant is a destination for river traffic, too. You can float to the bottom and walk up the bank. The dress code is casual. If you want to spend some time here, there are rustic little cabins and fishing (no permit required because it's a private lake). Cabins are $80; campsites are $10; RV parking is $20 without hookups. There are several combination packages for float trips, cabins, and dinner, so call for more information. Summer hours are 11:30 a.m. to 8:30 p.m. 7 days a week. The Cave is closed during the winter.

Fort Leonard Wood is the home of the US Army Corps of Engineers. It is also the home of the Army Engineering Center and the *US Army*

Engineer Museum. The fort covers about 63,000 acres in the Ozarks about 130 miles southwest of St. Louis on I-44 near Waynesville. A recipe for creamed chipped beef on toast, called SOS by the soldiers who had to eat it, is tacked on the wall of a restored mess hall, one of several "temporary" wooden buildings built during World War II. A field kitchen lists the fort's daily food requirements in 1943, including 4,750 pounds of bacon, 47 gallons of vinegar, and 105 gallons of syrup.

walkingonair

Eminence is the home of astronaut Tom Akers and his family. Akers, who has had four space flights to date, holds the record for the number of hours of EVAs (extravehicular activities, or space walks), most of that time accrued while helping to repair the Hubble Space Telescope.

Colonel Akers has experienced more than 800 hours of space flight, bringing his total EVA time to 29 hours and 40 minutes. He was a member of the first three-person EVA and the longest EVA—8.5 hours—in history.

The museum's oldest treasure is a signet ring that belonged to Lysimachus, an engineer general who served Alexander the Great in about 330 BC. The museum walks people through a chronological history of the corps. There are several specialized galleries. Many of the temporary mobilization buildings, two-story wooden barracks familiar to soldiers at every post in the world and built to last about 10 years, have been restored to create typical company areas. A supply room with a wood-burning stove, racks for M1 rifles and .45-caliber pistols, and entrenching tools would bring a tear to a supply sergeant's eye.

The history of the corps, however, dates from the Revolutionary War. There's a 1741 muzzle-loading cannon that the French lent to the Continental army, and a shovel and ax dating from the 1781 Battle of Yorktown, the first engineering victory of army engineers who built fortifications and trenches into British positions. The oldest unit in the US Army is the 101st Engineer Battalion of the Massachusetts National Guard, established in 1636 as the East Regiment.

Another display demonstrates low tide at Omaha Beach during the D-Day invasion of June 6, 1944, with an engineer disposing of German mines that would have been a danger to Allied ships.

Children can take the wheel of a restored pilothouse, US *Snag Boat No. 13,* which kept the Mississippi River clear for more than 50 years. Other hands-on activities include a land-mine detector. Gun enthusiasts will enjoy the 19th-century Gatling gun, an 1819 Flintlock rifle, an 1816 Springfield .69-caliber musket, and many small arms from more recent wars.

The museum is at the corner of Nebraska and South Dakota Avenues. Hours are 10 a.m. to 4 p.m. Mon through Sat. Admission is free but donations are accepted. Call (573) 596-0780 for more information.

St. Roberts is a popular tourist area for visiting military and families attending basic-training graduations at Fort Leonard Wood, which is the home of the Maneuver Support Center of the US Army.

Wander down Highway VV from Licking and enjoy the rugged countryside, which contains some of the largest springs in the world. The Jacks Fork River, Alley Spring with its restored **Old Red Mill,** and the Current River near **Eminence** provide year-round canoeing. (The spring water is a consistent 58 degrees Fahrenheit year-round.)

Highway 19 is a rustic stretch of the Ozark Plateau. The hills are steep and the road curvy, so your only choice is a slow drive across narrow bridges over gleaming waterways. You can't pass anyone on Highway 19, so you may as well relax and enjoy the view. This scenic highway has its share of people there just to see the towering pines that create a lush green canopy that shades the roadway. The highway snakes from near Hannibal to the Arkansas state line. You can drive from Hermann to Eminence while stopping at little shops for ice cream, sandwiches, and shopping. The views are enchanting, so take your time and slowpoke along.

Missouri's southwestern rivers—quick-running, spring-fed, and bone-chillingly cold—are so beautiful they bring a lump to your throat. In fact, the Current, the Eleven Point, and the Jacks Fork have been designated **Ozark National Scenic Riverways.** It is Missouri's largest national park.

Generations of canoeists and trout fishermen know these secluded waters. You can spend the day without seeing another soul, then camp on a quiet sandbar at day's end and listen to the chuck-will's-widows and owls call while your fire lights the riffles with bronze. Pick fresh watercress from these icy waters to garnish the trout that sizzles in lemon butter on your grill, and know that life gets no better than this. There are plenty of rental outfits; pick up brochures anywhere. Ask about Bluff Hole, a hidden swimming hole where the Jacks Fork River widens. There is deep water at the base of the rock shelf and gravelly shallows near the bank. The hole is hidden away at the end of a tree-shaded path and has been a favorite of swimmers for generations.

Springs gush from beneath solid rock, slowly carving themselves a cave. Early residents built mills here to produce flour, cornmeal, and sawn lumber. There's as much natural history as human history along these bright rivers.

The crystal-clear waters of the spring-fed Current River drift past rocky bluffs and shorelines thick with wildflowers. Schools of darters flash by in the cold water (water temperatures range from 53 to 57 degrees Fahrenheit year-round). This gentle wilderness is a favorite canoeing and tubing area for Midwesterners. Even beginners can navigate the waters without getting too wet except by choice. Paddle hard around the occasional rootwad, an area of ripped-up tree roots that may create some whitewater—or simply get out and push the canoe past it. Most stretches of the river are rated Class I, as easy as it gets. The gravel bars are fine places to pull out and have lunch or even to camp for the night. Only owls and the leaf rustle of small creatures break the silence. The tranquil moss-covered hillsides are a peaceful escape from the busy world back home. At some points along the river, the water turns a rich blue-green as it gets wider and deeper, sometimes as deep as 25 feet.

The half-day trip from Weymeyer put-in to Van Buren is an easy and beautiful route. A few miles before the Van Buren Bridge is Watercress Park, the site of a single Civil War battle—with trenches and grave sites—where the Union Army held the Confederates at bay across the river one cold night. At the pull-out spot just past the Van Buren Bridge, you can leave your canoe on the beach and let the outfitters know you are back.

Alley Spring Mill is called the most picturesque spot in the state. Some 80 million gallons of water a day flow through here, and the Red Mill has been restored to working order.

Big Spring is the largest concentration of springs in the world—a mystery to hydrologists, who do not understand the large volume of water. Beautiful rivers gush right out of the ground from the base of spectacular rock bluffs and create the most consistent, spring-fed, crystal-clear rivers in the country. Round Spring Cave is just off Highway 19.

If you have horses, *Cross Country Trail Rides* on Highway 19 East, Eminence, has a week planned for you. You can take the whole family on a cross-country trail ride from Apr through Dec. Jim and Jane Smith have spent more than 40 years perfecting the week's adventure. You will camp for the week on Jacks Fork River. The ride returns to the base camp every night, where 18 meals are served and entertainment is royal. Well-known country music performers entertain at a dance every night but Sun. There are horse shows, team roping events, and other sports to show off your steed. Jane says they fill up months in advance; to ensure a spot for you and your mount, call (573) 226-3492. This is a "BYOH" affair; no rental horses are available. Visit their website at crosscountrytrailride.com.

If you don't have your own horse, head for **Coldwater Ranch** (573-226-3723; coldwaterranch.com) on Highway 19 north of Eminence and turn right onto CR 208. Jim and Kathy Thomas have horses at their place and will arrange anything from an hour ride to a six-day pack trip. For the overnight trips, tents, sleeping bags, food, and beverages are provided, and your steed has a saddlebag for your personal stuff. Quarter horses and a few gaited horses range from mounts for the novice to those for the experienced riders. The ranch accepts all ages; they have had 4-year-olds and 80-year-olds. Horses are $40 per hour; overnight trips include three meals and about 10 hours of riding. Recent expansion on the ranch includes cabins and RV/camping). You can also bring your own horse and rent a stall.

A winding drive along US 160 takes you to the beautiful Eleven Point River, with its many natural springs and lovely spots for picnics. You will be surprised at the excellent roads through these wooded hills. The Between the Rivers section of the Ozark Hiking Trail covers about 30 miles. The northern entry point to this section is on US 60, approximately 3.5 miles west of Van Buren. Trailhead parking is provided for users at US 60 and at Sinking Creek Lookout Tower, about a mile west of Highway J.

The trail winds south for the first 13 miles across small tributaries that feed the Current River. Creeks with names such as Wildhorse Hollow, Devil's Run, and Big Barren flow through the area. Designed for both hikers and horses, the trail crosses a ridge that divides the Current River from the Eleven Point River along Gold Mine Hollow. The trail offers panoramic mountain views and deeply wooded areas to filter the summer sun. Deer gaze from the shadows, too. If you are a hiking enthusiast, this area is for you. Pick up a book with a listing of all the hiking trails on federal property, complete with maps, at the Federal Forest Service Office in Winona, grab your backpack, and head out.

Wooded Ozark roads stretch out before you now, with oak trees shouldering evergreens; the Doniphan Lookout Tower watches the national forest for fires here. Tune your AM radio to 1610 for Ozark Riverway information if you are headed for canoeing or camping at one of the many parks or rivers nearby.

If you have a carload of children and want a resort, the **River's Edge Resort** (573-226-3233; rivers-edge.com) is also near Eminence and offers not only rooms and cabins but also hot tubs, inner tubes, firewood, and lodging on the Ozark National Scenic Riverways at the Jacks Fork of the Current River. All of the rooms and cabins offer direct river access for floating, canoeing, fishing, tubing, swimming—whatever you want to do wet—as well as hiking, riding, cycling, picnicking, hunting, and even golfing. The river's edge has a private beach and under the shady canopy of old trees you will find a gallery of interesting iron sculptures that you won't forget. Relax is the key word, even if relaxing means doing something exciting.

Eminence Canoes, Cottages & Camp (573-226-3500 or 800-723-1387; eminencecanoescottagescamp.com) has everything you need for wilderness adventure. Rent a canoe and float on the 135 miles of the spring-fed, clear waters of the Jacks Fork and Current Rivers. Unwind in the informal cottages on 30 acres. These mini-homes have 1 to 3 bedrooms and fully equipped kitchens (and gas grills, free movies, and cable TV). Or you can camp out along the Jack's Fork River Valley in the family- and pet-friendly campgrounds.

Because of the number of campers who take this route to the wilderness, the little town of **Van Buren** on US 60 is the home of several neat shops and museums.

The **Hidden Log Cabin Museum** (305 W. John St.; 573-323-4563) is the darling of Ozark historian Wanda Newton. For many years she knew that a log cabin lay at the heart of the neat, ordinary frame house next door. She waited for the house to go on the market and spent the time buying antiques and refurbishing them. She also studied the history of the Ozarks and dreamed. Then in 1990, it happened. The old Bowen place was for sale, and she bought it and began removing decades of "improvements" from its interior.

A one-of-a-kind "yawning" fireplace of hand-cut sandstone with a huge arch rock was professionally rebuilt and the hearth made ready for cooking with a collection of early ironware. Layers of sheetrock, insulation, and ceiling tiles were removed to expose the original construction. Furniture and household goods from the 1800s were placed in the painstakingly restored home. By the spring of 1993, her work was complete. In addition to the original log cabin room, the museum also has a dining room, bedroom, kitchen, and summer kitchen, each room filled with artifacts and furnishings. But most important is the woman who has lovingly created its homelike atmosphere. Wanda knows every jewel in this jewel box. Many of the pieces of furniture are from families who lived here. The treasures span two centuries, from tools of the early 1800s, pre–Civil War books and toys, and willow furniture made by gypsies to a 1930s Zenith radio from the Depression years. Many of the items are dated—a rope bed is from 1838, and an immigrant trunk dates from 1869. Located in downtown Van Buren, the museum is a block west of the courthouse on the south side of the Float Stream Cafe at the corner of John and Ash. Hours are Mon through Sat 9 a.m. to 5 p.m. and Sun 1 to 5 p.m. Apr through Nov. There is a small admission fee.

The *Float Stream Cafe* (102 Main St.; 573-323-9606) is well worth a visit. Good food is served here. There is a special every day, 7 days a week. Friday is fried catfish day and Sunday has chicken and dumplings. The cafe is open from 5 a.m. until 9 p.m.

The main reason for being in the area is floating the Current River. There are plenty of places to rent canoes, tubes, and rafts, but one of the nicest is the *Rosecliff on the River Lodge* (1 Big Springs Rd., Van Buren; 573-323-8156; currentriverlanding.com), at the Van Buren Bridge. You can spend a full day on the river with the 22-mile Log Yard trip, which leaves at 7 a.m. Or you can take a two-day camping trip to Eminence on the Jacks Fork River. There are short 3-mile trips or longer half-day floats. Then there is the fun of tubing along Chilton Creek, and now rafts and kayaks are featured. But whatever you do, slather a lot of sunscreen on your body because you can get a world-class sunburn in an aluminum canoe on the brilliant water of the Current. The voice of experience is telling you this. Rosecliff Lodge has a good restaurant, the Blue Heron, which has a river view, as do all the rooms.

Big Spring Lodge (573-323-4423; bigspringlodgeandcabins.com) is about 4 miles from Van Buren; it is a National Park Service site on the Ozark National Scenic Riverways. Rustic log cabins with fireplaces that reflect a more relaxed pace and a dining lodge/craft shop were built by the Civilian Conservation Corps (the CCC, otherwise known as "Franklin Roosevelt's Tree Army") in the 1930s. The lodge is on the National Register, and rightly so; log, timber, rocks, and cut-stone materials and unique spatial arrangements make this an excellent example of the projects that brought work to so many in Depression-era America. Dining-room hours vary with the season.

Big Spring State Park is nearby, as are the Mark Twain National Forest and the Ozark National Riverways Tourist Information Station. Call (573) 323-4236 or write for an accurate list of trails and starting points (PO Box 490, Van Buren, MO 63965). Also, any Missouri tourism office can provide a list of hiking trails.

Big Spring is the largest single spring in the world, pouring out 277 million gallons of crystal-clear water each day—a breathtaking natural wonder you will want to photograph or draw.

The beginnings of ***Grand Gulf State Park*** (Missouri's answer to the Grand Canyon) in Thayer go back 450 million years to a time when sediment was deposited by ancient seas, forming dolomitic rock. As the area uplifted and the sea receded, water percolated down through cracks in the rock and began to dissolve passageways underneath. Streams cut their own beds on the surface of the soft rock. As air-filled caves formed and cave roofs collapsed, streams were diverted underground. The collapse of the Grand Gulf occurred within the past 10,000 years—fairly recent by a geologist's reckoning.

Today the gulf is ¾ mile wide with side walls 120 feet high. Part of the cave roof that did not collapse formed a natural bridge 75 feet high that spans 200 feet, one of the largest in the state. The park contains wheelchair-accessible overlooks with spectacular views of the chasm, a ¼-mile loop trail around the gulf, and a primitive trail across the rock bridge (don't look down). Call (573) 548-2525 for details.

West Plains is a starting point for canoeing on the North Fork River. Or you can strike off on foot into the wilderness of the Mark Twain National Forest. There's an Old Time Music, Ozark Heritage Festival (888-256-8835;

oldtimemusic.org) in June, so come to this historic downtown for music, hoedown dancing, and a jig dance competition. Of course there are the usual food booths and crafts.

Travel westbound from West Plains on US 160 to Highway 181 north to the little town of **Zanoni** if you want total peace, quiet, and privacy with nothing to disturb your sleep but the morning song of bluebirds and wrens.

Dawt Mill was established in 1897, and its water-powered buhr stone mill is still grinding grain. More than a century ago, teams of mules and horses would pull wagons filled with corn and wheat to the mill, and farmers would wait for their turn at the water-powered buhr stone mill. The cotton gin would be pumping out cleaned cotton ready to be sold or spun. While waiting for their grinding, the families would shop at the general store or use the blacksmith's skills repairing farm implements and shoeing animals. People gathered on the porch of the mill to play music in the evening and would fall asleep under their wagons while the mill ground into the wee hours of the morning.

Deep in the Ozark hills near **Ava,** a bell chimes in the early morning quiet. Trappist monks in white robes and cowls move quietly into the darkness of the chapel for morning prayers and meditation. A day begins at **Assumption Abbey** (417-683-5110; assumptionabbey.org), one of only 18 monasteries of the Trappist order in the country. The abbey is surrounded by 3,400 wooded acres. The monks seldom leave the abbey, and by their simple lives of prayer, labor, study, and solitude seek a deeper personal relationship with God. So why mention a monastery in a travel guide, you might ask? Well, although man cannot live by bread alone, a visit to the Assumption Abbey bakery is in order. To be self-supporting, as monasteries must, the monks discovered a market for fruitcakes. Now they produce more than 30,000 fruitcakes annually. Since the fruitcakes proved so popular, a new and larger bakery was added. Fresh fruit jellies and jams are also sold in the bakery store. Call the bakery at (417) 683-2258. Each cake weighs 2 pounds and is generously filled with raisins, cherries, and pineapple marinated in Burgundy. Each one is bathed with an ounce of dark rum for moistness and flavor. They bear no resemblance to the ready-made kind you get from your aunt at Christmas. They are sold by direct mail to customers throughout the US and are carried at prestigious stores such as Williams-Sonoma.

The abbey extends hospitality to men and women of all faiths. If you need a restful weekend, or counseling from the monks, you are welcome. Guests get home-cooked meals served family style by the brothers. A love offering helps defray the costs. Reservations for overnight stays are requested and donations help with the expenses. The simple quarters contain wash basins, twin beds, shared bath/shower, and a small homemade desk. Monks bring fresh soap and towels. It is a simple life. If you would like to spend a few days at this retreat, call or write Highway 5 Box 1056, Ava, MO 65608. The abbey is always closed during Jan for the monks' retreat and reflection.

Guest ranches are fun whether you are with a vanload of children or travel alone. If the abbey is too quiet for your tastes and you still want to get some brain-clearing time, mosey over to the ***Bucks and Spurs Scenic River Guest Ranch,*** also in Ava (HC71, Box 163, Ava; 417-683-2381; bucksandspurs.com), for a real Western experience. For all the details of this ranching vacation and the various packages offered, visit their website. The most popular package is the 5-night vacation Weekend packages are also available, as are family discounts. You can get some hands-on time on this 1,000-acre horse-and-cattle ranch by helping Cecil and Sonya Huff with the chores. Or you can float down Big Beaver Creek in an inner tube and study the clouds and treetops. The choice is yours. Four guest rooms sharing 2 baths are paneled in weathered barn wood. The dining room has a long table for chow time, or the Huffs will set up a picnic site when you ride the trails. Horses, tack, guides, and canoes are furnished. There's fishing and swimming or a turbulent game of horseshoes for excitement.

North on Highway 5 is tiny ***Mansfield,*** home of the ***Laura Ingalls Wilder–Rose Wilder Lane Museum and Home*** (417-924-3626; lauraingallswilderhome.com). Laura's home is just as she left it and the museum contains four handwritten manuscripts. Author of the now-famous (courtesy of television) *Little House on the Prairie,* among other books, Laura was encouraged to write by her daughter, Rose Wilder Lane, a well-known author in her own right from the early 1900s. They are buried in the Mansfield cemetery. Admission: adults $8, children up to 18 years old $4, seniors $6.

Head on to ***Mountain Grove*** for a great steak and baked sweet potato at the unusual ***Club 60*** (6773 US 60; 417-926-9954; club60steakhouse.com). The license-plate fence in front of this old 1946 tavern will catch your eye. Although drinks are served and there is a pool table, this is very much a family place. Co-owner Jim Alessi is confident to say "we offer the best steak you will ever have in Missouri." Of course he has also created over 500 specials (and still counting). Hours are Tues through Thurs 4 to 9 p.m., Fri and Sat to 10 p.m. Closed Sun and Mon.

Go west on US 60 to swing back into Springfield.

In the tiny town of *Miller,* there is an exquisite Victorian home known as *Maggie Mae's Tea Room* (206 W. 4th St.; 417-452-3299). As you partake of a wide array of luncheon specials consisting of homemade soups, salads, and entrees, save room for their special desserts. There is also a gift shop adjacent to the restaurant. Shop hours are Mon through Sat 9 a.m. to 5 p.m. Lunch is served from 11 a.m. to 2 p.m.

Mining Country

Head west on I-44 to Halltown, then slip onto Highway 96 west for *Carthage,* where the majestic 1895 Jasper County Court House stands proudly on the square, turreted like a medieval castle. Settled in the 1840s, Carthage was burned to the ground in guerrilla raids during the Civil War. The Battle of Carthage was fought July 5, 1861—16 days before the Battle of Manassas in Virginia—making it the first land battle of the Civil War. More than 8,000 men fought here, 1,000 of them German-American Union troops from St. Louis led by Colonel Franz Siegel. The rest of the soldiers were Southern sympathizers led by Missouri Governor Claiborne Jackson. Destruction of the town was total. The 1849 home named Kendrick Place, built by slaves, was one of the few homes left standing after the war. In the late 19th century, all-new homes were built here; there is an abundance of Victorian homes and more than 100 of them have been restored. This interesting piece of history can be researched more thoroughly at the *Civil War Museum* (205 Grant St., Carthage; 417-237-7060), open from 10 a.m. until 5 p.m., and at the *Victorian Era Powers Museum* (1617 W. Oak St., Carthage; 417-358-2667). The website for both the Victorian and the Powers Museums is carthage-mo.gov. The curator at the Powers Museum is Michele Hansford, and she is very knowledgeable about both the Victorian era in Carthage and the Civil War battles fought near here. Lead and zinc mines were developed after the war, and wealthy owners built magnificent homes away from the mining camps. Marble quarries provided Carthage gray marble for many large state and federal buildings. The fine old homes here bespeak prosperity. It's still a beautiful city—the courthouse, high school, and many of the churches and homes are built of the stone quarried here. (The stone is not technically marble, but a limestone that takes a high polish.) Both the courthouse and high school contain murals by Lowell Davis, one of America's best-known nature artists and a native of Carthage.

howtomake aspy

In her teens Myra Belle Shirley saw her town leveled by war. The Battle of Carthage was the first major Civil War battle, fought July 5, 1861. She became the infamous Confederate spy and outlaw Belle Starr.

Carthage has more than its share of well-known native sons and is becoming a center for artists in the area. About 18 resident artists call the city home. Internationally known zoologist and naturalist Marlin Perkins (remember *Wild Kingdom?*) was born here; you'll find a bronze sculpture of Perkins by artists Bob Tommey and Bill Snow in Central Park on Garrison Avenue.

Follow the historic-drive markers for a tour of Carthage's magnificent old mansions that have been kept so beautifully throughout the years. Innkeepers Don and Joy Sisco welcome you to their home, the imposing circa 1901 *Leggett House* (1106 Grand Ave.; 417-358-0683; bbonline.com/united-states/missouri/carthage/leggett.html). This magnificent home is in its glory again with stained glass, a mosaic-tiled solarium with a marble fountain, finely crafted woodwork, and—an elevator. Rates are $75–$180 a night, which includes a full breakfast served in the formal dining room. The best place to eat close by is the *Ranch House Restaurant* (2937 S. Grand Ave., Carthage; 417-359-5200). The father/daughter team of Susan Skaggs and Dick Fanning have something for just about any appetite, including big steaks. Hours are 11 a.m. to 9 p.m. every day but Sunday.

Jim and Jan O'Haro invite guests to join them at the *White Rose* (13001 Journey Rd.; 417-359-9253; whiterosebed-breakfast.com). The house was built in 1900 of Carthage marble and was originally a 1,000 -acre dairy farm. The front walk is 300 feet of Carthage marble leading to this beautiful three-story home. Rose, herb, cut-flower, and vegetable gardens lead you to the old carriage house. The White Rose is not an inn in the commercial sense, but a bed-and-breakfast of the European type. It is a private home open for guests to enjoy an atmosphere of warmth and comfort. As you might have guessed from the name, the family is proud of its Irish heritage. Not only do guests receive a full Irish breakfast, but tea is served at 4 p.m., and guests are given a complimentary beverage in the evening. Full-course dinners are also included in "Bed and Banquet" reservations, and ingredients used include both imported and those grown in the vegetable garden out back. The O'Haros describe it thus: "The idea is seductive and yet so simple. Who hasn't wished after a truly superb dinner . . . the kind that lingers in the memory . . . that you could just go upstairs and sink into bed instead of getting in a car and driving somewhere else? To keep the magic that surrounds the very best meals alive, you need to be able to linger, maybe to take your coffee in another room in front of a log fire, knowing that your bed is only a few steps away." Rooms are $89 to $105.

If you fancy colonial reproduction furniture, visit the **Colonial House Historic Reproductions** (348 Grant St.; 417-358-8454; colonialhousedecor .com), where every piece is authentic reproduction (is that an oxymoron?). This shop is unique to southwest Missouri. Hours are Mon through Sat 10 a.m. to 5 p.m.

Michael and Jeanne Goolsby have opened their 1893 Queen Anne Victorian to guests. The **Grand Avenue Bed & Breakfast** (1615 Grand Ave.; 417-358-7265 or 888-380-6786; grand-avenue.com) has four original stained-glass windows. All guest rooms have private baths, cable TV, telephones, and coffee service. Two have computer hookups. The first-floor room has a king-size bed and Jacuzzi for $99 (weekdays). On the second floor of this stately home, there's the Hawthorne Room ($119 weekends) with a two-person Jacuzzi, the Alcott Room ($77–$88 on weekends), and the Mark Twain Room ($88–$104 weekends), which can also be made into a suite. The Goolsbys also serve a full country breakfast (the specialty is orange nutmeg french toast) with sausage or bacon.

trivia

The town of Noel gets popular every year at Christmas—at least its post office gets popular—as people send letters and cards here for postmarks. It's actually pronounced "Nole." South of Noel is Bluff Dwellers Cave, a well-known tourist attraction that was 250 million years, give or take a million, in the making. It has drawn cave seekers since 1927.

Joplin is the end of the Missouri portion of old Route 66 and has been a stopping point on cross-country travel for many decades—in fact, since 1889, when Joplin City was named for the Rev. Harris G. Joplin, a Tennessean settler. The abandoned tailing piles and mine shafts scattered about the town and the elegant homes just west of the downtown area are reminders of the city's mining era. Mineral collectors are drawn to the abandoned mine dumps and chert piles and to the Tri-State Mineral Museum, one of the best museums of its kind in the state.

The Joplin Historical Society preserves much of the city's history at the **Dorothea B. Hoover Historical Museum,** located in Schifferdecker Park at the intersection of 7th Street and Schifferdecker Park, Joplin (and adjacent to the Tri-State Mineral Museum). Hours are Tues 10 a.m. to 7 p.m., Wed through Sat 10 a.m. to 5 p.m., and Sun 2 to 5 p.m. Call for holiday hours: (417) 623-1180 or (417) 623-2341.

On May 22, 2011, Joplin was hit by a powerful tornado that wiped out a large portion of the city, including the medical center. There were more than 900 injuries and 161 lost their lives. Joplin has made a good recovery and is now in business again. To learn more about the city of Joplin, visit its website at joplinmo.org.

Outside Joplin go east on County Highway V to Diamond. From Diamond drive 2 miles on V and then south about a mile to find the **George Washington Carver National Monument,** which commemorates a man who was more than an educator, botanist, agronomist, and "cookstove chemist." He was a man who wanted "to be of the greatest good to the greatest number of people," a man who refused to accept boundaries, who drew from science, art, and religion to become a teacher and director of a department at Tuskegee Institute in Alabama. He taught botany and agriculture to the children of ex-slaves and tried to devise farming methods to improve the land exhausted by cotton. Known as the "Peanut Man," Carver led poor, one-horse farmers to grow protein-rich and soil-regenerating soybeans and peanuts. The Carver Nature Trail leads from the birthplace site through two springs and ends at the Carver family cemetery.

Joplin is also the home of the **Spiva Center for the Arts** (222 W. 3rd, corner of 3rd and Wall; 417-623-0183; spivaarts.org). You can see the works of the artist of the month at the website. Gift shop hours are Tues through Sat 10 a.m. to 5 p.m. and Sun 1 to 5 p.m.

Just down US 71 is the ***Real Hatfield Smokehouse*** (7329 Gateway Dr., Neosho; 417-624-3765). Owner Chad Neece has a sparkle in his blue eyes as he talks about his "home-grown" hogs. "We smoke anything you can get from a hog," he says. Bacon, hams—you name it, he smokes it. He will mail hams anywhere in the US and even has a regular customer in London. The small smokehouse uses a special sugar cure and hickory logs to give meats a golden-brown finish and good flavor without as much salt as other smokehouses. Hours are 7:30 a.m. to 6 p.m. Mon through Sat. The smokehouse is closed Sun.

If you love ghost-storied and mysterious sights, visit "Spooksville," 11 miles southwest of Joplin. It is here that an eerie light has been appearing in the middle of a lonely road most nights since 1886. This almost supernatural spook light created panic in the small village of Hornet and is often referred to as the Hornet Ghost Light. Early settlers actually left the area in terror because of the giant ball of light bouncing over the hills and across the fields. Today the light seems to concentrate on one gravel road known as Devil's Promenade or Spook Light Road. The light has even been rumored to come right up to your car and land on the hood, then bounce off or go out and appear later behind you. It disappears whenever approached. If you have the nerve, take I-44 west from Joplin to Highway 43, then drive south on Highway 43 approximately 6 miles to Highway BB. Turn right. Drive approximately 3 miles to road's end. Turn right and drive another mile to a second dirt road to the left. If you haven't chickened out yet, you will now be headed west on Spook Light Road. The road is long. Park anywhere along the side of the road and wait. Try to find the darkest

trivia

Two major Civil War battles were fought in Newtonia—with total forces numbering in the thousands. The 1862 battle was one of very few encounters in which Native Americans fought on both sides. Southern forces had Choctaw, Cherokee, and Chickasaw soldiers, while other Cherokees fought with the Union forces. This was the first battle of Colonel J. O. (Jo) Shelby's famous Iron Brigade. The 1864 battle, also involving Shelby, was the last battle in the Civil War fought west of the Mississippi. A Civil War cemetery here houses the remains of 13 soldiers, including the famous (or infamous to the Confederates) Robert Christian. Many slaves and their descendants are also buried here. The earliest stone is from 1858.

spot about 2 miles down the road. You can even venture down some of the very dark side roads. There is no charge for this thrill except the years of therapy it will take to get over it.

Pierce City on Highway 37 has a couple of neat little places to stop for a rest. But this is only a rest stop, because what you really want to see is the *Jolly Mill.* You will be rewarded with a lovely wooded drive after you leave Highway 97 and turn onto US 60. Go 1⁹⁄₁₀ miles to a sign on FR 1010, then 1⁸⁄₁₀ miles across a creek with a bridge with no sides to FR 2025, past an old white church and churchyard, then ⁷⁄₁₀ mile to the park.

This park is sort of a secret spot that the locals enjoy. Its history is fascinating. In 1848 George Isbell built a water-powered mill to serve settlers with gristmill products (and spirits). The new village that grew up around him was called Jollification, and it was a rest stop and resupply point for wagon trains headed west to Kansas and Indian Territory. When the Civil War came, the area was ravaged, and two cavalry battles raged here. Bushwackers terrorized and burned the village but, here's a surprise, the distillery was spared.

A new village rose from the ashes and the distillery resumed operation. In 1872 a railroad was built to Indian Territory, eliminating wagons. At the same time George Isbell refused to pay the new tax on spirits, stopped making whiskey (much to the regret of travelers), and turned his attention to milling flour. The village faded and by 1894 the mill stood alone with the schoolhouse. But the mill prospered; flour was milled here until the 1920s, and gristmill products were ground out here for 50 more years.

A community effort was made to have the mill placed on the National Register of Historic Places, and the mill was rehabilitated. It is once again a working mill. The water still rushes by picnic tables, the covered bridge, and another wooden bridge. It is worth the drive to see.

Webb City's claim to fame, the *"Praying Hands,"* is in *King Jack Park.* This 32-foot concrete-and-steel structure is atop a 40-foot-high hill. The park is named for the ore called "jack" that made the city rich in the 1870s. There are no signs inviting the visitor to stop to see the huge sculpture; it just suddenly appears. The hands were created by Jack Dawson, an art instructor at the Webb City schools, and he intended it to be just a quiet reminder for people to turn to God. Webb City is off US 71.

When you get enough of sitting around indoors, you outdoors folks can go west on US 59 at Anderson to enter canoe heaven. US 59 runs along the Elk River, and the sudden appearance of the famous overhanging bluffs makes you want to duck as you drive under them.

Tri-Lakes Area

The last town on Highway 76 before you enter the Mark Twain National Forest is *Cassville.* Highway 76 is a long and winding road through the forest, so if you arrive at this point after dark, you might as well spend the night.

The *Devil's Kitchen Trail* winds from the valley to the top and down again, giving a close-up look at the geology and history of the area. Eleven of the park's 14 caves are found along the rocky bench here. Shelters like these were used by Ozark bluff-dwelling Indians who lived here about 10,000 years ago. Artifacts such as food and fragments of clothing have been found to date this culture. The Devil's Kitchen was named for the stone formation that provided a hideout for Civil War guerrillas. As you head south on Highway 112, softly winding roads, tree-lined hills, and spectacular views pop up as you crest hilltops in this lovely national forest.

Roaring River State Park is the fountainhead of the Roaring River. There is a hidden spring in a cave filled with crystal-clear aqua-blue water that stays a constant 58 degrees Fahrenheit year-round. More than 20 million gallons a day are pumped into the river. Here the state maintains a trout hatchery and stocks the river daily in season.

The biggest day of the year happens on Mar 1, when the whistle blows early in the morning to open trout season. Anglers stand shoulder to shoulder in hopes of catching a lunker or their limit. Friendly competition abounds to catch the biggest trout. If you skip work to make opening day, try to avoid all the press who are waiting to snap pictures of the annual event. If you catch a big fish, you might just end up on the front page of the local newspaper . . . and then you will have some explaining to do when you get back to work.

The park runs the *Roaring River Inn* (417-847-2330 or 800-334-6946; roaringriverstatepark.com). The inn, made largely of wood and stone, has 26 rooms and a view of the river valley below. Other accommodations are available outside the park and in the town of Cassville.

The **Parkcliff Cabins** (417-236-5902; parkcliff.com) are log cabins with loft, deck, fireplace, full kitchen, and two bedrooms for $155 for the first two and additional $10 for each additional person. This is the perfect romantic winter getaway if escape is what you are looking for, but then the nearness of Branson, Table Rock Lake, and Eureka Springs, Arkansas, also make it a perfect family getaway, as well. There are also several campgrounds in the Mark Twain National Forest, and about 20 miles east of the state park is the **Big Bay Campgrounds** (877-444-6777; reserveusa.com). Big Bay is on the shores of Table Rock Lake on the border of Missouri and Arkansas. It has bathrooms and water and is geared mostly to tent campers. A red cedar and hardwood forest shades the campground and separates the campsites for privacy and a natural environment. The lake is visible from most campsites and there are walking paths to the water. The clear water is home to bass, catfish, crappie, and sunfish. Rates are $10 a night. RV sites are available with electric hookup. There is no drinking water at this camp. It has bathrooms and water and is geared mostly to tent campers. Rate is $18 a night.

Roaring River State Park is part of the White River basin. From a geologist's point of view, the basin tells a fascinating story. The White River has cut into the flat Springfield plateau, creating deep, steep-walled valleys and exposing varied layers of rock—shale, limestone, dolomite, and chert.

Pastures fringed with woods are found along Highway 76 East through the Piney Creek Wildlife Area. Mile after mile of ridge roads and startling views unfold until finally, over the crest of the last hill, beautiful Table Rock Lake appears before you. It feels like the top of a Ferris wheel from this vantage. The occasional small farm or Ozark stone cottage dots the roadside.

trivia

Unlike Huckleberry Finn, you don't have to play hooky to go fishing in Cassville because school is officially closed on Mar 1 every year so residents can grab a fishing pole and open trout season. It has been a school holiday in this Ozarks town near Roaring River State Park for as long as anyone can remember. Many spend the night along the stream to secure a good spot. There can be as many as 4,000 anglers vying for spots along the stream. In 2005 Missouri Secretary of State Robin Carnahan fired a pistol at 6:30 a.m. to officially open the 6-month season.

Valleys with pastures, ponds, or a lone barn sitting starkly against the sky are the only traces of civilization.

At the town of Cape Fair you can turn right on Highway 76 to Table Rock Lake or turn left to **Reeds Spring.** Because of the proximity of Silver Dollar City, quite a few artists are in residence.

Fred and Beth Hickeman's family shows a diverse run of art at the newly opened **Gallery at the Spring** (81 Spring St.; 417-272-0430), downtown just behind the spring. Fred does fine woodworking with oak and other woods. Beth is a painter in watercolor and acrylic. Their son Nathan and his wife, Dori, are an artistic duo who share a love of art. He does pottery and she is a photographer. Beth says they will be open "probably" during the daytime 6 days a week. Call for hours.

At **Omega Pottery Shop** (417-272-3369; omega-pottery-shop.com) on Highway 248 East (at the south edge of town), Mark Oehler crafts each piece of wheel-thrown stoneware and finishes it in a gas-fired kiln at 2,350 degrees—that makes it safe for oven, dishwasher, micro-

missouridivided

By the time the Civil War was approaching, Missouri was warring within itself. The governor and many legislators favored secession but were outvoted at the convention called to decide the matter. The governor's faction fled south to Cassville, where they signed an ordinance of secession and affiliation with the Confederate States of America.

wave, and moon missions. He travels occasionally but says it's "too much of a bother to pack everything up and move it." He would rather stay here in Reeds Spring. "Pottery is a craft that needs space to display it," he says. "That's why potters have studio-galleries." Mark enjoys doing custom work—such as lamps, sinks, and dishes. He points to other craftspeople— Tom Hess, another potter; Lory Brown, a pine-needle basket maker—all in the Reeds Spring area. Omega Pottery is open from 10 a.m. to 5 p.m. every day except Wed. Winter has him closing at 4 p.m. and sometimes taking Sun off. So call or visit his website not only to see his wares but also to learn how pottery is made.

Hess Pottery and Baskets on Highway 413 North, a mile north of Reeds Spring (417-272-3283; hesspottery.com), is where potter Tom Hess and basket maker Lory Brown have built a unique 12-sided Mongolian yurt for their workshop and gallery. The natural surroundings offer the perfect atmosphere to enjoy the work these two fine artists produce. Tom's pottery is handmade, using natural red clay. Each piece is sealed with a coating of very fine clay and then fired in a kiln, and his red clay pie plates make a perfectly browned pie crust that releases easily, so they are not just another pretty face but a valuable kitchen necessity—a good reason to stop in and shop here. The plates are ovenproof and dishwasher safe, and can be used in a microwave.

Lory's pine-needle baskets are made with 18-inch southern yellow pine needles and 10-inch ponderosa pine needles. These baskets must be seen to be loved. Each coil of pine needles is stitched with raffia palm leaf to the preceding coil using closely spaced stitches. The finished baskets are sturdy and durable and retain their wonderful pine scent. The shop is open from 10 a.m. to 5 p.m. in the summer and "most days" in the winter.

And if riding a zip line over the treetops is on your bucket list, you have come to the right place. **Zip Line USA** (3335 Hwy. 160; 417-559-5398) is the number-one attraction of Reeds Spring. If you have never done a zip line, you really have to try it. Flying over the trees at bird level is just a thrill you will not regret and you can talk about it for months—whether you are a kid or a senior citizen.

The **Museum of the Unexplained** (22183 Main St.; 417-272-9620) has a NASA display and real proof of UFOs, as well as information on Area 51 and even Bigfoot. It might make a believer of you.

Table Rock State Park is one of the most popular (meaning crowded) state parks in Missouri. Off the beaten path here means wilderness, on the path means bumper-to-bumper in summertime. As in most resort areas in the state, early spring and late fall are perfect times to roam without the huge crowds summer brings.

Author Harold Bell Wright came to these hills for his health in the early part of the 20th century and was so taken by the beauty of the area that he settled in to write. *The Shepherd of the Hills* is his best-known and most-beloved book; it captured the imagination of generations and even became one of John Wayne's early movies (which, incidentally, borrowed only the name from the book—the script was unrecognizable!).

US 65 is an old-fashioned, uncrowded Ozark highway. You can still see the view as you crest hills here, but the **Shepherd of the Hills Inspiration**

Tower offers an incredible one. The tower's first observation level is at 145 feet; the tower is 230 feet, 10 inches tall, with 2 elevators or 279 stairs to the top. But rest assured it is stable. It is designed to withstand 172 mph winds (gusts of 224 mph), and it cost $1.5 million to build; this is not surprising since it contains 92,064 pounds of steel and is set in 43 truckloads of concrete. It also contains 4,400 square feet of glass, for a breathtaking view from the highest point around the Tri-Lakes area.

If you've heard of Silver Dollar City (and you will if you stay in Missouri for long), you've heard of *Branson.* Once a quiet little town pocketed in the weathered Ozark Mountains near the Arkansas border, the town has seen business pick up considerably of late.

Branson has changed in the past several years from the strip of country music "opries" and related foofaraw crowded cheek-by-jowl along Highway 76 (known as "the strip") to the country-music capital of the Midwest,

trivia

The Shepherd of the Hills Theater is the longest-running theater in the country. It began with a stage with its audience on blankets on the hillside, upgraded to folding chairs, and now is an outdoor amphitheater that seats around 2,500 people. The year 2009 marked its 50th year of nonstop operation. In 1998 there was a big fire in the dressing rooms and it was announced that there would be no show that year. People poured in with stage props (antique guns, for example) to help, and the theater was up and running in time for the annual performance.

giving Nashville a run for its money. Twenty-seven theaters in town now feature such stars as Loretta Lynn, Mel Tillis, and Elvis. No, really. Elvis is alive and well and living in Branson. Elvis (Ehlert) does an uncanny impersonation of the King. And possibly the most popular show in town is Japanese hillbilly fiddler Shoji Tabuchi.

Branson is trying to keep up with the demand of more than 4 million tourists a year, but as you would suspect, about an hour before the matinee or evening shows begin, the traffic is much like a long narrow parking lot. How bad is the traffic? Well, women have been seen leaving their husbands behind the wheel on Highway 76 while they get out and shop, buy things, and rejoin their spouses in the car a block or so up the street. We are talking gridlock here. The secret to getting around is learning the back roads.

Just knowing that the quickest route is not 76 Country Boulevard (a road to avoid if at all possible) can save you enough time for dinner.

There are other little secrets, too. The chamber of commerce will give you a free, easy-to-read map showing the shortcuts from one end of the 5-mile strip to the other. The recently repaved back roads can make life a little easier, even though you can't avoid the traffic altogether. The city now has a trolley system on the strip and that helps a bit.

trivia

Children can attend several shows, such as the Osmonds and comedian Yakov Smirnoff, at no cost. If you wait until after 3 p.m. to visit Silver Dollar City, you get in free with the same ticket the next day.

Do flea markets interest you? You're in the right place; downtown Branson has five of them. If you don't find something in this lineup, you aren't looking very hard, or you have a good deal more self-discipline than most of us.

Innkeeper Glen Cameron is a native of the Ozark Mountains. For several generations his family has lived in the Ozarks of Missouri and Arkansas. You met Glen back in the Southeast section of this book. He runs the Ozark Mountain Country Bed and Breakfast Reservation Service. His home near Branson can be your home, too, while you visit this busy town. ***Cameron's Crag Bed & Breakfast*** (417-334-4720 or 800-933-8529; camerons-crag .com) has 3 beautiful rooms for your enjoyment. The Highland Rose Suite is a romantic hideaway and is a favorite for honeymoon or anniversary couples. The private spa room features a sunken hot tub for two. Sliding-glass doors open to a private deck with a fantastic view of the lake and river valley. A comfy king-size bed and reclining love seat add to the appeal. There is a private entrance, a private bath (tub/shower), refrigerator for your champagne, and microwave, coffee bar, Wi-Fi, and cable TV. That should cover everything you might want for a honeymoon, shouldn't it? The suite is $135. The Around the World Suite also has a hot tub on a deck overlooking Lake Taneycomo. It also has a private entrance, king-size bed, sitting area, refrigerator, microwave, coffee bar, cable TV, and CD player as well as a large private bath (tub/shower) with a dressing room. The decor has a sort of international flavor. It costs $125. You can enjoy a spectacular view from your suite and from the hot tub on your private deck overlooking the lake and valley in the Bird's Eye View Suite, which encompasses an entire level of the detached guesthouse. This spacious suite includes a king-size bed, living/dining area with queen-size sleeper sofa, and a full kitchen. The private bath features a shower and deluxe whirlpool bath for two. This suite also has a private entrance and cable TV. It costs $145. The Grandview encompasses the entire upper level of the guesthouse. (The Bird's Eye View Suite is the lower level.) If you want the best for your Branson getaway, the Grandview is it. This 3-room suite includes a bedroom with king bed and sitting area, combination living/dining room with built-in library and plenty of windows to enjoy the view, full kitchen including dishwasher and laundry facilities, and a spacious bath with whirlpool tub for two and a separate shower. A wraparound deck offers a private hot tub and a panoramic view over the valley and the Branson skyline. There's also cable TV in the bedroom and living room, as well as a DVD and CD player. This most requested suite costs $165 a night for two. A sleeper sofa in the bedroom can accommodate up to two additional guests with an added charge. You can take a virtual tour of the suites at the website.

You probably had breakfast at the B&B, so think brunch now and order a three-egg omelet at the *Hard Luck Diner* in the Grand Village Shops (2800 76 Country Blvd.; 417-332-0150; restaurantsbransonmo.com) and have someone sing a country song. The singing waitstaff makes sure your day begins with a song. Hours are 11 a.m. to 8 p.m. every single day. Another great place for "off the beaten path" dining is *Sugar Leaf Treats* (417-336-6618; sugarleaftreats.com) in Branson's Grand Village. There are handmade cakes, cookies, and other goodies, along with soups, salads, quiches, coffee, and more.

Because Branson is in the throes of a building boom and the traffic can be a genuine pain, the best thing to do is to find a bed-and-breakfast somewhere away from Branson and then just go in when you are psyched up to do it. (Avoiding the whole place might be more to your liking.) But you've come this far, so the first order of business is to get that map (the chamber of commerce and many hotels have them) and use all the traffic shortcuts you can. The side roads that loop off Highway 76 do reduce travel time and frustration. If you are not attending a show, stay off the streets around the 7 and 8 p.m. curtain times, when about 1,500 people per theater are all on Highway 76 and the local police are issuing tickets for driving in the center turn lane. Branson traffic lulls roughly before 8:30 a.m., between 10 and 10:30 a.m., and from around 2 to 2:30 p.m. Branson drivers are very courteous, though, and it won't be long before someone lets you pull out in front of him onto the strip.

One of the most interesting things to do when you hit Branson is to head to the old downtown area, which sits on the banks of the Taneycomo River. Here you can visualize what the town was like before it became an entertainment center. The riverfront and downtown area is going through a renaissance, and many changes are under way. To acquaint yourself with some of the improvements planned, visit branson.com, which is the website of the Downtown Branson Main Street Association (417-334-1548). To take the pulse of the town, you must visit **Branson Cafe** (120 W. Main St.; 417-334-3021; thebransoncafe.com), the oldest restaurant in town. A big country breakfast with all the trimmings and friendly, charming waitresses await you when you slide into a red upholstered booth and kick back to enjoy. The waitresses are a wealth of information about where to go and what to see that is "hot" in Branson. The cafe has a daily luncheon special posted in the window. All the homemade favorites appear there on a weekly basis. For dinner you might try some of the freshly caught trout from the Taneycomo River. Be sure to save room for some homemade cobbler or pie. Hours are from 6 a.m. to 8 p.m. daily; closed Sun.

There are many gift shops on Main Street, but one of the "don't miss" ones is Dick's 5&10 Cent Store (103 W. Main St.; 417-334-2410; dicksoldtime5and10.com). You truly do take a walk back in time to the good old days when you could have a quarter and shop to find just the right toy to delight your child's heart. You can find such things as those gadgets that mooo when you turn them over or paper dolls, the kind we used to play with for hours. They also have an assortment of old-time dime-store items.

The ladies who like lovely things will not want to miss **Patricia's Victorian House** (101 W. Main St., Branson; 417-335-8000). Patricia's exquisite shop is packed with French and Italian reproduction furniture, Victorian dolls, jewelry, paintings, and decorator items. All of this brings out the visitor's romantic side and makes one think of a dream bedroom. It is truly a "fantasy" shop of beautiful things. Hours are 9 a.m. to 6 p.m. every day.

Keep going another block east, across the railroad tracks, and you will find the **Branson Scenic Railroad** (206 E. Main St.; 417-334-6110; bransontrain

.com). Here you can book a tour of the Ozarks countryside. The train leaves from the historic Branson Depot. You might want to call ahead for schedules and packages; the train doesn't run from Dec to the first week in Mar.

If you are in a mood to do some trout fishing on Lake Taneycomo, check with ***Scotty's Trout Dock*** (395 Lake Dr., Branson; 417-334-4288; scottystroutdock.com). They can supply you with all the necessary items and good advice on how and where to catch "the big one." They rent tackle, boats, and even pontoons, and they will supply a guide if you want one. Or maybe all you need is a driver, so you can stretch out and catch some rays on the back of the pontoon—definitely a "little slice of heaven." Hours are 7 a.m. to 5 p.m.

Head west on 76 ("the strip"). You can stroll along the strip and take the trolley. Then you can leave the driving to someone else and have fun with your friends. You and the kids can "Ride the Ducks," vintage WWII amphibious vehicles that go along the strip, through an outdoor military history museum, and then splash into the lake.

The Branson/Lakes Area Chamber of Commerce will send you information packets. The one to ask for is the *Branson Roads Scholar: Mastering the Back Roads of Branson*. It contains a map of alternative routes and traffic tips. Call (800) 214-3661 or visit bransonchamber.com.

The most exciting part of visiting Branson is how easy it is to get up close to the stars—the music legends who are playing golf (10 a.m. Wed at Pointe Royale Golf Course on Highway 165 often has stars like Mel Tillis and Moe Bandy teeing off together) or shopping at the grocery store. That constellation of stars is only the beginning. Other stars are scheduled to shoot through Branson for performances, too.

So you never know whom you will see sitting in one of the many restaurants (most of which are down-home sorts of places, not exactly low-calorie eateries) in town. For the best ambience, though, drive across the lake to the ***Candlestick Inn*** (127 Taney St. on Mount Branson), where the food is more upscale. The atmosphere is romantic, the view of downtown Branson is sensational (especially during the Christmas season's Festival of Lights), and you never know who will be at one of the tables. The menu features such delicacies as crab-stuffed trout. You can see the humongous neon candle sign (it says steak and seafood) from downtown, but it's tricky to find if you don't know to just follow Highway 76/68 across the bridge. Call (417) 334-3633 for reservations or visit the website at candlestickinn.com. Hours are lunch Wed through Fri 11 a.m. to 3 p.m., dinner Sun through Thurs 5 to 8 p.m., Fri and Sat 5 to 10 p.m.

Needless to say, there are many motels around Branson. You can escape the motel rut with a bed-and-breakfast if you plan ahead a little. Plus, the people in the B&Bs tend to know their way around the town and can give you the shortest, fastest routes to wherever you are planning to go. Call Ozark Mountain Country Bed & Breakfast Service at (800) 695-1546 and let Kay Cameron find you one of the more than 50 B&Bs in the Tri-Lakes area near Table Rock Lake, Lake Taneycomo, Branson, Silver Dollar City, or just across the border in Arkansas. She has about 100 bed-and-breakfast inns to direct you to in the Ozarks, from cozy hideaways for couples to family-friendly accommodations, some with their own hot tubs or swimming pools. Kay also has the number of a show service that will deliver tickets to any bed-and-breakfast inn for you.

The easiest way to reach Branson is from US 65, which runs through the east end of town. The West Missouri 76 exit will put you on the strip, where you will watch pedestrians speed by your slowly moving car. Or you can use the back entrance and take Highway 248 to the Shepherd of the Hills Expressway to the west side of town, where things will not be much better. You can reach the Branson/Lakes Area Chamber of Commerce at (900) 884- BRANSON for a guide that lists the shows in town and the ticket office phone numbers. There is a $1.50 per minute charge for that call (average three minutes), and you get a recording to leave your name and address. It is sometimes cheaper to call the visitor information number at (417) 334-4136, but that line is often busy and you can be put on hold for about 10 minutes. They have a computerized service listing the hotels and motels with vacant rooms. For show tickets you can call BransonTix, a private company that handles about a dozen theaters, at (800) 888-8497.

And don't leave town without having biscuits and gravy at **Billy Gail's Cafe** (5291 Hwy. 265; 417-338-8883). Blue gas pumps stand in front of this former gas station/log cabin. Inside owners Billy and Gail Blong serve up really good food in a comfy casual, 10-seat dining room with red-checkered tablecloths.

The **Stone Hill Wine Company** (417-334-1897; stonehillwinery.com), at the junction of Highway 165 and Green Mountain Drive, 2 blocks south of Highway 76 West, is one of the state's oldest wineries and a very popular attraction. Visitors may tour the winery where they watch the winemaking process and enjoy the aroma of sherry being aged in oak. At the end of the tour visitors are invited to taste a selection of wines and juices. The hours vary with the month, so it's best to call ahead or go to the website. The gift shop also sells sausages, cheese, and wine-related items. Slow down 2 miles outside town and turn west onto Highway V. There's something here you won't want to miss: the *School of the Ozarks* (417-334-6411; cofo.edu) in *Point Lookout.*

It's a college campus, all right, but wait. What's going on here? Everybody looks so . . . busy. This is a different kind of college—a fully accredited, four-year school where each full-time boarding student works at one of 65 campus jobs or industries to pay in part for his or her tuition. It calls itself "the campus that works." The rest is provided through scholarships. The campus fruitcake and jelly kitchen is open during business hours weekdays. Student workers bake some 20,000 fruitcakes a year and produce delicious apple butter and many flavors of jelly.

Students built the college itself—it's a pretty one—and run the Ralph Foster Museum and the Edwards Mill (a working replica of an old-time gristmill) as part of their tuition. If you're hungry while you're here, stop at the student-run *Dobyns Restaurant* on Point Lookout. It is more than just a restaurant. The dining hall seats 275 people in an elegant and relaxed rustic lodge design with handmade furnishings and magnificent landscaping—and all the cooking is done by the students. There is even a gourmet bakery with fresh pastries and desserts. A gift shop—with student-made stained glass, jellies, fruitcakes, pottery, and freshly milled grain products—is inside. What more could you want? Well, okay, there's a hotel facility as well. Prices for these luxury rooms (which have king- and queen-size beds and fireplaces with balconies overlooking the campus) are moderate and many of them sleep 6, with 2 bedrooms and pull-out couches. The School of the Ozarks campus is beautiful, perched on its hill; don't miss the view from Point Lookout. Stand here at dusk when the bells of the carillon roll out over the mist-shrouded river below, if you want goose bumps up and down your arms. When the sun slides down the sky, that sound of bells on the crisp evening air is unforgettable. Williams Memorial Chapel is a fine place to stop for a moment; the tourist bustle slows to a halt here and there's room to breathe.

Say you want to get out of Branson for a while: Take US 65 North toward Springfield, then left onto Highway 176 West, then left toward Day Road, and continue straight to ***Copper Run Distillery & Lounge*** (1901 Day Rd., Walnut Shade; 417-587-3456; copperrundistillery.com). The distillery makes whiskey, rum, vodka, and moonshine. Yep, moonshine—something that has been made in these Ozark hills for generations. But now you don't have to be a bootlegger and worry about the Volstead Act, because these are "hand-crafted spirits" (to use their words, which sound better than "hooch" or "white lightning"), and this is the first legal distillery opened in the Ozarks since Prohibition in 1933. And to be honest, distilling whiskey and rum is

On a Very Personal Note

My husband and I had driven to the Branson area to see Willie Nelson and Wayne Newton. I pointed out a tattoo shop to him and told him I wanted to go back the next day to interview the owner for the book. He went off to play golf that day, and when he came home I proudly showed him a new tattoo of a butterfly on my, uh, hip.

He was not amused. In fact, he was not pleased at all. He began to get surly about it. Then he smiled and accused me of getting a "stick-on" tattoo. He led me into the bathroom to rub it with soap and water. It did not come off. I expected him to tell his golf buddies about it the next day, but he never mentioned it to anyone. He was truly embarrassed for me. Every night when I undressed, he glared at me. Now mind you, I had just turned 50 years old and we had been married nearly 25 years. To say he did not like surprises is putting it mildly. He is very conservative.

Of course, so am I. The tattoo was not done by a shop but purchased in the five-and-dime downtown. But I was having so much fun I decided to carry on with the fiction. Before the butterfly began to wear off, I used alcohol to remove it and applied a new one—on the other side this time—and waited for him to figure it out. He didn't. This went on for four weeks—first on the right, then on the left—the butterflies remained on my backside, and impossibly, he did not notice their change of address. But the good news was that on the fifth week when I replaced the butterfly with a dragon, he did notice.

It was probably the best practical joke I have ever managed. My husband believed me; my best friends and my mother believed me. Only my dad (who never saw it) never believed it. He said he simply knew me too well to believe I would have a butterfly permanently placed on my derriere. Now, the dragon maybe. . . .

much more complex than one would think. (Moonshine is just unaged whiskey, consumed before it is placed in barrels to mature.)

Owner Jim Blansit studied brewing and distilling for many years before returning home and embarking on this adventure at the family farm. He and his father built this bar out of old barrels and barn beams. There is an antique stove that belonged to his grandfather, and materials for the ceiling came out of a 105-year-old barn. He has been making small-batch spirits since 2009. There are free tours on the hour of the distillery including a sample of the spirits. The lounge area has great live music with local musicians. Copper Run is open Mon through Sat from 10 a.m. to 7 p.m. and Sun from 11 a.m. to 7 p.m.

Big Cedar Lodge (612 Devil's Pool Rd.; 800-BCLODGE; big-cedar.com) in **Ridgedale,** 9 miles south of Branson, is off the beaten path literally, but is very well known by people throughout the country. You can stay in the lodge itself or in private cabins, and there is a Jack Nicklaus–designed executive golf course called **Top of the Rock.** It is an Audubon Signature Course, the first in the state and only the sixth in the country. The distinction means the course meets Audubon's environmental guidelines on natural habitat and water life. Big Cedar also has a fine trout stream and waterfalls all over the place. Devil's Pool Restaurant offers a level of dining not found easily in the Ozarks—maple-glazed quail with white bean ragout, prime rib, and a champagne brunch on Sunday.

January is spawning season at **Shepherd of the Hills Fish Hatchery** (417-334-4865), 6 miles southwest of Branson on Highway 165 in the White River valley, just below Table Rock Dam. The Missouri Department of Conservation produces 1.2 million fish annually, 80 percent of which go into nearby Lake Taneycomo. There is a visitor center filled with exhibits and aquariums, and 4 trails ranging from ³⁄₁₀ mile to about 1½ miles. Hours are Sept through June 9 a.m. to 5 p.m., Memorial Day to Labor Day until 6 p.m. 7 days a week (except Thanksgiving, Christmas, and New Year's Day). Visit on the last Sat in Feb for "Vulture Venture" (noon until 6 p.m.) and see hundreds of vultures enjoying their winter roosting spots. There are fun activities for the kids, too. Visit mdc.mo.gov and type in "Shepherd of the Hills Fish Hatchery" for more information.

If you want luxury in the European style, the **Chateau on the Lake** (415 N. Hwy. 265, Branson; 888-333-LAKE; chateauonthelakebranson.com) is high-dollar elegant. This 10-story hotel sits on a hill right next to Table

Rock Lake and has 302 rooms and suites. A standard room with a mountain view begins at $139 and goes higher if you want to see the lake. It has a world-class day spa, too. The murals that decorate the ballroom are of castles in Europe, and you can scuba dive, parasail, water-ski, fish, play tennis, or work out in a 24-hour fitness center. There's a Sweet Shoppe and a deli, and even a free movie theater. The Chateau Grille offers fine dining.

Long Creek Herb Farm (417-779-5450; longcreekherbs.com) is nestled deep in the woods on the Long Creek arm of Table Rock Lake. Jim Long calls it an "old-fashioned working herb farm in the heart of the Ozarks," and that describes it pretty well. Guests sip herb tea on the shady porch and listen to the tree frogs. On the 27-acre farm, skullcap, foxglove, and horehound are grown, and goats, chickens, guineas, geese, and steers are raised. Jim grows 400 cultivated and native herbs; many of them, such as sweet goldenrod and horsetail, are unique to the Ozarks.

There is a meticulously groomed demonstration garden with winding paths and a bentwood gazebo. After 20 years as a landscape architect, Jim decided that his love of plants needed a new outlet, and he wanted to share the experience of herbs with people.

He also has a gift shop where you can buy about 80 products, including seasonings, teas, and herb blends both medicinal and culinary. You can buy a Dream Pillow to induce dreams that are relaxing, romantic, or action-packed, depending on the herb blend.

The farm is open Wed in the summertime (May through Oct) and other days by appointment. You must call first. You will need directions or a map to find the place, because you must cross two state lines and three county lines to get there.

The *Golden Pioneer Museum* in *Golden* (417-271-3300; goldenpioneermuseum.org) can be found between Branson and Eureka Springs on Highway 86. The owner of this museum is Winfred Prier, and the curator is Murry Carmichael. The museum is home to Arlis Coger's collections from the Trail of Tears Museum, which used to be in Huntsville. The 5,200-square-foot museum contains clay pots (800, to be exact), weapons, tools, and clothing made by the Arkansas Osage Indians and found in the War Eagle (Arkansas) mounds. Here is the largest collection of Dalton points (more than 1,000), arrowheads knapped around 8000 BC by Native Americans living along the White River south of Huntsville. On display also is the world's largest collection of Tussinger points. The extensive mineral collection includes the world's largest quartz and crystal cluster—4,200 pounds—found in Hot Springs and displayed in its own glass case, as well as the world's largest turquoise carving, weighing in at 68 pounds. Other displays show rocks that look ordinary until ultraviolet light reveals the vibrant fluorescent color within them. There is also an incredible collection of baseball cards. The guns on display include one of only three or four derringers like the gun that killed President Abraham Lincoln. The museum also has one of the largest collections of carnival glass in the Midwest: more than 72 collections, and still growing. There is a gift shop, too. Call to arrange for a tour (open Apr through Oct, Tues through Sat, 10:30 a.m. to 4:30 p.m.).

Dogwood Canyon Nature Park (417-779-5983; dogwoodcanyon.com) on Highway 86 West and Highway 13 near *Lampe* is the dream come true of Johnny Morris, founder of Springfield's Bass Pro Shop. This 10,000-acre property preserves an Ozark wonderland that Morris now shares with the public. Three creeks flow through the canyon—Dogwood Creek, Little Indian Creek, and Hobbs Creek—creating one of the best trout streams in the Midwest. Strategically placed weirs, or dams, and a series of short spillways form terraces in the stream and aerate the water. Each dam creates a pool for the trout. Wet-season, spring-fed waterfalls from bluffs above the stream bank were made year-round attractions by the addition of pumps to recirculate water to add oxygen for the trout. Stone walkways and wrought-iron railings built by Bass Pro's staff blacksmiths guide visitors, and 6 miles of paved road pass the most interesting sights in the canyon. There are 29 stream crossings on the property, and most fords are located at the base of a weir so that passengers in vehicles can view cascading water at eye level. Other crossings include stone bridges built by a local mason and a post- and beam-covered bridge built by Amish craftsmen. The park is open to the general public year-round and for tram tours from mid-Mar to Christmas. Horseback trail rides are offered, and bicycle tours are also available. Try a half-day guided trophy fishing excursion on Dogwood Creek (ages 13 and older) or two hours of unguided fishing. Tour guides relate the history of the area during the 2-hour tram ride, pointing out caves where workers discovered ancient burials. One site high on a bluff contained the remains of a Native American who died more than 1,000 years ago—predating Missouri's Osage tribe. Remains (a child and two adults) at another site were dated to 6000 BC by scientists—making them the oldest human remains ever found in the state. The tour crosses into Arkansas and travels among herds of bison, longhorn cattle, and elk. The visitor center has Civil War and Indian artifacts. Reservations are required for tram tours, trail rides, and fishing excursions.

Just a mile east of US 65 on Highway 14, the town of *Ozark* is a haven for antiques buffs. The largest collection is housed at the *Maine Street Mall* (1994 Evangel; 417-581-2575), a warehouse along US 65 and home to 108 antiques dealers. There are even antique cars inside. The mall is open 7 days a week from 9 a.m. to 6 p.m. (5 p.m. in the winter). You will find a couple dozen more shops—filled with a gazillion items—in the town of Ozark itself. This town, 15 miles south of Springfield and near enough to Branson to draw its crowds, is a mecca for folks who love old stuff.

Dear's Rest Bed and Breakfast (1408 Capp Hill Ranch Rd., Ozark; 417-581-3839 or 800-588-2262; dearsrest.com) is tucked in a beautifully natural Ozark setting where you can enjoy unexpected visits from deer, raccoons, and wild turkey, and birdsong will wake you in the morning. The rustic house was built for innkeepers Allan and Linda Schilter by local Amish builders and is filled with family antiques and old toys. The great room has a cozy fireplace, and since the home is open to only one family at a time, it becomes your fireplace, too. The all-cedar home has art-stenciled walls. The broad deck, hot tub, and covered porch are ideal places to enjoy the woodsy view or take your breakfast. You can hike on the old ranch roads and come back to steam away the cricks in a large hot tub in the woods. Birders enjoy the beautiful mountain views and the 250 varieties of birds that have been sighted in the area. There is a resident bluebird that frequents the water provided there. The pristine, spring-fed creek provides the perfect spot for "stream snorkeling" and the Schilters will provide the snorkel gear. Dear's Rest is actually 12 miles south of Ozark in the Mark Twain National Forest, so there is a world of outdoors waiting.

The bedroom contains 2 full-size beds and can accommodate parties of 2 to 6. The additional people in your party will share a bath and sleep in a cozy loft for an additional $15 for each child and $25 for each adult. The room with a private bath is $149. Allan and Linda will fix you a full country breakfast in the morning and send you on your way to nearby Springfield or Branson. To find the house, take Highway 14 to Highway W and then follow the road to Logan Ridge.

Places to Stay in Southwest Missouri

*has restaurant
**most hotels in the Branson area have specials

SPRINGFIELD

Holiday Inn
2720 N. Glenstone Ave. 3
(417) 865-8600 or
(800) HOLIDAY
Inexpensive

Lamplighter Inn
2820 N. Glenstone Ave.
(417) 869-3900 or
(800) 707-0326
Inexpensive

Lamplighter Inn & Suites
1772 S. Glenstone Ave.
(417) 882-1113 or
(800) 749-7275
Inexpensive

Super 8 Motel
3022 N. Kentwood Ave.
(417) 833-9218 or
(800) 800-8000
Inexpensive

VAN BUREN

Smalley's Motel
Business 60
(573) 323-4263 or
(800) 727-4263
(tube floats leave from motel)
Inexpensive

WEST PLAINS

Holiday Inn Express
1605 Imperial Dr.
(417) 257-3000
Inexpensive

Regency Inn Suites
Highway 61 and Highway 160
(417) 256-8191
Inexpensive

LEBANON

Best Western Wyota Inn
1225 Millcreek Rd.
Business Loop 44, exit 130
(417) 532-6171 or
(866) 996-8246
Inexpensive

Holiday Inn Express
1955 W. Elm St.
I-44 and Highway WW Corner
(417) 532-1111 or
(800) 315-2621
(800) HOLIDAY
Inexpensive

EMINENCE

Shady Lane Cabins and Motel
509 N. Main
(573) 226-3893
shadylanecabins.com
Inexpensive

CARTHAGE

Best Budget Inn
13008 E. Highway 96
(417) 358-6911 or
(800) 357-4953
Inexpensive

Carthage Inn
2244 Grand
(417) 358-2499 or
(800) 325-2525
Inexpensive

*Econo Lodge
1441 W. Central
(417) 358-3900
Inexpensive

*Precious Moments Best Western Hotel
2701 Hazel St. (northeast corner of Highways HH and 71A)
(417) 359-5900
Inexpensive

JOPLIN

*Holiday Inn
3615 Range Line Rd.
(417) 782-1000
Inexpensive

REEDS SPRING

Mountain Country Motor Inn
14930 Business 13
(417) 739-4155 or
(800) 753-2755
mountaincountrymotorinn.com
Inexpensive

BRANSON**

Econo Lodge
230 S. Wildwood
(417) 336-4849 or
(800) 542-3326
Inexpensive

Dockers Inn
3060 Green Mountain Dr.
dockersinn.com
(417) 334-3600 or
(800) 324-8748
Inexpensive (breakfast
included)

Radisson Hotel
120 S. Wildwood
(417) 335-5767
radisson.com/branson
Moderate

Places to Eat in Southwest Missouri

SPRINGFIELD

Nonna's Italian Cafe
306 South Ave.
(417) 831-1222
Inexpensive

Bangkok City
1129 E. Walnut St.
(417) 799-1221
Moderate

Patton Alley Pub
311 S. Patton
(417) 865-4255
Moderate

WINONA

Flossie's Apple Barrel
Highway 19 N
(573) 325-8273
Inexpensive

WEST PLAINS

Colton Steak House & Grill
1421 Preacher Roe Blvd.
(417) 255-9090
Moderate

EMINENCE

Ruby's Family Restaurant
101 Main St.
(573) 226-3878
Inexpensive

KIMBERLING CITY

The Bearded Clam Lounge and Eatery
Highway 13
(417) 739-4440

FINDING HELPFUL VISITOR INFORMATION

Branson
branson.com
(888) 903-2929 or (417) 334-2360

Kimberling City
kimberling-city.net
(800) 595-0393

Springfield
springfieldmo.org
(800) 678-8767 or (417) 881-5300

Van Buren
seevanburen.com
(573) 323-0800

Welcome to America's Heartland, where the Mighty Mo marks the end of the glaciated plains, and hill country begins. Remnant prairies tucked between the hills remind us that once these seas of grass covered a third of the state. In this area there are not one but three big lakes, and from Kansas City to the Lake of the Ozarks lie tiny towns built on gentle ridges, waiting to be discovered. Rough gravel roads wind through dogwood forests, along tentacled lakeshores and into towns that seem to have been protected from the rush like the wild morel hidden under a leaf. The big city here is Kansas City: the birthplace of jazz, the homeland of barbecue, and the Heart of America.

Lake of the Ozarks is not only a tourist area, it is a second homesite for people from both Kansas City and St. Louis. The eastern shore, known as the St. Louis side, has million-dollar homes in the Land of the Four Seasons resort area. Six Mile Cove (the 6-mile marker means you are 6 miles from Bagnell Dam) is called Millionaires' Cove by boaters and has some of the most opulent homes in the Midwest. A houseboat business has sprung up on that side, and visitors can now cruise the lake and see both shores

without the long drive around the lake. There is also a toll bridge that connects east to west at Osage Beach.

The Heart of America

Describing **Kansas City** as a city with "manure on its feet and wheat in its jeans" was a fair assessment at one time. Its two major industries were meat and wheat—all because a man named Joe McCoy convinced the local powers-that-were in 1871 that the newfangled "bobwire" (barbed wire) made it impossible to herd Texas cattle east. A central shipping point was needed, and the Kansas City stockyard was born. A fine steak house, the **Golden Ox Restaurant,** is within sniffing distance at 1600 Genessee Street (816-842-2866; goldenox.com). This old vintage steak house has been serving the best steaks in the world since just after World War II. It is the oldest steak house in a city famous for its beef. Owners Stephen Greer and Bill Teel are justifiably proud. "We've spruced the old gal up," Teel says. Greer adds, "This is the real reason Kansas City is famous for steak." The two have pushed into another famous KC food arena by adding a state-of-the-art barbecue smoker. This is still a steak house in the best tradition, though. Prime rib, Ox Club salad, and its famous bourbon pecan pie make it worth the trip. Hours are Mon and Tues from 11 a.m. to 9 p.m., Wed through Fri until 10 p.m., and Sat from 4 to 10:30 p.m. This fine restaurant is in walking distance of Kemper Arena, where many sporting events are held. In the fall the American Royal, a longtime cattle and equine event, is held here.

Kansas City is known as the "Heart of America," not because of its location in the center of the country

trivia

The Kansas City strip steak originated in Kansas City at the Golden Ox Restaurant (in the stockyards) in 1949.

but because of the people who call it home. Kansas City has a symphony, a lyric opera, the Missouri State Ballet Company, baseball's Royals, and football's Chiefs. Fountains and sculptures grace its wide avenues. Enclosed in the very heart of the city is Swope Park, the second-largest city park in the nation, with quiet, tree-shaded picnic areas and a modern zoo now upgraded to world-class. If you haven't been to KC lately, be sure to drive

TOP RECOMMENDATIONS IN CENTRAL MISSOURI

Cascone's Grill, p. 117

Dutch Bakery and Bulk Food Store, p. 142

Harling's Upstairs, p. 123

Lyceum Repertory Theatre, p. 138

Piano Room Lounge, p. 127

by the futuristic Bartle Hall sculptures at night, beautiful in a strange, space-age way.

Another must-see but not exactly off-the-path is the **Kauffman Center for the Performing Arts** (1601 Broadway; 816-994-7200; kauffmancenter .org). Tours of the Center are $5 a person and reservations are required (816-994-7222, ext. 3), but the best way to see it is to enjoy a performance in this remarkable theater.

The Nelson-Atkins Museum owns one of the finest collections of Oriental art in the world and has a beautiful outdoor sculpture garden. The museum proves that "everything's up to date in Kansas City" with a new wing and underground parking, and the *Kansas City Star*'s new printing facility is a huge landmark in the downtown loop. The Kansas City Museum has a planetarium and an old-fashioned ice-cream parlor where you can order a phosphate or a sundae. The Kansas City studio of artist Thomas Hart Benton is now a state park.

Kansas City has more fountains than any city except Rome, and most of them are on the **Country Club Plaza.** Built in 1922 and modeled after Seville, Spain, the Plaza's Mediterranean architecture and charming fountains give this suburban shopping center something no other has. Walk around the more than 100 designer shops, cafes, restaurants, and bars lining the wide streets. The Segway store offers guided tours during the day and at night, too. Brush Creek's wide meander through this charming area is broken by a fountain and stone pedestrian bridges right in the middle of the creek. Small boats carry visitors up and down the water. But the Plaza offers more than simply shopping—much more—especially during the winter holiday season after Thanksgiving night, when most of the fountains are turned off but the holiday lights are turned on. After dinner, there is a mass migration to see the famous Plaza lights twinkle on across the entire 15-block area, where each and every building is outlined in sparkling lights. The most popular building looks like Cinderella's enchanted pumpkin. Taking grandchildren through this wonderland has become a holiday tradition in many families. Bundle up and bring along a thermos of hot chocolate. The most romantic way to see this is in a horse-drawn carriage. Dreams are made here on snowy nights as the holiday season begins, with the flip of a switch, in Kansas City.

yardbirdatrest

Charlie "Yardbird" Parker's grave site is in Lincoln Cemetery, at 8604 Truman Road. The road to the bedraggled cemetery is narrow and unmarked. There is an entrance from Blue Ridge Boulevard. But off the beaten path could be a bit risky here, so if it's really something you want to visit, be careful. Go at high noon and take a bunch of buddies.

The first question most visitors ask when they get off a plane at Kansas City International Airport is "Where's the best barbecue?" Whether you like it to the sweet side or a bit spicy, that's for you to judge: The oldest contenders are *Arthur Bryant's Barbecue* (1727 Brooklyn; 816-231-1123; arthurbryantsbbq .com) and *Gates and Sons Bar-B-Q* (1221 Brooklyn; 816-483-3880; gatesbbq.com). Both offer carryout, so you can do comparison tests with their different sauces until you are all "pigged out."

Gates's and Bryant's owe their fame, in part, to the fact that they used to be situated next to the old Kansas City Royals baseball stadium. Not only were they favorite places to eat before and after games, but the announcers would also be happily noshing barbecue and talking about it during the games. Then writer Calvin Trillin, a KC native and New York writer, declared KC the barbecue capital of the planet and made Bryant's even more famous. Trillin claims Bryant's is the best restaurant in the world! But no one comes here for the ambience unless you like bright lights and cafeteria-style service. The hunk of meat wrapped between two pieces of white bread is a leader in the best-barbecue-in-town contest. Gates's has the comfy high-back booths and a tangier sauce. The only way to make a decision here is to try both. But there are between 100 and 150 barbecue restaurants in the Kansas City area, and most of the best are just joints tucked away somewhere, and "best" is defined by what kind of sauce you favor. **Danny Edwards Blvd BBQ** (2900 Southwest Blvd.; 816-283-0880), for example, has a sign in the window that reads eat it and beat it, which tells you something about its size, popularity, and attitude. Open for lunch only Mon through Fri from 10 a.m. to 2:30 p.m., **B.B.'s Lawnside Bar-B-Que** (1205 E. 85th St.) is a fun spot with wooden floors that slope and old blues posters on the walls. There is a definite Louisiana influence in the food there—great gumbo as well as some of the best barbecue in town. B.B.'s is as famous for the blues jam sessions as it is for the food. The owner has a slogan: "B.B.'s restaurant is where barbecue meets the blues." Thursday nights are the best jam sessions, with John Paul's Flying Circus playing live blues music. Wednesday through Sunday nights local, regional, and national blues acts may be found. They play a two-hour set that may turn into a "jam" session with others joining in. The music is loud, the food fantastic, the crowd enthusiastic, and it is just more darn fun than you can stand. Call (816) 822-7427 to see who is playing tonight or to check the menu, or visit bbslawnsidebbq.com.

Fiorella's Jack Stack Barbecue, in the old train station freight house at 22nd and Wyandotte (816-472-7427; jackstackbbq.com), is definitely worth looking for. The appetizer Rack and a Half (10 huge onion rings served stacked on a stem) will start you off. Also not to be missed are the Fire Kissed Prawns. These are served slightly charred on skewers after being rubbed with the Fiorella brand of sauce, which imparts its own unique hint of garlic and cayenne pepper. The architecture in the Freight House is spectacular. A beautiful high roofline ceiling of natural wood, brick walls, and dynamic artwork set off the magnificent arched windows. There are intimate booths where you can get lost in the atmosphere. The menu is extensive, and fresh seafood is flown in every day. Although the barbecue is what many come here for, Fiorella's also offers beef, pork, and lamb ribs. The Cheesy Corn Bake is one of the sides; it consists of fresh corn kernels and a cheddar cheese sauce that are baked to perfection. The Hickory Pit Beans are as good as they get. Portions are extremely generous, and great service tops off this dining experience. Hours are 11 a.m. to 10 p.m. Mon through Thurs, to 10:30 p.m. Fri and Sat, and 11 a.m. to 9 p.m. Sun.

Stroud's Restaurant is located north of the Missouri River, just off I-35 and Brighton (5410 NE Oak Ridge Rd., Kansas City; 816-454-9600;

TOP ANNUAL EVENTS IN CENTRAL MISSOURI

MARCH

St. Patrick's Day Parade
Lexington
(660) 259-4711

JULY

Fireworks on the Water
Osage Beach
Tan-Tar-A Resort/Four Seasons Resort
(800) 826-8272

AUGUST

Village of Laurie Annual Hillbilly BBQ Cook-Off
Laurie
(573) 374-8776

Missouri State Fair
Sedalia
(660) 530-5600

Community Fair (third week in August)
Lexington
Old Fiddlers and Skillet-Throwing contest

SEPTEMBER

Santa-Cali-Gon Days Festival
Independence
Celebrates the Santa Fe, California, and Oregon Trails
(816) 252-4745

Annual Fall Festival of Color
Hot Air Balloon Race
Osage Beach
(573) 365-6663

OCTOBER

American Royal Barbecue
Kansas City
300 teams of BBQers, music, dancing, and food
(816) 221-9800

Annual Old Tyme Apple Festival
Versailles
(573) 378-4401

Plattdütscher Low German Theatre
Cole Camp
(573) 668-4970

Annual Lake of the Ozarks Dixieland Jazz Festival
Lake Ozarks
Country Club Hotel & Spa
(573) 392-1731

Annual Missouri State Buddy Bass Championship
Sunrise Beach
(573) 374-5500

Apples, Arts & Antiques Festival
Lexington
Scarecrow contest with more than 40 unique scarecrows on the lampposts downtown

NOVEMBER

Plaza Lighting Ceremony
Kansas City
(816) 274-8444

stroudsrestaurant.com). The motto stated on the waiter's T-shirts is "We choke our own chickens." Be prepared for a wait, but it is worth it. This picturesque farmstead is a walk back in time. You can stroll the garden, take a walk down to the lake to see the swans, or have a seat in an old buggy and contemplate the big family-style chicken dinner you are about to enjoy. Meals come complete with green beans, mashed potatoes and gravy, and homemade cinnamon rolls that melt in your mouth. There are plenty of things on the menu, but the fried chicken is what keeps people coming back for more.

As long as you are north of the Missouri River, take I-35 north to I-29 North to the Barry Road exit. Go left (west) and take a right into **Zona Rosa,** a neighborhood of shops, restaurants, and condos. There are plenty of well-known names along with some homegrown ones. Go to the Zona Rosa website to see what else is in store for you: zonarosa.com.

Want to have a real Kansas City steak? This is a personal favorite for steak, promise you, a steak you will remember. The **Hereford House** (8661 N. Stoddard Ave.; 816-584-9000; herefordhouse.com) has been a local tradition for more than 50 years. Probably the first restaurant KC natives remember (from Prom Night, say) and still one of the best places to have a KC steak cooked just right. It used to be downtown but now has moved to the 'burbs, with a location in Zona Rosa, but the quality has not changed a bit. Hours are lunch Mon through Fri 11 a.m. to 3 p.m., Sat and Sun noon to 3 p.m. Dinner Mon through Thurs 3 to 9 p.m., Fri and Sat until 10 p.m., and on Sun from noon to 9 p.m. In fact, Zona Rosa is a pleasant way to spend an evening strolling after eating a steak.

Now for dessert: Back in 1817 the Stam family owned a bakery in the Netherlands that was famous for pastries and chocolates. In 1913 Jacobus Stam decided to specialize in chocolates and the bakery became **Choco-laterie Stam** (8747 NW Prairie View Rd.; 816-256-3317). Now the Dutch tradition of fresh cream and nut-filled chocolate bonbons as they were made in the Netherlands has come to Kansas City. Stop by and indulge yourself in one sweet bonbon or buy a box for someone you love (love yourself).

Here and there, drowsing on old streets, pocketed in small shopping centers, crouching behind buildings, or even tucked inside buildings, you're likely to find places that definitely qualify as out of the mainstream. After barbecue, Kansas City is famous for jazz.

Eighteenth and Vine in Kansas City was really jumping from the 1920s to the 1950s. There were smoky joints filled with baseball players from the Kansas City Negro League team, the Monarchs, and jazz musicians signing autographs for fans and talking and laughing over drinks. There were restaurants and nightclubs there—the Mardi Gras, Blue Room, and Subway Club—and baseball and jazz are forever linked in Kansas City. An untouched memory of that time can still be found at the **Mutual Musicians' Foundation** (1823 Highland Ave.; 816-471-5212; thefoundation-jamson.org), in the old Musicians' Union Hall—a hot-pink bungalow in the historic jazz district around 18th and Vine. It is, in fact, the only building inside the city limits that is on the National Register of Historic Places. Tours are available, but the place really jumps on Friday and Saturday nights when musicians from throughout Kansas City gather here to jam after their regular gigs around the city. The traditional jazz jam starts at midnight. There is no cover charge, but donations are always welcome to keep this place open.

trivia

Kansas City has more fountains than any city except Rome and all of them are turned off in the winter except one. The Northland Fountain at the intersection of North Oak Street Trafficway and Vivion Road in Kansas City North becomes a gigantic ongoing ice sculpture, never the same, as the water cascades and melts throughout the winter. Surrounding the fountain are a walk path and park, but the enormous fountain is visible from both Vivion Road and North Oak Street Trafficway.

Now the area is coming alive again, and the link is still strong. At the **American Jazz Museum** (1616 E. 18th St., Kansas City; 816-474-8763; americanjazzmuseum.org), visitors can listen to the music of such greats as Louis Armstrong, Julia Lee, Duke Ellington, Ella Fitzgerald, and Charlie "Yardbird" Parker. In fact, the museum is the final resting place of Yardbird's saxophone. The museum has an extensive exhibit honoring Ella Fitzgerald, "The First Lady of Song," with 30 of her most identifiable personal effects, including her famous cat-eye, rhinestone-covered glasses and silver pumps.

This is one of the most interactive museums in the country. Music fills the air as the story of jazz is told through sight and sound. Visitors can listen to performances while a giant video wall projects early performances by some of these famous artists. The museum offers something for every level of jazz understanding. You can putter in a mixing station and create your own mix of sounds or enter the Wee-Bob children's activity center. Shop for a CD, T-shirt, or poster in the Swing Shop.

trivia

While you are downtown in Kansas City, look for the "cow on a stick." The huge bull used to be atop the American Hereford Association, but the organization has since moved. Now the giant bovine watches over the area from his perch on a pylon above Argus Health Systems. They decided to keep it so folks could find them easily.

Museum hours are Tues through Sat from 9 a.m. to 6 p.m. and Sun from noon to 6 p.m. Admission to the museum is $6 for adults, $2.50 for children, or you can buy a combination ticket to both the jazz and baseball museums for $8 for adults, $4 for children younger than age 12; kids younger than age 3 are free.

Kansas City's *Negro Leagues Baseball Museum* (816-221-1920 or 888-221-NLBM; nlbm.com) is at 1616 E. 18th St., too, and it remembers the other half of the jazz and baseball love affair—the league that played in the 1920s and 1930s before the all-white major leagues would accept black players. Black players formed their own league, and some of the best athletes ever to play the game got their start there: Satchel Paige, Ernie Banks, Josh Gibson, "Cool Papa" Bell, and Buck O'Neill. Do these names sound familiar? How about Willie Mays, Hank Aaron, Roy Campanella, or the incredible Jackie Robinson? The Kansas City Monarchs were considered the Yankees of black baseball. The Negro National League drew more than 50,000 spectators from coast to coast. Then in 1947 a guy named Jackie Robinson stepped up to bat for the Brooklyn Dodgers and smashed the color barrier right over the fence. The rest is baseball history.

The museum is more than just a collection of pictures and memorabilia: It re-creates the look, sound, and feel of the game in the heyday of the league. Its centerpiece main gallery has a three-station interactive computer module with video games, historical vignettes, and coaching tips. The museum covers the history of black baseball from its beginning after the Civil War through the end of Negro Leagues play in the 1960s, and it features a custom-designed database to search for the play-by-play of league games. The gift shop features autographed baseballs, Louisville Slugger bats, T-shirts, caps, and jackets. Hours are Tues through Sat 9 a.m. until 6 p.m., Sun noon to 6 p.m. Admission is $6 for adults and $2.50 for children younger than age 12.

Right across the street is the historic *Gem Theater Cultural and Performing Arts Center* (1616 E. 18th St.). As early as the 1920s, Kansas City's vibrant theatrical community was known around the world. This reconstructed theater still has the trademark neon marquee hanging outside and once again presents first-class entertainment. The latest in lighting, sound, and acoustical design have been added. The Alvin Ailey Dancers perform here along with renowned jazz groups and theater ensembles. Call the ticket office at (816) 474-6262 for a schedule filled with multimedia events.

At 2033 Vine is the *Black Archives of Mid-America,* where you can find documents, artifacts, paintings, and exhibits that explore the lives of African Americans in Kansas City, including musicians, artists, writers, and

Something Old, Something New

Although not off the beaten path by any means, there's something old and something new in Kansas City. The old Kansas City Union Station—site of an infamous gangster massacre and formerly one of the largest and busiest rail centers in the country—at 2300 Main St. has been restored to its glorious original beauty and is now an urban plaza and entertainment center. There are several restaurants, evening entertainment at City Nights with live performance theater, motion pictures, and laser and magic shows as well as music and theater performances. There are also shopping areas and, best of all, especially for the kids, Science City, featuring more than 50 hands-on environments for all ages to explore. Science City is a city-within-a-city on multiple levels with streets and alleyways. Each exhibit is a realistic environment that offers interactive experiences with costumed citizens who live and work in the "city's" Festival Plaza, Uptown, Downtown, Southside, and Old Town. You can even explore an excavation dig site in prehistoric Kansas City or assist a surgical team in the Operating Room. Want a chance to be on TV? You can broadcast news from the television station. You can bake a cake in the test kitchen or try your hand at being an astronaut in the space center. Or you can board a real locomotive located just outside the station. Science City's website is at sciencecity.com. Science City is open daily. Call (816) 460-9372 or (800) 556-9372 for times and shows.

leaders in many other fields. The first-floor exhibit features the Tuskegee Airmen of World War II, and the second floor is dedicated to the Buffalo soldiers of the Civil War. Hours are Mon through Fri 9 a.m. to 4:30 p.m. Visit blackarchives.org.

Downtown (way downtown near the Missouri River) is the *City Market,* where you can shop outdoors with a big wicker basket for just-picked produce in the wonderful atmosphere of a European marketplace. You can buy everything from morel mushrooms in early May to late-harvest turnips in October. There are always fresh eggs and fresh or even live chickens, and on Saturday mornings local farmers and buyers meet over the freshest produce this side of the garden. The area by the Missouri River has undergone restoration, complete with a riverboat museum.

The year was 1856 when the steamboat *Arabia* set out for the West, loaded with trade goods and passengers. As the folks at the *Steamboat Arabia Museum* (400 Grand, Kansas City; 816-471-4030; 1856.com) say, you'll find everything from axes, awls, and augers to zillions of other treasures restored to near-mint condition. How did they manage to amass all this in one place? Well, the *Arabia* hit a cottonwood snag in the Missouri River and sank like a stone. There it rested from 1856 to 1988, a time capsule waiting to spill its treasures, both everyday and exotic, into the present. But, of course, even the everyday from more than 100 years ago is exotic now. You'll find spurs, tinware, perfume (that retained its scent after its sojourn under 45 feet of mud and water), wine, whiskey, and champagne (still bubbly), canned goods, hair pins, inkwells, and clothing.

The Hawley family excavated the boat and spent untold hours painstakingly restoring the artifacts they found. To our good fortune, rather than selling off the bounty, they opened a museum, and this treasure trove now tells casual visitors, schoolkids, scholars, living-history reenactors, and just plain history buffs volumes about what life was like on the frontier; civilization was built with the bits and pieces of trade goods carried by packets like the *Arabia.* A short film introduces you to the museum and to the excavation and restoration process. See what frontier life was like. Adults $14.50, seniors $13.50, children 4–12 $5.50, free for younger kids. Hours are Mon through Sat 10 a.m. to 5:30 p.m. (last tour begins at 4 p.m.), and Sun noon to 5 p.m. (last tour begins at 3:30 p.m.). Winter hours, Jan through Mar, close at 4:30 p.m. and last tour begins at 3 p.m.

Wearin' o' the Green—Italian Style

The North End is where I grew up. We lived with my grandmother, "Nana" Randazzo, until I was about 12 years old. I went to the Catholic school a couple of blocks from our home—Holy Rosary School—and rarely left the neighborhood. My grandma spoke Sicilian, my parents were bilingual, and I grew up knowing just enough Sicilian to stay out of trouble with my Nana. Everyone in the neighborhood was Italian. There was a penny-candy store on one corner, an Italian bakery on the other, and a park with a bocce court and a swimming pool a half block away. A good restaurant served the area, and we could open fire hydrants on hot summer days and play kick-the-can in the streets. Yelling "first light!" when the street lights came on was a nightly contest. We even had lightning bugs. Why would anyone want to leave a neighborhood so wonderful? It was safe. It was home.

But one of my earliest childhood memories, kindergarten or first grade, was of walking to school on March 17—a day that meant absolutely nothing to my family—and finding everyone else dressed in green. Now remember, this was an Italian neighborhood. There was not a drop of Irish blood anywhere for miles. Suddenly everyone was Irish, and I was the one who got pinched dozens of times—for not wearing green—before the bell rang to begin classes. I was terrified, and when the lunch bell rang, I took off for home with my lunch tucked under my arm like a football. (We wrapped our lunch in newspaper; sacks didn't exist for us.) When I arrived home unexpectedly, crying, my Nana couldn't understand what the problem was. I refused to go back to school until she found me something green to wear. When she saw that I was adamant, she began to rummage in the closets muttering "manacia l'America!" under her breath. (That is phonetically spelled and is some sort of Sicilian-American *slanguage*. It means "blame it on America" and was used whenever American things got to be too much for her.) I returned to school wearing green but not understanding why. I noticed that nobody pinched Sister Mary Margaret. Although she was wearing black, she had a green shamrock pinned to her habit.

Across from the 5th Street market building is ***Cascone's Grill*** (17 E. 5th St.; 816-471-1018), where the market crowd eats. The Cascone family cooks up the most amazing early morning Italian breakfasts (Italian-breaded steak, Italian sausage, fried eggs, hash browns, and Italian-bread toast) and late-in-the-day lunches featuring Vita Cascone's own spaghetti sauce. They open and close seasonally with the rhythm of the market crowd, and lines can be long to get in (always a good sign food-wise since there are several good restaurants in the market area). But Tues through Sat 6 a.m. to 2 p.m. will usually find them open.

Catty-corner from the market, across the street at 513 Walnut, is **Planters' Seed and Spice Co.** (816-842-3651; plantersseed.com). Step inside this old building and inhale the wonderful odors of fresh bulk herbs and spices, the scent of old wood, the aroma of exotic teas and coffees, and the clean smell of seeds. Need a watering can? They've got 'em. Want to buy a pound of dried bay leaves? Look no further. It's a delightful place.

Just down the street from the City Market is a French bistro—admittedly a most unlikely spot to find such a place—but it is as authentic as it can be, with an outdoor cafe in the alley just as they are in Paris. **Le Fou Frog** (400 E. 5th St.; 816-474-6060; lefoufrog.com) isn't really faux at all (it means "the crazy frog"), as owner and chef Mano Rafael will tell you. He is from Marseilles and made his reputation as head chef in some New York hot spots (Petrossian and Casanis). He met and married Barbara Bayer from Kansas City, and the rest is history.

The real test of a French bistro is the *soupe a l'oignon gratinée* with a bubbly top of Gruyère cheese. This one passes with gold stars. Of course, it is impossible to taste everything on the menu, but give it a good try. The *poulet aux olives et herbes de Provence* (whole baby chicken roasted in a fragrant sauce of olives and fresh herbs and served with garlic mashed potatoes) is a personal favorite. Seasonal menu changes daily. Entrees range from $19 to $42—and are worth every franc. Le Frog is open for dinner only Tues through Thurs 5:30 to 10 p.m., Fri and Sat 5:30 to 11 p.m., and Sun 5 to 9 p.m. Sunday nights feature live music. There is an excellent wine list with some very good and inexpensive wines available, just as there should be in a bistro.

Keep going east on 5th Street to Harrison, and on the corner is a restaurant that has changed hands a few times but has always been Italian, because this is a neighborhood simply known as "the North End." It is the Little Italy that many big cities have. Here Mass was said in Italian at nearby Holy Rosary Catholic Church in the old days. Now the neighborhood had blended into a more Vietnamese/Italian mix, but it still has the feel of the streets we played on as children—where opening a fire hydrant was the coolest thing that happened on a hot summer day—and that ambience is still there. **Garozzo's Ristorante** (526 Harrison, Kansas City; 816-221-2455;

garozzos.com) has soft music by Frank Sinatra, a lively bar, and really, really huge servings of pasta. Do not, repeat, do not order spaghetti and meatballs unless you want to eat it for a week or can share it with several other people. The other dishes are more moderately proportioned but excellent. If you like, no, love garlic, order some olive oil to dip your Italian bread into and you will get a bowl of oil smothered in garlic and Parmesan cheese. Hours are Mon through Thurs 11 a.m. to 11 p.m. and Sat 4 to 11 p.m.

St. Mary's Episcopal Church (1307 Holmes; 816-842-0975) is a grand old church in downtown Kansas City. The redbrick church has been there forever (since 1888) and as with many old churches, it has some interesting history and a good ghost story. Amazingly, the building was spared when the neighborhood around it was razed during urban renewal in the 1960s. It is a wonderful Sunday morning experience to follow the sound of the carillon and to hear the organist make the huge pipe organ sing for the Solemn High Mass celebrated every Sun at 10 a.m., complete with incense and bells. The congregation is an interesting and varied collection of people from the urban area as well as suburban people who make the drive into the city every Sunday. Call for the times of other services.

KC Power and Light District downtown offers nightlife and more (800-767-7700; visitkc.com). People from Kansas City remember when

The Ghost of St. Mary's

The ghost of St. Mary's is believed to be that of Father Henry Jardine, who was rector of St. Mary's in 1879. A crypt was built under the altar for Father Jardine's body before his death. Because he suffered from a painful facial nerve disorder, he took laudanum (tincture of opium) and used chloroform to help him sleep. One night he died from the combination. The bishop declared it a suicide, and therefore Father Jardine's body was buried in unconsecrated ground rather than in his beloved church. There have been several ghostly incidents. When one acolyte arrived at the church, he saw a priest, in vestments, who stood facing the altar. He hurried to the sacristy thinking he must be late, only to find the rector waiting for him there. When they went back to the sanctuary, no one was there. Several people have sensed a presence in the gallery where his restless ghost hovers. St. Mary's rector, Reverend Dr. Bruce Rahtjen, is attempting to have Father Jardine's remains moved from the cemetery to the church's columbarium, perhaps allowing his spirit to rest in peace at last.

downtown was the go-to place. There was jazz, there were parties, it was alive with rhythm and blues, and one of the places remembered fondly is still tucked away in the historic Hilton President Kansas City hotel, within walking distance of the Power and Light District. *The Drum Room* (1335 Baltimore; 816-303-1686; drumroomkc.com) has been open since 1941 and still has the flavor of old KC. You can feel the presence of Frank Sinatra, Benny Goodman, Sammy Davis Jr., Tommy Dorsey, Glenn Miller, the Marx Brothers, and Patsy Cline, who have all played this venue. There is live entertainment still on Fri and Sat night from 9 p.m. until 1 a.m. Happy hour is 4:30 to 6:30 p.m. and is the perfect time to try one of their infamous 9-ounce martinis. Lunch is served from 11 a.m. to 4 p.m. (try the sweet potato fries), when dinner begins (go for the paellas named after Sinatra and his Rat Pack) and is served until 10 p.m.

Along Southwest Boulevard the scent of chile peppers fills the air. This is Kansas City's Hispanic neighborhood, and the restaurants here are very popular, especially at lunchtime.

If you are looking for homemade tamales wrapped in corn husks, go to *La Posada Grocery* (728 Southwest Blvd., Kansas City; 816-421-0715). They sell about any Mexican ingredient you could want—chiles, spices, corn husks, even Mexican coffee. Speaking Spanish will ease the shopping queries here. Hours are Mon, Tues, Thurs, Fri, and Sat 8 a.m. to 6 p.m. and Sun 8 a.m. to 3 p.m.

There is always some discussion about which, exactly, is the best Mexican restaurant in the Southwest Boulevard area. It just depends on whom you ask. One favorite of people who work downtown and eat there often is *Manny's* (207 Southwest Blvd.; 816-474-7696; mannyskc.com). The Lopez family has been here for years and years—about 30, actually. They bottle their salsa to take home because there is such a demand for it. If you have never tasted real Mexican pork chili, it should go to the top of the list. Manny's is open for lunch and dinner Tues through Sat and makes a mean margarita. Another favorite is *Ponak's Mexican Kitchen* (2856 Southwest Blvd.; 816-753-4886; ponaksmexicankitchen.com). This place has great margaritas on tap and a covered outdoor dining patio. There is a special every night and a personal favorite is the spinach enchilada on Wednesday—no, wait, maybe it's the Mexican pork tips stew cooked slow in a tomato-jalapeño-garlic sauce on Thursday. Maybe everything at Ponak's is good. You decide.

The Hallmark Crown Center (2450 Grand Avenue; crowncenter.com) is a little city of its own with luxury residences and hotels and several levels of shopping. It even has an outdoor ice-skating rink. This is not off the beaten path, though; it is one of the city's most popular areas. Across the street—or over the skywalk if the weather is bad—is Union Station.

You *can* buy the ***Best of Kansas City*** (816-842-0200; thebestofkc.com) at the shop of the same name at Crown Center. Everything from art to Zarda barbecue sauce is sold here. Order gift baskets at (800) 366-8780. Hours are 10 a.m. to 9 p.m. (Sun until 5 p.m.).

There is a little-known museum under a well-known tower standing sentry on a hill across from Crown Center. ***The National World War I Museum at Liberty Memorial*** (100 W. 26th St.; 816-888-8100; theworldwar .org) is in a new complex and uses interactive technology to bring alive the history of this "war to end all wars." Then ride the elevator to the top of the tower for a breathtaking view of Kansas City.

This is an old industrial area with some pretty good eating places hidden away in it. One of them, ***Lidia's*** (101 W. 22nd St.; 816-221-3722 for reservations; lidias-kc.com) is located in a converted warehouse. Lidia's is very well known around town—there are three in New York—and beautifully done. The food, of course, is quite good, as is the wine list. Hours are 11 a.m. to 2 p.m. weekdays for lunch and 5 to 9:30 p.m. for dinner. Sat dinner hours are from 4:30 to 10:30 p.m.

This area is the up-and-coming art district of KC. The ***Crossroads Art District*** is situated between Crown Center and downtown, just behind Union Station. A hundred-year-old railroad trestle bridge was moved from the river, through downtown KC, and placed at Union Station, and now is used as a walkway from the station to the nearby art district. The amazing move was filmed and shown on the History channel. For a really fun evening, join the

trivia

The Crossroads Art District began in the 1980s when a professor from the Kansas City Art Institute bought an old building in the warehouse district and turned it into lofts where young artists could afford to live. Their rent subsidized the gallery downstairs, where their work was displayed. Today that building is the Leedy-Voulkos Art Center (2012 Baltimore Ave.; 816-474-1919; leedy-voulkos.com), and many other galleries and lofts have made this a popular urban art community.

6,000 other people who flock to First Fridays, the city's monthly art walk, from 7 to 9 p.m. Shops and galleries stay open late and the restaurants tease you with scents of wonderful food to nibble as you walk.

Christopher Elbow Artisanal Chocolate (1819 McGee St.; 816-842-1300; elbowchocolates.com) is where every piece of chocolate is a work of art. Christopher's signature Stiletto vodka chocolates compete with strawberry balsamic caramel (from Modena), rosemary caramel (locally grown rosemary), caramel with *fleur de sel* (a soft ganache infused with French sea salt) or a personal fave, the bourbon pecan (with dark chocolate making it very healthy). This famous chocolatier is open Tues through Sat from 10 a.m. to 6 p.m. *Black Bamboo* (1815 Wyandotte St.; 816-283-3000; black-bamboo.com) carries Asian antiques, Chinese pieces dating from the Qing Dynasty (1644–1911) and carefully restored by craftsmen in that country, along with modern furniture chosen to complement the Asian antiques. Hours are Tues through Sat 10 a.m. to 5 p.m. One of the most interesting to visit is *Webster House* (1644 Wyandotte; 816-221-4713; websterhousekc .com), a circa 1885 schoolhouse restored and filled with antiques, gifts, and home goodies. It is also a favorite place for lunch.

The perfect place to cool off on a sweltering summer day used to be the corner drugstore in any small town. It was a great spot to meet your favorite sweetie and the only place to get a fizzy chocolate phosphate, an ice-cold cherry Coke, or a tall ice-cream soda. *The Kansas City Museum* (3218 Gladstone Blvd.; 816-460-2020; kcmuseum.org) is in the process of renovation. No tours are available for Corinthian Hall (originally the carriage house) in the foreseeable future; however, museum programming continues on the site, in other buildings. Visitors are welcome daily. The museum visitor center can provide an introduction to the Long family, who owned the home, and the history of Kansas City. History-themed films, such as the pre-Civil War epic *Bad Blood,* are shown frequently in the StoryTarium. The new exhibition *The Long Family and Corinthian Hall* has opened, on colorful informational panels, around the perimeter of the estate.

The museum has re-created that corner drugstore for the children of the city. What the heck's a phosphate? A combination of flavored carbonated water and ice. Why is that chocolate-covered dip of vanilla called a sundae? Old "blue laws" made it illegal to sell soda water on Sunday, so it had everything an ice-cream soda had except carbonated water. Most soda pops were originally hawked as health tonics. In fact, Coca-Cola was invented by a pharmacist. The cherry-wood pharmacy dates from 1886, the marble-topped soda-fountain counter and stained-glass lamps with spigots from about 1910. All came from the Kirby Drugstore in Modena. The museum hours are 9:30 a.m. to 4:30 p.m. Tues through Sat, and noon to 4:30 p.m. Sun. Regular museum admission is $2.50 for adults and $2 for kids and seniors.

The 39th Street area of Kansas City is a wonderful old area in which to stroll. There are antiques shops, crystal shops, and just a lot of interesting places. The area also is home to some of the city's best restaurants. Now, before we get all fancy-schmancy with the new bistros, let's talk about ***Sosa's 39th Street Diner*** (3906 Waddell; 816-531-7672) just past downtown Kansas City. It is replacing the old Nichol's Lunch, which was everybody's favorite place to eat at odd hours. Like a real old-fashioned diner, it was just always open. Always. 24/7. The location at 39th and Southwest Trafficway made it handy for the late-night people doing the downtown Kansas City jazz and blues clubs to eat breakfast before trying for home after the bars closed at 1:30 in the morning. Sosa's opened in 2013 and is a celebration of Kansas City in its decor, lots of black-and-white vintage photos of Kansas City, and a combination of American and Mexican comfort foods (huevos rancheros for breakfast!). He plans freshly baked breads, house-made cinnamon rolls, and for lunch and dinner we're talking about chicken-fried steak, fried chicken, pork tenderloin, beef burritos . . . what's not to like? Worth giving it a go, wouldn't you say? Sosa says they are "considering" doing the 24-hour thing in the future if the restaurant takes off as planned.

Around the corner, about a half mile away, is the ***Genghis Khan Mongolian Barbecue*** (3906 Bell St.; 816-753-3600; gkbbq.com), an eat-all-you-can meat, seafood, and vegetable grill that is well worth its modest prices. Don't be misled by the name. It is not a barbecue in the KC sense of smoked ribs. This is fresh raw meat cooked before your eyes on a huge griddle-type cooking area. You choose your shrimp, calamari, meat, veggies, whatever and they throw it on the grill and stir fry it while you watch. Hours are Mon through Fri 11 a.m. to 9:30 p.m., Sat noon to 10 p.m., closed Sun.

Drive on toward Main on 39th Street and you will dead-end at an old art deco building, and the only clue you will have that you have found the right place is the occasional neon beer sign in the second-floor windows. You have found ***Harling's Upstairs*** (3941-A Main St.; 816-531-0303). The best time to search out Harling's is between 1 and 6 p.m. on Saturday, when Diane "Mama" Ray and her blues band pour their heart into a jam session that packs the house every week. A long list of Kansas City jazz and blues musicians join her to jam on any given Saturday. Stay put once you are there; if you give up your seat, you will never get it back. There are other things going on at Harling's at night, including Irish music on Thurs. But Mama Ray is worth the trip on a Saturday afternoon, and if you love the blues, you will get there early and stay through the entire session.

There is more good jazz and blues in Kansas City than anywhere in the country. Pick up a copy of *Jam (Jazz Ambassador Magazine)*, with listings of all the jazz clubs in town and who is playing where. Then you can search out nightlife at such places as the ***Levee*** (16 W. 43rd St.; 816-561-2821; thelevee.net), with wonderfully loud rock 'n' roll to dance to on Saturday afternoons until 8 p.m.

In case you are cruisin' on your Harley (or even if you're not) and want to experience an upscale "biker-bar atmosphere," check out Frank Hick's ***F.O.G. Cycles & Knucklehead's Saloon*** (club: 816-483-1456; office: 816-483-6407; knuckleheadskc.com). It's a honky-tonk blues bar next to FOG bike shop at 2715 Rochester in the East Bottoms just off I-435 and Front Street. Live bands play that cool Kansas City blues music. When weather permits, you might find yourself at an outdoor street party. Wear your leathers if you want to fit right in. Knucklehead's is open Wed from 6 p.m. to midnight, Thurs from 6 p.m. to 1 a.m., Fri from 6 p.m. to 1:30 a.m., Sat from noon to 1:30 a.m., and Sun from 1 to 6 p.m. It is an over-21 club, so minors must be with their parents. Check the website for upcoming shows and show times. Tickets can be ordered online or by calling the club or office phone numbers. The saloon took some top honors for blues clubs and is the premier club for that venue in KC. It has been awarded Best of KC by *Pitch,* a Kansas City newspaper, and the "Keepin' the Blues Alive" award.

At Knucklehead's, you can have the usual hamburgers, tacos, or sausage, of course, but you gotta try the Knuckle Sandwich. Don't ask what's in it, just order it. (Okay, if you must know, it's fried bologna.) From downtown Independence Avenue (east of Prospect), go north on Chestnut. Go to the stoplight at Nicholson Avenue and turn left. Turn left onto Montgall. Turn left one more time onto Rochester and you are there.

At the corner of the block at 1700 Summit, the **Bluebird Bistro** (816-221-7559; bluebirdbistro.com) serves lunch Mon through Sat—great home-made soups and interesting sandwiches on crunchy sunflower-seed bread. This corner cafe is much larger than it looks from the outside, but it fills up quickly at lunchtime. The tin ceilings and antique cabinets make the high-ceilinged rooms cozy. A long bar along one wall is a fine spot to wait for a table. Lunch is available from 11 a.m. to 2 p.m. Mon through Sat. Dinner is served Wed through Sun from 5 to 10 p.m.

Historic Westport, some 40 blocks south of downtown, was the whole city at one time. Some of us think it still is. **The Broadway Cafe** (301 Westport Rd; 816-531-2431) and the **Broadway Roasting Co.** (4106 Broadway; 816-931-9955) are just two neighborhood coffeehouses in Westport. There is a blackboard where colorful chalk lists today's beverages and baked-today scones, biscotti, and cakes (their famous apple cake, for example). Sara Honan and Jon Cates invite you to taste samples of that day's baked goods and have a cup of one of the more than 20 types of coffee they roast every day (Ethiopian Harrar, for example). The coffee is roasted at the roastery on Westport Road, but you can still smell the coffee roasting "when the wind's right" at the other address, too. Why two cafes so close together? They like the Westport area. And so will you. Visit their website at broadwaycafeandroastery.com. The cafe is open daily 7 a.m. until 9 p.m. and the Roasting Company is open Mon through Fri 7 a.m. until 5 p.m.

The **Classic Cup,** owned by John Meyer, has moved to 47th and Central (301 W. 47th St.; 816-753-1840; classiccup.com). The all-time favorite entree here is the raspberry–Dijon mustard sauce on grilled pork tenderloin (sometimes it's blueberry–, blackberry–, or tart cherry–Dijon sauce). Hours are Mon through Fri from 8 a.m. to 10 p.m., Sat from 8 a.m. to 11 p.m., and Sun from 9:30 a.m. to 10 p.m.

> ## hasanyoneseen dan'snephew?
>
> **Kelly's** in historic Westport (500 Westport Rd.; 816-561-0635) is a good place to sip a brew. This has been a very popular Kansas City nightspot for more than 30 years. In fact, Daniel Boone's nephew used to hang out here. Well, he once ran a trading post in the building, which is the oldest in Kansas City. He hasn't come in lately.

Three Dog Bakery (602 W. 48th St.; 816-753-3647; threedogbakery .com) has tasty-looking cookies arranged in a bakery case. You might be tempted to buy a bagful to munch on as you walk. What you need, however, is a doggie bag, because owners Mark Beckloff and Dan Dye are serving freshly baked treats for your pooch. You can buy your canine a pupcake or a cheese pizza. For the vegetable course there is "collie-flower," and for dessert there are "snickerpoodles," always a favorite. A portion of the price goes to help abused dogs. The treats have no salt or chemicals and are low-fat (your dog will thank you). You can also order your loving pet its own specially decorated birthday cake to share with other dogs on the block. Three Dog Bakery has grown from its origins here in KC to a franchise that has tongues hanging out around the world. They use only human-grade ingredients, so you can join your pup for a snack if you are so inclined. You can order treats online not only for your dog but for your cat as well. But there is only one feline product, a freeze-dried salmon treat called We Pity the Kitties. Hours are 10 a.m. to 7 p.m. Mon through Sat (Thurs until 9 p.m.) and 11 a.m. to 5 p.m. on Sun.

Let's get small. If you love tiny things (or if you haven't quite grown up), don't miss Kansas City's *Toy and Miniature Museum* (5235 Oak St.; 816-235-8000; toyandminiaturemuseum.org). Childhood friends Mary Harris Francis and Barbara Marshall started the museum in a Mediterranean-style mansion built in 1906. It has been expanded to 21,500 square feet. The mansion and the surrounding property are owned by the University of Missouri–Kansas City, but the toys and miniatures belong to a private nonprofit foundation. Miniatures are not toys; scale is important in a miniature—everything in a miniature room must look exactly like a full-size room. Toys are a separate collection.

Tucked upstairs is a Victorian nursery with a brass cradle made in Paris in 1850. It has been in Mary's family for several generations. Barbara's father, Hallmark Cards founder Joyce C. Hall, had a dollhouse built for his daughter at a local high school. When it was time to pick it up for Christmas, it was too big to take out of the school, so she did not get her dollhouse. Now they have a museum recognized as one of the largest miniatures museums in the world. There are more than 85 antique furnished dollhouses at least 100 years old, scale-model miniature rooms, and toys. The museum is open Wed through Sat 10 a.m. to 4 p.m. and Sun 1 to 4 p.m. It is closed for two weeks following Labor Day. Admission is $7 for adults, $6 for seniors and students, and $5 for children. Every Saturday at 1 p.m. you can enjoy storytellers, and at 2:30 p.m. on the first Sat of the month there's a magician to entertain you.

The Crestwood Shops around 55th and Oak Streets lure antiquers. *Charlecote* (337 E. 55th St.; 816-444-4622; charlecoteantiques.com) specializes in 18th-century English furniture from Queen Anne to George Hepplewhite, when craftsmanship was at its height. *Pear Tree* (303 E. 55th St.; 816-333-2100; peartreeantiqueskc.com) is open 10 a.m. to 5 p.m. and is full of really cool stuff—really nice, albeit not inexpensive, antiques from the world over, plus accessories, lighting, mirrors, and decorative arts for both home and garden. If you want it, it's probably here and fun to search for, too. Look at the website to see some examples of what you will find.

If you have children along, you might want to swing by *Brookside Toy & Science* (330 W. 63rd St.; 816-523-4501; brooksidetoyandscience .com), where a fine display of bugs under glass and an array of toys not to be believed will keep the kids busy for a while. Next door is the *Reading Reptile* (328 W. 63rd St.; 816-753-0441; readingreptile.com), a well-loved kids' bookstore, which is open Mon through Fri from 10 a.m. until 6 p.m. and on Sat until 5 p.m., and Sun noon to 5 p.m. And just to prove that reading is fun, click onto their website and read the funny story of how owners Debbie and Pete and the kids have survived the Bookstore Wars since 1999.

For the grown-ups, a well-named place called *Stuff* (316 W. 63rd St.; 816-361-8222; pursuegoodstuff.com) is packed with the same: stuff such as antiques, collectibles, fine art, and gifts.

The piano bar seems to be a dying breed of nightclub, which is what makes *Piano Room Lounge* (8410 Wornall Rd., Kansas City; 816-363-8722) such a great find. This is a comfortable neighborhood bar in a strip mall. But don't be fooled by its quiet storefront: The Piano Room is a one-of-a-kind, traditional piano bar that opened in 1978 and was originally called Inge's. This intimate space is frequented by customers who are always welcomed to the microphone by Kansas City Jazz Hall of Fame piano player Dave McCubbin. Dave seems to be able to play almost any tune ever written. His book ranges from standards and Broadway to pop and rock. Dave is also an accomplished vocalist, as are the bartenders and many longtime customers. He even played, just on request, "Happy Birthday" to the tune of the

"Song of the Volga Boatmen" so I could sing it for a friend's birthday. The guy's a genius.

Singers and music lovers alike are always welcome at this unique Kansas City venue. This is not a karaoke bar, however, and the people who come up to stand by the mic are regulars and, for the most part, have the voice and style of professionals. There is no recorded backup music or words on screens; this is the real thing. Open Mon through Sat from 10 a.m. to 1:30 a.m.

The city of *Independence,* just east of downtown Kansas City on I-70, could be a day trip in itself: There's Harry S Truman's home, now a national park, and the *Truman Presidential Library,* at US 24 and Delaware (816-268-8200 or 800-833-1225; trumanlibrary.org), is open 9 a.m. to 5 p.m. Mon through Sat and noon to 5 p.m. Sun (closed Thanksgiving, Christmas, and New Year's Day). There's a special program night on Thursday, when the museum is open until 9 p.m. Admission is $7 adults, $5 seniors, $3 children ages 6 to 18, children younger than age 6 admitted free. Self-guided tours.

strange as it seems

Want to see the mantel Jackie Kennedy started a feud over? When Harry Truman moved this mantel to the Truman Library in Independence, the former first lady had a fit and wanted it returned to the White House.

In Independence you'll also find the world center for the Reorganized Church of Latter-Day Saints and the RLDS Auditorium. There are also Civil War battlefields, as well as the beginnings of the Santa Fe Trail, still visible in the worn earth. (Sometimes it seems as if half the towns on this side of the state claim the trail, but in Independence they still celebrate the Santa-Cali-Gon, where the Santa Fe, California, and Oregon Trails jumped off into the wilderness.) The National Frontier Trails Center is a fine place to learn more about the hardships and adventures of those who dared to leave civilization behind and strike out across the wilderness to a new life. It's in the historic Waggoner-Gates Milling Company building. Call (816) 325-7575 or (800) 810-3900 or visit visitindependence.com for further information about the city.

The *Rheinland Restaurant* (208 N. Main, Independence; 816-461-5383; rheinlandrestaurant.com) serves a scrumptious *Zigeunerschnitzel*

(Gypsy Schnitzel), a pork cutlet with a spicy pepper sauce and a side of *späetzle* (tiny dumpling or noodles). A large dark beer will help the digestion. Heinz and Rosie Heinzelmann are the owners, and they suggest the *Jaegerschnitzel* (hunter-style), which is less spicy and covered with a creamy burgundy-mushroom sauce. These and the *Rouladen* with *Rotkoiil* (beef filled with bacon, pickles, and onions, served with red cabbage and späetzle) are available for dinner only; however, the lunch crowd can try the *Schnitzel à la Holstein* or many kinds of sandwiches (the Strammer Max is a favorite—thin-sliced Black Forest ham on rye topped with a fried egg). The Rheinland is open Tues through Sat from 11 a.m. to 9 p.m. and on Sun from 11:30 a.m. to 2:30 p.m. Fri and Sat night there is live music—on Fri it's sing-along accordion music and from a hammer dulcimer and guitar on Sat night.

There are antiques stores, bed-and-breakfasts, and dandy places to eat in Independence—in short, there's entirely too much to include in a single volume. We've narrowed it down to these few, which are off the beaten path by virtue of location, arcane historical significance, or ambience. Of course, the best tenderloin in town is at the **Courthouse Exchange** (113 W. Lexington; 816-252-0344; courthouseexchange.com). The portion is huge. The pie list will make you weep. Along with the ordinary kind of pies hide pies from your youth: sweet potato, pecan, old-fashioned raisin, gooseberry, Dutch triple berry, and the list goes on—27 kinds of pie at last count—and you can order a whole pie to go. Sweet. Hours are 11 a.m. to 9 p.m. Mon through Thurs, and until 10 p.m. on Fri and Sat.

Don't miss **Clinton's** (816-833-2046; clintonssodafountain.com) on the square, at 100 West Maple. When he was on the campaign train in Independence, President Bill Clinton visited here; they have photos and a thank-you letter to prove it! (He's wearing a Clinton's sweatshirt.) Just how long has it been since you've had a real chocolate soda or cherry phosphate? While you're there, ask them to make a chocolate-cherry cola; it's like a liquid, chocolate-covered cherry with a twist. This is a real old-time soda fountain, complete with uniformed soda jerks and a marble counter with a mirrored back; the malts still whir in those tall, frosty metal containers as they did when we were kids. Clinton's is open Mon through Sat 8:30 a.m. to 5 p.m.

And if all this hedonistic revelry doesn't get you, maybe the historical angle will: Truman's very first job was at Clinton's. You don't have to be a soda jerk first to be president, but maybe it helps. Harry was one of our most popular commanders in chief.

Visitors to the historic Independence Square can now experience the excitement and charm of Scandinavia. Just a few steps from the Harry S Truman Home ticket office, **Scandinavia Place** (209 N. Main; 816-461-6633) in downtown Independence features a smorgasbord of traditional Scandinavian gifts complemented by a splash of the unique and the unexpected. In addition to the wide selection of items from Denmark, Sweden, Norway, Finland, and Iceland, a shopper can also find an assortment of gifts from other European countries, especially packaged gourmet foods. Gift wrapping and shipping are available. Come and browse the many fine foods and gifts and visit with Nina, the Icelandic owner. Hours are 10 a.m. until 6 p.m. Mon through Sat and from noon to 4 p.m. on Sun.

You think celebrity prisoners in our jails are pampered now. When Frank James, Jesse's brother, was held at the jail in Independence, his cell sported an Oriental carpet; he had guests in for dinner and served them fine wines. For that matter, so did William Quantrill when he was incarcerated here.

Although the dank cells with their monolithic stone walls were decorated when company called, they were still jail. More than 135 years after the fact, the cells are still dark, forbidding holes that look impossible to escape. The 1869 **Jail, Marshal's Home and Museum** (816-252-1892) are at 217 N. Main, Independence. The two-story, brick, federal-style Marshal's Home continues to front N. Main. What you don't see (until you surrender a small admittance) is the Jackson County Jail . . . huge limestone jail cells that are situated at the back of the Marshal's Home. The home and the lockdown were both constructed beginning in 1859. As the 12 new limestone jail cells were opened, hostilities between free-state and proslavery forces were reaching a boiling point in this area. By 1854 Congress had passed the Kansas-Nebraska Act, which opened the Kansas Territory to settlement. The result of this act was violent guerrilla fighting that terrorized local populations on both sides of the Missouri–Kansas line as abolitionists poured into the Kansas Territory. The state of Missouri was held in the union by martial law even though the elected governor and legislators had voted to secede from the Union, so the history is very interesting here. The museum is open Apr through Oct, 10 a.m. to 5 p.m. Mon through Sat, 1 to 4 p.m. Sun; Nov,

Dec, and Mar, 10 a.m. to 4 p.m. Tues through Sat, 1 to 4 p.m. Sun; closed Jan and Feb. Admission is $6 adults, $3 ages 6 to 17, and free for children age 5 and younger.

Several interesting B&Bs are in Independence. ***Serendipity Bed & Breakfast*** (116 S. Pleasant St.; 816-833-4719 or 800-203-4299; serendipitybedandbreakfast.com) is a step back in time. This three-story 1887 brick house is full of Victorian details. An authentic-looking iron stove hides an electric range, and tall glass-door cabinets are full of antique food containers and plates. Even the brick-edged flower beds in the garden are alive with color from spring through fall. The most modern item is the 1926 Studebaker in the carriage house, which is driven to take guests on a tour of Independence. Rates are around $95, which includes a full breakfast in the dining room. Longer-stay discounts and economy rates without breakfast are available. If there are 6 or more in your party, you can arrange for a Victorian tour and tea.

Perhaps you remember the 19th-century painting of two trappers in a long wooden canoe. A big black animal—perhaps a bear—sits in the bow gazing enigmatically at the viewer. Or maybe *The Jolly Flatboatmen* is more your style, with the rivermen dancing at the dock, playing instruments, and generally raising a ruckus. Artist George Caleb Bingham painted both, along with many others depicting life along the western frontier.

Bingham made his home in Independence for a time at the elegant ***Bingham-Waggoner Estate*** (313 W. Pacific, Independence; 816-461-3491; bwestate.org), where he watched two Civil War battles rage across his front lawn (not conducive to painting a decent picture. Think what that would do to your concentration!).

Visit from Apr through Oct, Mon through Sat from 10 a.m. to 4:30 p.m. and Sun 1 to 4 p.m. to find out how "the other half" lived in the 19th century—or rent the mansion for a festive event and make the past your own. The mansion is also open from late Nov through Dec for the Christmas season; they decorate all 26 rooms. Admission is $5 for adults, $4.50 for senior citizens, $2 for children ages 6 to 16, and free for children younger than age 6, with slightly higher winter fees to defray the cost of all those decorations.

Another beautiful visit is to the ***Vaile Mansion*** (1500 N. Liberty, Independence; 816-325-7430; vailemansion.org). Built in 1881, the Vaile stands as one of our nation's premier examples of Second Empire Victorian architecture. This 31-room mansion includes painted ceilings, flushing toilets, 9 marble fireplaces, and a wine cellar. But that is just the beginning of the story of over a century of history that has unfolded in this house. It is open Apr through October, Mon through Sat from 10 a.m. to 4 p.m. and from 1 to 4 p.m. on Sun. Admission is $6 for adults and $3 for children ages 6 to 16.

There is great antiques shopping in this region. Independence was the jumping-off point for pioneers heading west, so this is as far as a lot of their furniture got. Schlepping across the country with a wagon full of sideboards and armoires didn't seem practical, so Independence is where many pioneers began jettisoning large pieces of furniture. (Rocking chairs often made it as far as the Platte River.)

National Frontier Trails Center (318 W. Pacific St., Independence; 816-325-7575) exhibits commemorate the Santa Fe, California, and Oregon Trails, all of which passed through or began in Independence. The center doesn't feel like a museum, because it presents the trails through the words of the pioneers who traveled them. The layout of the center is patterned after the trails. At one point, a fork in the path forces visitors to choose between taking the Santa Fe or the Oregon-California routes. One route dead-ends, so if you choose that route, you have to go back and try again. Voice-activated boxes tell stories of how the West was settled, and the murals by Charles Goslin show how it was accomplished. There are many pioneers' journals, which make fascinating reading, and there is a theater with a trails film. Hours are 9 a.m. to 4:30 p.m. Mon through Sat, 12:30 to 4:30 p.m. Sun. Closed Thanksgiving, Christmas, and New Year's Day. A small admission is charged.

The ***Woodstock Inn Bed & Breakfast*** (1212 W. Lexington; 816-886-5656; woodstockinnmo.com) was originally a doll and quilt factory. It features 11 uniquely and beautifully appointed guest rooms. Innkeepers Todd and Patricia Justice have

whatgoesaround comesaround

William Clark returned from the historic expedition with Meriwether Lewis to become administrator of the Missouri Territory. Respectful and frail, Clark was accorded similar courtesies by the tribal chiefs, sparing the state some of the woes brought upon other areas by mismanaged dealings with the Native Americans.

completely refurbished the place, which now features a fenced-in courtyard and garden area, thermo-massage spa tubs, fireplaces, and a wealth of fine collectibles, rare antiques, and priceless artwork from around the world. Rooms range from $125 to $205 and all rooms have private baths.

Every town tries to have the weirdest little museum, and *Leila's Hair Museum* (1333 S. Noland Rd.; 816-833-2955; hairwork.com/leila) gives Independence a lock on that title. (Ow! Sorry!) It is the only hair museum in the country. You can see a 14-inch-high tree made of human hair. The museum is inside Leila Cohoon's Independence School of Cosmetology. Her collection of more than 2,000 wreaths, brooches, watch fobs, bracelets, and buttons (all made from human hair) began in 1956 when she found a little square frame made of hair. She was a hairdresser then and it piqued her interest. Hair art was a reminder of a loved one before cameras were invented. You have to see the wreaths (she has more than 300 now), which are created by carefully weaving hair over fine wires to make tiny flowers. Her oldest piece is a finely detailed brooch from 1680, brought to this country from Sweden. The museum is open from 9 a.m. to 4:30 p.m. Tues through Sat. Admission is $5 for adults, $2.50 for seniors and children.

Independence is the center of the *Community of Christ International Headquarters.* Belonging to what is known as the Reorganized Church of Latter-Day Saints, the temple is something to behold. Inside the 1,600-seat sanctuary at 201 S. River is a 102-rank, 5,685-pipe organ built by Casavant Frères Limitée in Quebec, Canada. That is only the beginning. The rest you have to see for yourself. It is truly magnificent. The building is open to the public for guided tours from 9 a.m. to 5 p.m. Mon through Sat and from 1 to 5 p.m. on Sun. You can attend free organ recitals at the auditorium from 3 to 3:30 p.m. daily from June through Aug, and on Sun only during the remainder of the year. Also open to the public is a daily prayer for peace at 12:30 p.m. in the temple sanctuary. At the old RLDS auditorium, the one with the green dome at 1001 W. Walnut, Independence, you can take your children to the nondenominational *Children's Peace Pavilion.* There they will have a good time playing in the "DO TOUCH" museum. Inside are games that help them build self-esteem and learn cooperation and communication. The Peace Pavilion is on the fourth floor; admission is free. Call (816) 521-3030 for information. Hours are 9 a.m. to 5 p.m. daily; closed Christmas and New Year's Day.

Just outside Independence is the town of *Sugar Creek,* where you can have dinner at *Salvatore's* (12801 E. Hwy. 40; 816-737-2400; salvatores.us). Try some of the excellent spiedini and a glass of Chianti. Remember Garozzo's in Kansas City's North End? Well this is the same family: owner Mike Garozzo's cousin and godson Sam Garozzo. It's open for lunch and dinner.

Historic River Section

How about a day trip back in time? It's 1803, the year of the Louisiana Purchase: Imagine Missouri nearly empty of "civilization," as it was when it became part of the US. Early fur trappers traded necessities—such as tobacco, tomahawks, blankets, fabrics, and cookware. The Osage peoples were the most common Indians in this area, and they did business amicably with both French and American trading posts.

East of Independence you'll explore *Fort Osage* (816-650-5737; jacksongov.org/fortosage), a National Historic Landmark and the westernmost US outpost in the Louisiana Purchase. Its site was chosen by Lewis and Clark; construction was originally supervised by William Clark himself. Strategically overlooking the Missouri River, the fort was reconstructed from detailed plans preserved by the US War Department. The factory building stands today on its original foundation. Artifacts unearthed during the excavation are on display in the visitor center.

You may find a living-history reenactment in progress, complete with trappers and military men, Indians, explorers, storytellers, and musicians. Clothing displayed is authenticated down to the last bit of trim, and guides learn their alter egos' life and times so thoroughly that you forget you are only visiting the past. Sit inside the blockhouse looking out at the river, watch arrowheads being made from local flint, or visit the gift shop to purchase unique items with a sense of history (such as real bone buttons).

Rustle up a group to enjoy one of the after-hours programs offered by the Jackson County Heritage Program. You can reserve a place at a hearthside supper in the factory's dining rooms, for example. Enjoy an authentic 19th-century meal by candlelight; then cozy up to the fireplace and savor the entertainment.

Several weekends a year, special events such as the Sheep Shearing (May) or Militia Muster and Candlelight Tour (October) are offered, or spend the Fourth of July as our forebears did—the fort's a great place for it. To find Fort Osage, take US 24 from Kansas City east to Buckner; turn north at Sibley Street (Highway BB), and follow the gray signs through the tiny town of Sibley. The fort is open year-round on weekends from 9 a.m. to 4:30 p.m. You can explore on your own Wed through Sun, Apr through Nov. Admission is $7 for adults and $3 for senior citizens, $4 for children.

A more historic (and scenic) route between Fort Osage and Lexington will take you down the Highway 224 spur through Napoleon, Waterloo, and Wellington. This is Lafayette County—beginning to get the picture here? Must have been history buffs around this area since dirt was young. The road runs along the Missouri River, sometimes almost at water level, other times from a spectacular river-bluff view. Don't miss the turnoff to tiny downtown Napoleon. A bit farther on is Waterloo, just between Napoleon and Wellington—the obvious place, don't you think? There's not much here but a sign and a few houses, but it would be perfect even if it were only the sign! A great photo op.

On the way into *Lexington,* watch for colorful sights guaranteed to make you smile, like the A-frame wedding chapel overlooking the river, the old Peckerwood Club, and a grain silo painted to look like a lighthouse—and that glorious old river.

Once you enter historic Lexington, soak up the antebellum ambience. The homes along US 24 and on South Street are wonderful examples of Victorian charm—and remember, we're not just talking 1890s gingerbread here. The Victorian era began

rideonby

The Pony Express house at 1704 South St. is not open to the public, but it is interesting that one of the founders of the Pony Express, William Bradford Waddell, built it, and family members have lived there ever since. The person who now occupies the house—Katherine Bradford Van Amburg—is his great-great-granddaughter. Members of the Waddell family have lived in the house since 1840.

in the 1840s. You'll itch to get inside some of these beauties; check with the chamber of commerce for dates and times of historic homes tours. Lexington has 4 national historic districts and 110 antebellum and Victorian homes and shops. There are several good B&Bs, too.

The *Victorianne* (1522 South St.; 660-259-2868; thevictorianne.com) is the labor of love of Mary Ault. This lovely Victorian was built in 1885 by the town banker. It has 13 rooms and 10 beautiful fireplaces. Mary has done a lot of renovation and added an enclosed gazebo and hot tub in the garden. There's a carriage house with one room and a private bath. It is almost like an apartment, with a refrigerator filled with soft drinks and a sitting area with a wicker couch and television. Two more rooms are in the main house. Rates are $85 and $100 with continental or full breakfast.

Owned by Shirley Childs and Katherine VanAmburg, *Riley's Irish Pub and Grill* (913 Main St., Lexington; 660-259-4770; rileyspub.net) is a pub tucked into a historic building, a pub in the real sense of the word—families gather there to eat and the bar is open until closing time. There is an Irish menu as well as food cooked on the grill, so it is an interesting place to stop. It is open Wed through Sat from 11 a.m. until 10 p.m.

The area around the courthouse has plenty of places to browse in. At the *Velvet Pumpkin Antiques* shop (920 Main St., Lexington; 660-259-4545; thevelvetpumpkin.com), owner Georgia Brown keeps regular hours Mon through Sat from 10 a.m. to 5 p.m. and Sun from noon to 4 p.m. There are a couple of nice shops for the ladies in town. Georgia also owns *Gigi's Boutique* (922 Main St.; 660-259-4050), in the historic 1880s Eagle Building. Hours are Mon through Sat 10 a.m. to 5 p.m.; Sun noon to 4 p.m.

There are about 20 shops in the downtown area, so it can be a day trip from Kansas City to enjoy the over 100 antebellum homes and historic structures.

The Battle of Lexington was fought in September 1861 when General Sterling Price moved his Confederate troops north after the Battle of Wilson's Creek and the fall of Springfield. After 52 hours of fighting, Union troops surrendered to the invaders. General Price took 3,000 prisoners and broke the chain of Union-held posts along the Missouri River. Remnants of the battle endure; a cannonball remains lodged in a pillar of the courthouse. You can still find earthworks out behind the *Battle of Lexington State Historic Site* (660-259-4654; mostateparks.com) overlooking the Missouri River. This redbrick house served as headquarters and hospital for both sides and is now a Civil War museum.

andthestate mottois

The state motto is a quotation from Cicero: "Salus popali suprema lex esto." (Let the welfare of the people be the supreme law.)

· Along US 24 toward **Waverly,** the land undergoes a change from fenced, row-cropped fields to orchards. The peach crop is always at risk in Missouri's unpredictable weather. Blossoms are often teased out early by a mild February to be punished by an April freeze. It is a dangerous business, but the area around Waverly perseveres. The best peaches from this area are huge and sweet and dripping with juice. A bad year for the peach business is when the fruit is too big, too juicy, and not nearly plentiful enough to make shipping profitable. This is bad for orchard owners but wonderful for anyone lucky enough to be driving through.

US 24 is the old Lewis and Clark Trail along the river. Now it is filled with markets where orchard owners sell their bounty to travelers. Pick up peaches and apples or honey, homemade sausages, cheese, and cider along this scenic drive.

The Santa Fe Trail ran through here at one time, and it is still a trail of sorts for people living in the area: It is Missouri's apple and peach country. The Santa Fe Trail Growers Association is made up of 17 members in the area. On a drive along US 24 you will see a bountiful expanse of apples, peaches, nectarines, strawberries, raspberries, and blackberries—and all for sale if the season is right. Schreiman and Burkhart are just two of the orchards you will pass along the road. Greenhouses along the way are filled with vegetables, sweet corn, cider, and honey. In July **Peters Market** (petersmkt.com) is worth the drive from Kansas City for many people.

Pioneers stopped at historic **Arrow Rock** on their way west; it was a Santa Fe Trail town, a river port, and a meeting place for those who shaped history. More than 40 original buildings remain. Arrow Rock is still a real town, with permanent residents, a grocery store, a gas station, and a post office, but it is also a state park and historic site. The population numbers only 70 (and the historic district is so tightly controlled that someone has to die before someone new can move in, they say) but the place is packed in the summertime when the Lyceum Theatre is active. Arrow Rock looks like a normal town, but normal for a long time ago. Arrow Rock became a town in 1829 but for generations before that it was known as *"pierre a fleche,"* literally translated as "rock of arrows." In the 1820s the Santa Fe Trail crossed the river and travelers filled their water barrels at Arrow Rock. In 1829 the town was founded and named Philadelphia. But, thank goodness, the name was changed in 1833 to match the landmark for which the town was known. Streets and gutters are made from huge blocks of limestone; board sidewalks clatter with footsteps. The old bank acts as ticket office for the Lyceum, and the tiny stone jail still waits for an inmate. You may camp at Arrow Rock State Park; sites are available for groups or individuals. Visit the website at arrowrock.org.

Today the *Lyceum Repertory Theatre* (660-837-3311) offers performances throughout the summer in an old church building; it's Missouri's oldest repertory company. Call ahead for a list of plays and their rotating dates, or visit lyceumtheatre.org.

Borgman's Bed and Breakfast (706 Van Buren; 660-837-3350; visitarrowrock.com/Borgmans) is a 19th-century inn with 5 bedrooms and a common game room. Play a quick round of Scrabble, or enjoy a fireside chat with owner Kathy Borgman, who did much of the restoration work herself; take a look at the fascinating "house book," which shows step-by-step what's been done. After a generous breakfast, Kathy will give you a tour of the town—she's an official Arrow Rock guide. Additional meals are available if you make prior arrangements. A cat and bird are in residence, so no other pets are welcome. Rates are $60 to $65 for a double.

Artist George Caleb Bingham's home is here (remember him from Independence?), as is the home of Dr. John Sappington, one of the first to use quinine to treat malaria. Kathy Borgman will tell you all about it.

Historic *J. Huston Tavern* (305 Main; 660-837-3200) dates from 1834, when Arrow Rock was a thriving river port. The most ordered item on the menu is the specialty of the tavern, fried chicken. And why not? This recipe, like many others here, has been handed down for generations. Ole-time hominy salad, bread pudding, and fudge pie are included in those hand-me-downs. Blueberry cobbler, and wonderful bread pudding make people come back again and again. There is more, too. The 170-year-old tavern (that word was synonymous with hotel then) was home to travelers on the Santa Fe Trail or people bound for Independence and the Oregon Trail. Some died here of the cholera and typhus that stopped the westward trek of many. And so, the place is haunted. Beds used in exhibits on the second floor have been found mussed, quiet voices have been heard as well as the cries of a child whose mother died here, photos show strange images that are not really there, and once, a mysterious cloud of smoke appeared in the manager's upstairs bedroom. They seem to be friendly spirits, though. The museum is upstairs. The restaurant opens Easter and serves Sunday lunch only through May 12, when regular season begins: lunch Tues through Sun 11 a.m. to 2 p.m.; dinner Sat 5 to 8 p.m., and Wed and Fri 5 to 8 p.m. if there is Lyceum performance. There are seven B&Bs in Arrow Rock. It is quite a draw for Missourians in the summertime when the theater is going. ***Bucks-nort Trading Company*** at 802 Main St. has to be mentioned just because the name should be noticed. It is a store as unusual as its name. It carries southwestern, western and unusual gift items. It is open April through Dec, Wed through Sat from 10 a.m. to 5 p.m.; Sunday noon to 5 p.m. Call 660-837-3224 or visit arrowrock.org for a complete list of shops in town.

Nearby ***Blackwater*** has another B&B. ***Aunt Jody's Farmhouse Bed and Breakfast*** (8498 Springs Rd.; 660-846-2018) gets you out of town and into the country. The spacious 1918 prairie-style farmhouse is tucked under large old maple trees. There is a front porch swing, homemade breakfast made with eggs from the farm, and dining areas outside and inside. There are 4 guest rooms, 3 shared bathrooms, a claw-foot tub, and plenty of room for families. It is located 8 miles south of Arrow Rock on Highway 41.

At ***Boonville,*** following the river east, the western prairie meets the Ozarks. The town was settled in 1810 by the widow Hannah Cole, who with her nine children built cabins on the bluffs overlooking the Missouri River. During the War of 1812 the settlement was palisaded and named Cole's Fort. It became the main river port for all of southwestern Missouri.

The older residential section of Boonville has an unusually well-preserved collection of antebellum brick residences with wide halls and large rooms. Modest neoclassical homes are mixed with more flamboyant Victorian ones; many are on the National Register of Historic Places.

While in Boonville visit the ***Old Cooper County Jail and Hanging Barn*** (614 E. Morgan). The jail was built in 1848 and used until 1978 when public hanging was declared cruel and unusual punishment.

cupid'sarrow indianstyle

Legend has it that the town of Arrow Rock was named after a bow and arrow competition between Indian warriors vying for the hand of a chief's daughter. One arrow—the winner's, no doubt—shot from a sandbar in the river flew so far that it lodged in a distant bluff above the river.

Prisoners' quarters resemble dungeons, where the inmates were sometimes shackled to the wall with metal rings. Outside the jail is the hanging barn where 19-year-old Lawrence Mabry was executed in 1930, the state's last public hanging (as told in historian Bob Dyer's folk song "The Last Man to Hang in Missouri").

Thespian Hall (522 Main St.; friendsofhistoricboonville.org/thespianhall.html) is the oldest theater still in use west of the Alleghenies. Originally built in 1857, it has been used as an army barracks, Civil War hospital, and skating rink, among other things. It featured gymnastics, opera, and movies in its day and is now home to Boonville Community Theatre.

If you have come to town for one of Boonville's many bluegrass festivals—where musicians play everything from harmonicas to paper bags—Thespian Hall is the center of the activity. The folk-music tradition lives on here through the efforts of the Friends of Historic Boonville. If you can, try to coordinate your visit with one of these festivals. The Big Muddy Folk Festival is in Apr, and the Missouri River Festival of the Arts is in Aug.

If you are out walking around, search out ***Harley Park,*** where Lookout Point sits atop a bluff over the Missouri River, and get a feel for what early townsfolk saw along the long bend of the river. An Indian burial mound surmounts this high point; imagine the prospect of immortality with such a view.

In nearby ***New Franklin*** the ***Rivercene Bed and Breakfast*** (27 CR 463; 660-848-2497 or 800-531-0862; rivercene.com) will take you back in time to the 1869 home of a riverboat captain, Joseph B. Kinney, who ran a line of 21 stern-wheelers up and down the Missouri River. The three-story brick Second Empire, or Baroque, revival home has survived flood after flood because of Kinney's understanding of the river and the architect's foresight in building the house upon a pyramidal, floating foundation that kept water away from the first floor. Marble fireplaces warm the rooms, and hosts Jody and Ron Lenz wake the guests in the 7 rooms each morning with the aroma of breakfast. You can spend the day on one of several porches watching the birds and wildlife or take off on the KATY Trail. If you do, one of the rooms has a Jacuzzi, which feels fine after a day on the trail. Rooms are $119 to $135+.

The mid-Missouri area was the site of many of the key battles of the Civil War. The first land battle of the war was fought 4 miles below

Boonville on June 17, 1861. State troops under the command of Confederate Colonel John S. Marmaduke were defeated by federal forces led by Captain Nathaniel Lyon. Military historians consider this victory important in preserving the Union.

Jefferson City, Missouri's capital, is smack in the center of the state on US 50, handy to legislators and lobbyists. Built on the steep southern bluffs of the Missouri River, the city and the surrounding rural landscape offer considerable scenic variety. Large streams are bordered with steeply sloping and heavily forested hills. Bottomland here is rich with alluvial and yellow loess soils that don't look the way you expect fertile topsoil to look but support more wheat and corn than any other section of the Ozarks.

Here also is Jefferson Landing, one of the busiest centers of the 19th century. It's still busy; the Amtrak station is at the landing, as are the Lohman Building, the Union Hotel, and the Maus House.

The state capitol is certainly on the beaten path; however, once inside the House Lounge, you will find a mural painted in 1935 by Thomas Hart Benton. This mural stirred controversy in 1936 because some of the legislators said it lacked refinement. Always quick with an answer, Benton retorted that he portrayed "people involved in their natural, daily activities that did not require being polite."

Central Dairy (610 Madison St., Jefferson City; 573-635-6148; centraldairy.biz) still has old-fashioned ice cream and old-fashioned ice-cream prices. This is a must-stop place for people on the KATY Trail on a hot summer's day and for everyone else, for that matter. Hours are Mon through Sat from 8 a.m. to 6 p.m. and Sun from 10 a.m. to 6 p.m. One of the specialties is called the Rock and Roll. It's like a banana split but with four, count 'em, four flavors of ice cream and toppings. Betcha can't eat one!

Arri's Pizza (117 W. High St., Jefferson City; 573-635-9225; arrispizzaonline.com) is a favorite with the members of Congress in the capital city. Hours are 11 a.m. to 10 p.m. Mon through Sat until 10 p.m. and 4 to 10 p.m. on Sun.

Native Stone Winery (4317 Native Stone Rd. near Jefferson City; 573-584-8600; missouriwinecountry.com/wineries) is a 300-acre estate through which Lewis and Clark passed in 1804. They noted a rock formation in their journals and called it "Bull Rock," hence the name *Bull Rock Brewery.* The 19th-century farmhouse is the tasting room and gift shop and restaurant.

There are covered decks, sunny patios, and lawns. The winery is open Thurs through Sat 11:30 a.m. to 9 p.m. and on Sun until 6 p.m., serving lunch and dinner and providing tours of the winery and microbrewery and vineyards.

Missouri's Melting Pot

Head west to **California** (that's California, Missouri) on US 50, and go south on Highway 87, 2.5 miles to **Burgers' Smokehouse** (32819 Hwy 87; 573-796-4111; smokehouse.com.), if you fancy a ham to carry home. It is open from 7:30 a.m. to 5 p.m. This family-owned smokehouse has been in business for more than 25 years and is one of the largest country meat-processing plants in the US, producing 200,000 hams annually. You can take a tour of the plant any day but Sun between 7:30 a.m. and 4 p.m. There is a toll-free number for ordering a ham: (800) 345-5185.

What you wouldn't expect to find here are the seasonal dioramas, which show the beauty of the Ozarks with great care for botanical and zoological detail. These scenes by artist Terry Chase depict the influence of Ozark geography and changing seasons on the process of curing meat.

Leave California on Highway 87 and travel about 12 miles to **Jamestown** and, if it's between June and fall, pick some berries at **Missouri Highland Farms** (17071 Garrett Rd.; 660-849-2544; missourihighlandfarm .com). Growers Dan and Mary Brauch begin the year with asparagus and follow it up with berries of about any color you might be craving: blackberries, blueberries, and raspberries in three colors (black, red, and yellow). Hours are from 8 a.m. until about 5 p.m. in the summer and from 10 a.m. in the fall when the raspberries are ripe. To find the farm, turn right off Highway 87 in Jamestown and follow "Y" Road (the one next to the post office) to the end.

US 50 will take you to the town of **Tipton.** Follow the signs to the **Dutch Bakery and Bulk Food Store** (709 US 50; 660-433-2865). Located on Highway 5 and US 50 at the west end of Tipton, the shop is owned by Leonard and Suetta Hoover. Old Order Mennonites, they came here from Pennsylvania and speak Pennsylvania Dutch when alone in the shop with just family. Her pies are baked from homegrown berries and fruit; fresh vegetables from their garden are available in season. Homemade breads (a favorite is a wonderful oatmeal bread) and rolls fill the shelves along with bulk foods. But the primary reason for stopping here is the "Dutch letters"—crisp, thick pastry rolled and filled with almond paste and shaped into letters. They are cheaper if you buy five, and you might as well so you won't have to turn around and come back in an hour. Open 6 a.m. to 6 p.m. Mon through Sat.

While in Tipton try to visit the circa 1858 **Maclay House** on Howard Street and Highway B (660-433-2068; tiptonmo.com/maclay.htm), which is open on the second or fourth Sunday of each month for a modest fee of $3 for adults and $1 for kids under 12. This beautiful old three-story house has been restored and contains the original furniture. It is the site of the annual Fourth of July ice-cream social and features dinner and entertainment in September. The first Saturday in July is called Super Saturday around here and draws a thousand visitors for the barbecue contest, volleyball, and three-on-three basketball contests. Call the Tipton Chamber of Commerce (660-433-6377) for more information about the Maclay House and Super Saturday. Be sure to notice the "eight-ball" water tower; there's a Fischer's Pool Table manufacturing plant in town.

Hooray!! It's back! **The Wheel Inn** was a must-stop place on the way to the Lake of the Ozarks for Kansas City people. It closed, and all were disheartened. A landmark had disappeared—where else could you get a Gooberberger? Sigh. The Gooberberger is delicious. It is a heart-stopping (perhaps literally) combination of good old-fashioned hamburger, Miracle Whip, and peanut butter with lettuce and tomato. Yes, you heard that right: peanut butter. Sooo good the kids start cheering when they see the Sedalia city-limit sign. The Wheel Inn is at a new location now, 2103 S. Limit Ave., but the burger is the same. You gotta stop and try one just to tell people about it. The number is (660) 826-5177.

If you're in the mood for some really good barbecue, turn south on US 65 where it intersects with US 50 and drive to 1915 S. Limit to **Kehde's Barbecue, Sedalia** (660-826-2267), where John and Chelsea Kehde (pronounced K.D.) serve the best barbecue in the area. But that's not all. Kehde's also has jalapeño fries (french fries dipped in some kind of spicy coating) and a grilled tenderloin sandwich that is as good as the fried kind but without all the fat. Kehde's is a regular stop for folks headed to or from the Lake of the Ozarks and Kansas City. Kehde's added a railroad dining car to the building to handle the extra crowds from the state fair and the summertime Lake of the Ozarks crowd. It's fun to sit up in the old dining car and watch the traffic go by while enjoying the best barbecued ribs in the area. Take home a bottle of the sauce. In fact, take a couple or you will have to send for more when you get home. To find out more about Sedalia, go to mysedalia.com.

If you drive into Sedalia on US 65, you will probably pass (off to your left and way up) a beautiful stone mansion overlooking the highway. It is Stonyridge Farm in **Bothwell State Park,** 19350 Bothwell State Park Rd. Bothwell chose limestone as his primary building material for the lodge and cliff house. There are more angles to this place than a Chinese puzzle—it must have driven the roofers crazy. The original carriage road rises almost 100 feet but in a gentle ascent, with the lay of the land; hand-laid stone culverts allow water to pass under the road. Take the first left after you pass the house on US 65 going toward Sedalia (or, driving north, watch very carefully for the small sign marking the turn or you will have to turn around and go back when you finally see it). It is worth the trouble to find; there are spectacular views and wonderful walking trails near the house.

There are several antiques malls in Sedalia, but remember that in August this is the home of the **Missouri State Fair,** which attracts more than 300,000 people. The path gets beaten smooth, but it leads to midway rides, big-name entertainment, livestock shows, and car races—good, clean, all-American fun.

In the little community of **Georgetown,** just outside of Sedalia on Highway H (22166 Route H), stands a three-story girls' school built in 1842 by General George R. Smith, who founded the town of Sedalia. He built the girls' school for his own two daughters and other young ladies in town. The 10-room, white-brick beauty now houses Lorene Downing's **Georgetown Inn Bed and Breakfast.** Three (or four) guest rooms, two with private baths, come with a big "farmer's breakfast" and are priced at $100. You can call Lorene at (660) 826-3941 or visit visitmo.com/george-town-inn-bed-and-breakfast.aspx.

There's another B&B in Georgetown, too, just 3 miles north of Sedalia. **Georgetown Country View Estate** (22378 Hwy H) is on 80 acres of Missouri farmland and has an outdoor porch and swing just like a farmhouse built in 1869 should. Private baths and the two-person jetted tubs make it much more modern than the old-fashioned farmstead, but the antique furniture keeps the mood right. It went from being a country home for a banker to the county poor farm in 1894 when the banker died. It's a beautiful outdoor setting (great for weddings) and has a swimming pool as well. Visit the website georgetowncountryviewestate.com for prices and more information or call (660) 826-3941.

The **KATY Trail** snakes along the river from Clinton to Machens for 237.7 miles, burrowing through tunnels and also treats you to the only Missouri River railroad bridge near Franklin, and then it goes past glittering Burlington limestone bluffs containing millions of fossils from the sea. The Mighty Mo has been out of banks twice since the trail was begun, once in the Great Flood of 1993 and again in the almost-great flood of 1995, but work is progressing to connect the trail here with its other end in St. Charles. When the river is behaving, you can look "across the wide Missouri" and have a magnificent view of the river traffic of barges and boats.

Western Missouri waited a long time for a botanical garden; St. Louis, in the east, has one of the finest in the country. Finally, after much hemming and hawing among folks in the greater Kansas City area and those just over the Kansas border, the people of **Powell Gardens** (1609 N.W. US 50; 816-566-2600; powellgardens .org) couldn't wait any longer and began their own. Hurrah for private initiative! This almost 25-year-old garden is a beautiful 915-acres of blooms

thekatytrail

The KATY Trail is named for the MKT (Missouri-Kansas-Texas) Railroad tracks laid down more than a century ago. The MKT came out of Fort Riley, Kansas, in the mid-1890s and shot into Indian Territory. It was the heart of the area, rumbling in and bringing the lifeblood of freight, newspapers, and passengers needed to make the Midwest part of the Industrial Revolution. By 1892 the KATY had a direct route to St. Louis and connections to the eastern seaboard. Many of the small towns along the trail were born—and died—with the railroad.

and a natural resource center where you can wander among the flowers and indigenous plants, learn about "S-s-s-s-snakes!," make an all-natural wreath, or learn how to plant, prune, and harvest your own backyard botanical garden—you get the idea. The size sounds a bit overwhelming, but this oasis has free trolleys to help you cover the ground. Notice the hen and chicks, and the sedum and other plants peeking out from the crevices of a

600-foot-long stone wall in the Island Garden. Take time to visit the secret sunken garden where floating lotus blossoms glisten in the dappled sunlight. The Hummingbird Garden calls these little creatures in droves and although pockets of blooms pop up around every corner, find the Perennial Garden, which has 1,200 kinds of flowers covering 3.5 acres. The stunning redwood and glass Marjorie Powell Allen Chapel at the gardens was designed by E. Fay Jones, a nationally honored and recognized architect who built Thorncrown Chapel in Arkansas. The Garden is food for the soul as well as the tummy. You can see a Missouri Star quilt pattern planted in vegetables, a demonstration kitchen, and a kitchen garden. Powell Gardens has opened the 12-acre Heartland Harvest Garden, where everything is edible and visitors can learn about the path of food from seed to plate. Hours are from 9 a.m. to 6 p.m. daily May through Sept, and until 5 p.m. Oct through Apr. Workshops and seminars are scheduled year-round. There are also a cafe and a gift shop, which opens at 10 a.m. Admission is $12 adults, $10 seniors, and $5 for children 5 to 12 years old. Powell Gardens is just south of US 50 in *Kingsville.*

Watch for signs from I-70 (or Highway 291) for *Fleming Park* and *Lake Jacomo.* You'll find the usual sailing, swimming, and fishing as well as the *Burroughs Audubon Society Library* in *Blue Springs* (7300 SW West Park Rd.; 816-795-8177; burroughs.org). Learn about the birds, take a hike, browse through the books, and discover how to turn your backyard into a wildlife sanctuary. The library offers not just viewing but free Wi-Fi access, nature photography, bird seed and feeders, and gifts and cards. The library is open from 1 to 5 p.m. but closed on Mon and Wed.

Stop in your tracks. The world is moving altogether too quickly, but there's an antidote: *Missouri Town 1855* in Fleming Park in *Lee's Summit.* Managed by the Jackson County Parks Department, one of the two largest county parks departments in the US, it is a collection of original mid-19th-century buildings moved on-site. They now make up a brand-new old town founded in 1960.

A wide variety of architectural styles add to the historical significance of the town. It's just that sort of progression from rugged log cabins to fine homes that would have taken place in the 19th century as settlers arrived and commerce thrived. You'll find antebellum homes, a tavern, a schoolhouse, a church, a lawyer's tiny office (apparently the law was not quite so lucrative then), and the mercantile, where settlers would have bought outright or bartered for their goods. It has even been the setting for several movies, including the television version of *Friendly Persuasion* and the more recent movie *Across Five Aprils,* a story of a family split by the Civil War.

If the buildings alone aren't enough to pique your interest, this is a living-history experience. You're liable to see the blacksmith at work, watch oxen tilling the soil, or be followed by the resident flock of geese. You can wander around a real herb garden and discover how many herbs were used as medicinals in the 19th century—hospitals were rare in those days, and medical insurance was unheard of.

Missouri Town 1855 is at 8010 E. Park Rd. in Lee's Summit, on the east side of Fleming Park. Take Colbern Road east to Cyclone School Road. Turn north (left) and follow the signs 2 miles to the entrance. Admission for adults is $3 and $1 for youths, and children younger than age 4 get in for free. The town is open Tues through Sun from 9 a.m. until 4:30 p.m. March 1 through November 15 and on weekends only 9 a.m. to 4:30 p.m. from November 16 through Feb.

what'sinaname

In 1868 when 51 pioneer families settled in the area, they applied for a post office and name for their town. Excelsior was suggested, but it was already taken. More names were sent, and more had already been assigned. Finally the frustrated citizens of this settlement on the east branch of the Grand River sent one last request: "We don't care what name you give us, so long as it is sort of 'peculiar.'" Well, that's exactly what they got: Peculiar, Missouri.

Ray Julo's place is always full of ice-cream connoisseurs, people who know how special frozen custard is. **Custard's Last Stand** (308 SE 291 Hwy) has been in town since 1989, and business is fine even with the competition. Frozen custard is a super-premium ice cream with one-third less air than regular ice cream and is served at 28 degrees Fahrenheit instead of 10 degrees Fahrenheit like regular ice cream. It doesn't freeze your taste buds. And, Ray points out, it has eggs in it, which makes it creamier and very thick—so thick it is handed to you upside down.

Custard's Last Stand was voted best ice cream in the Kansas City area two years in a row by a local magazine. There are 45 flavors to choose from, including peanut butter, bubble gum, and the ever-popular Berry, Berry,

Berry (a combination of strawberry, blueberry, and raspberry). Call a member of the Julo family (there are three generations working there) at (816) 347-9922. Hours are from 11 a.m. to 10 p.m. (10:30 p.m. on Fri and Sat) and from noon to 10 p.m. on Sun. Visit the website at custardslaststand.com.

Ciao! Bella Ristorante (235 SE Main; 816-554-2442; ciaobelladowntown.com) in the middle of Lee's Summit serves southern Italian food in an upscale setting—hardwood floors, brick walls, tablecloths—and reservations are a good idea. It is open Mon 4 to 9 p.m., Tues through Thurs from 11 a.m. until 9 p.m., and Fri and Sat from 10 a.m. until 10 p.m. Closed Sun,

Once upon a time there was a little village named Cockrell on Old US 50, and in that little village was an old mercantile general store. But that was more than 115 years ago. Today the vintage village is known as **Cockrell Mercantile Company** (30003 E. Old US 50; 816-697-1923; cockrellmercantile.com) between Lee's Summit and Lone Jack. Proprietors Chris and Becky Glaze have made the five cottages and barns home to five unique shops. The Mercantile carries gadgets galore—aprons, tea towels, glassware, pots and pans—and treats you to a free cup of coffee or tea while you shop. The Fiesta Cottage has the largest selection of Fiestaware in this part of the country. The Morton House features bakeware and most anything a baker could need, including King Arthur Flour products. Cockrell Cottage is filled with home decor items, barbecue supplies, gift books, candles, and the line of Aromatique products. There are butcher blocks, pot racks, and gourmet foods throughout the village, and gift wrapping is complimentary. Then last—but certainly not least if you are a gardener—is the Cockrell Annex, an outdoorsy shop full of surprising garden accessories. To find the village, travel east on US 50 through Lee's Summit and go ¾ mile past the Highway 7 exit. Turn right at the Cockrell sign and follow the road for a half mile. The store is on the right. Hours are Mon through Sat 10 a.m. to 6 p.m. and Sun noon to 5 p.m.

Lake Lotawana is a fine place to be on a warm summer night. If you are out in a boat it's even better. Float up to the docks at *Marina Grog and Galley* (22 A St.) and enjoy great food and a view to match. The circa 1934 building has been renovated. There are four dining options, and all are elegant. The main dining room overlooks the lake on one side and a 1,500-gallon saltwater aquarium on the other. The upper deck features 2 fireplaces and provides a cozy atmosphere for dining. On a warm summer night you can sit on the outer deck, right at water's edge. The newest addition is the luxurious Marina Bay Club, a private dining area available by reservation Sunday through Friday. The cozy dining room with fireplace overlooks the lake and seats only 12 to 16 guests at one hardwood table. A sunken bar and over 200-bottle wine list make this a fine dining experience. Guests are invited into the kitchen to watch the chef and sous chef prepare the courses. Only USDA prime dry-aged steaks are offered, as well as Alaskan king crab legs. The house specialty is deep-fried lobster. From the intersection of Colbern Road and Highway 7, drive east 1.5 miles to Gate 1 (#1 is on the sail on both stone pillars). Take a right, travel ¼ mile down the lake road, and the lake is before you. The Marina is on your right before the dam. Call (816) 578-5511 to get directions by car or check the web at marinagrogandgalley.com for detailed directions from other places. They are open 6 nights a week Tues through Sun.

Take Highway 7 from the Lake Lotawana area to E. Colbern Road and then south to 9515 S. Buckner Tarsney Rd., in Grain Valley, and pig out, so to speak, at *Porky's Blazin' BBQ*. This barbecue comes highly recommended by weekend bikers—businessmen, lawyers, doctors, etc. disguised in leathers—who really know how to find good food on straight roads. Hours are from 11 a.m. until 8 p.m. Fri and Sat and until 5 p.m. on Sun. Call (816) 566-0203.

Unity Village, on US 50 just west of Lee's Summit, is an incorporated town with its own post office and government. It's a peaceful setting with an old-world feel; spacious grounds contain a natural rock bridge, Spanish Mediterranean–style buildings, and a formal rose garden with reflecting pools and fountains. In the past few years the fountains have been stilled and the pools sit empty awaiting repairs but people of all faiths still use the resources for holistic healing at Unity. The restaurant, bookstore, and chapel are open to the public, and you can arrange an overnight stay at the "spiritual life center" by calling (816) 524-3550 or going to unityvillage.org.

Little *Greenwood* is just south of Lee's Summit on Highway 291, then east on Highway 150. This was once a bustling place with not one but two train stations. It was a major shipping center for cattle and lumber. It still has two explosives factories and a rock quarry nearby, accounting for the heavy trucks rumbling through this sleepy town.

An old wooden bridge marks the end of downtown proper; watch for signs to find any number of little antiques stores and factory outlets. ***Greenwood Antiques and Country Tea Room*** (502 Main St.; 816-537-8434; thegreenwoodcountrytearoom.com) is a mall-type operation by the railroad bridge and just full of small booths. More than 70 shops occupy 15,000 square feet of space. The food is excellent; add your name to the waiting list when you go in the door, and they'll find you. Hours are 11:30 a.m. to 2:30 p.m. Wed through Sat.

Then there is ***Perazzelli's Italian Ristorante*** (812 W. Foxwood Dr.; 816-537-9997; perazellis.com) in ***Raymore.*** If your name ends in a vowel, then comfort food means dishes like pasta fagiole (an Italian beef stew with pasta, beans, and vegetables), and pasta is the first course of every important meal—especially Thanksgiving, since Italians are thankful for pasta—and Perazzelli's understands this. "Lite" would mean a pizza Margherita with fresh basil, tomatoes, and mozzarella cheese. Hours are Tues through Thurs 11 a.m. to 9 p.m., Fri and Sat until 10 p.m., Sunday brunch from noon to 2 p.m., and Sunday dinner from 3 to 8 p.m.

Lone Jack is another unlikely spot for a winery. ***Bynum Winery*** (13520 S. Sam Moore Rd.; 816-566-2240) is 3 miles east of Lone Jack at the intersection of US 50 and Sam Moore Road. The Bynum family was among the earliest settlers here in 1836. Mr. Bynum's great-great-uncle George Shawhan was a well-known whiskey maker before Prohibition. Carrying on the family tradition, Floyd Bynum opened the winery in 1989. Bynum Winery is a 6-acre vineyard, tucked in Missouri's rolling hills, with plans to develop over 30 acres in time. Both red and white wines, along with fruit wines, are made here. The winery is open 7 days a week. Hours are Mon and Wed noon to 4 p.m. and Tues and Thurs through Sun noon to 5:30 p.m. Visit missouriwinecountry.com/wineries, which is a good resource if you want to visit wineries along any route in the state.

If you still haven't gotten enough of the War Between the States, head south and east of ***Warrensburg*** to ***Cedarcroft Farm*** (431 SE County Rd.; 660-747-5728 or 888-655-9830; cedarcroft.com), a farm getaway bed-and-breakfast where Bill and Sandra Wayne have an 1867 farmhouse on 80 scenic acres. The house was built by Sandra's great-grandfather, who was a Union soldier. Bill is a Civil War reenactor and historian who can tell you a lot about the history of this area. He even has a uniform you can try on and a musket he will teach you to shoot. Bill and Sandra have added a secluded romantic cottage with spa, fireplace, and king-size bed; it costs from $179 to $229 a night. They will even pick you up at the Amtrak station. Horseback riding is available nearby, too.

The farmstead is on the Historic Register and dates from the 1860s. The basement barns for the horses are unique because the horses sleep downstairs and the loft is at ground level. This prominent farmstead has what Sandra calls "a little Garden of Eden on the back 40," so consenting adults can walk in the woods, play in the creek, and "do some smooching." It's a good place to get away from the kids for the weekend. As you might suspect, this cottage goes quickly, so call early. Sandra can direct you to the nearby Amish community in Windsor and lots of other interesting places in the area.

Warrensburg is the home of University of Central Missouri. It is a fair-to-middlin'-size city now as it grows with the university. The website for Warrensburg is warrensburg.org.

The *Camel Crossing Bed and Breakfast* (210 E. Gay, Warrensburg; 660-429-2973; bbonline.com/mo/camelcrossing) belongs to Joyce and Ed Barnes. It is a lovely turn-of-the-20th-century home in the residential area near the university. Tastefully decorated with Middle Eastern and Oriental accents gathered while the couple lived in Saudi Arabia, the place has a unique flavor, including a collection of several hundred camel figures. A camel-crossing sign is used as their logo. Rates are $70 to $90 with private bath.

Bristle Ridge Winery, between Warrensburg and *Knob Noster,* is a half mile south of US 50 at Montserrat and produces high-quality wines that range from subtle, dry whites to bright, sweet reds. It sits on a hill with a panoramic view, the perfect spot to picnic with a bottle of wine, bread, cheese, and summer sausage—all sold at Bristle Ridge. Open Mon through Sat 10 a.m. to dusk and Sun 11 a.m. to dusk. Winter hours vary. Call (660) 422-5656 or (800) 994-WINE, or visit brvwine.com.

Look up while driving through Knob Noster, because there are interesting things in the air above Whiteman Air Force Base. The previously very, very, top-secret Stealth Bomber calls this base home, and its eerie Batman-like silhouette can be seen low in the sky on approach to the base's runway. If you see it, you might as well pull off to the side of the road—as everyone else is doing—to watch it land.

North of Knob Noster on Highway 23 is the town of **Concordia,** where they take their German heritage very, very seriously. The **Plattdutsch Hadn Tohopa** (Low German Club) of Concordia has an annual Low German Theater at the Concordia Community Center at 802 Gordon Street. This lavish fall production is compiled and written by people of the town. Saturday night offers a dinner theater serving German delights such as peppered beef and bratwurst. Sunday is usually matinee theater only. Call (660) 463-2212.

Concordia's rich German heritage draws thousands of visitors each year for the annual **Concordia Fall Festival** (concordiafallfestival.com) in September. There are exhibits, carnival rides, and German food and beer at the "Heidelberg Gardens" in one of the two beautiful parks in town. Visit the website or send an e-mail to concordiafallfestival@gmail.com for more information.

The Ozarks

Cole Camp is a tiny town that would be easy to miss, but don't. The first place to stop, if you have planned this right and it is lunchtime, is **Gartenfest Tea Room** at the four-way stop in the heart of town (101 S. Maple)—you can't miss it; the town is small. This European bistro cafe has a fireplace to keep you warm, in the fall and winter and a trickling fountain to keep you cool in the spring and summer. Everything is made from scratch—quiche with blends of cheese and homemade crust, salads, soups, and croissants. The tearoom serves from 11 a.m. until 2 p.m. Mon through Sat. Handel Haus, the building that houses the tearoom, was built in 1920 as the Cole Camp Mercantile and now is filled with antiques, art, pottery, linens, and quilts. You can rummage through the treasures Mon through Sat from 10 a.m. to 5 p.m. and on Sun from noon to 4 p.m. The phone number (660) 668-9952 works for both businesses. If you decide to stay in Cole Camp, check out **Harris' Gästehaus** at 106 W. Butterfield Trail (800-301-2329 or 660-668-4432). It's a cozy private place to stay with an outdoor patio. The cottage is a reasonable $67 a night. Pick up a copy of the *Antiques and Shop Guide* and stroll through town. You will find many, many places to poke around.

Nearby (everything is nearby) in the historic Bellview Hotel is the **Maple Street Cafe and Bakery** (124 S. Maple St.; 660-668-3028). Chef

Michael Decker turns out breads and pastries ranging from focaccia to fruit turnovers and cinnamon rolls. Every dish he creates is special. Breakfast and lunch are served Mon through Sat 8 a.m. to 3 p.m.

The **Eichenberg Winery** is in Cole Camp (103 N. Olive; 660-668-3511; eichenbergwinery.homestead .com), 1 block north and 1 block east of the only stoplight in town. Eichenberg means Oak Hills, which describes the hills covered with varieties of oak trees. Rodger and Theila Luetjen are the proprietors. It started as an idea to give their grandkids a chance to play among the grapes as Rodger did as a child, the grapes from Germany, where Rodger's ancestors grew them. He became a craftsman of the art and now brings each variety to a perfect finish. There is the Norton, a full-bodied red, and the Baco Noir, which is light and spicy. Try the Weiswein, a medium white, or Seyval, a light semisweet wine. If you prefer sweet wines, the Concord, Rosawein, and Liebersaft will pleasure your sweet tooth. Hours are Fri 3:30 to 7 p.m., Sat from 11 a.m. until 6 p.m., Sun 1 to 5 p.m. For more places to visit, check colecampmissouri.com.

trivia

Cole Camp was at the hub of four major roads at the time of the Civil War. It became the site of one of the first battles of the war on June 19, 1861. A force of around 700 Home Guards was mobilized on June 13 and had its "baptism by fire" that same week. The pro-Confederate Missouri governor, Claiborne Jackson, was retreating from his defeat at Boonville, but the Union Home Guards were blocking his escape route, which would have brought him through Cole Camp. A force of Confederate sympathizers was organized at Warsaw and on June 19 launched an early morning attack on the Home Guard encampment. The Home Guard was routed and the way cleared for Governor Jackson to escape, adding another bloody footnote to Missouri's Civil War history.

Highway 52 runs into Highway 5 at the city of **Versailles** (pronounced just as it looks, not the French way). Versailles is the gateway to the Lake of the Ozarks area. Here you make the decision to go east on Highway 52 to the St. Louis side of the lake or southwest on Highway 5 to the Kansas City side.

Just half a block southeast of the square in Versailles, a brick walkway leads to a two-story white Victorian home that has become the **Hilty Inn Bed and Breakfast** (206 E. Jasper; 573-378-2020; hiltyinnbedandbreakfast

.com). This elegant home built in 1877 has 4 rooms with private baths. Owner Doris Hilty knows her way around the area and can guide you in your shopping or lake fun. If a quiet afternoon is what you want, though, there is a sitting room. The east bedroom has a private front porch, and there is a screened side porch with swings for the other guests. A good breakfast with gourmet coffee and tea is part of the package. Doris also serves dinner in the dining room of her home—lovely candlelight gourmet dinners. Simply call her 24 hours in advance to reserve a seat any night of the week. She can accommodate parties as large as 20 people or as small as 2. Rates are $119–$139.

World Craft and Thrift Shop (123 E. Newton St., Versailles; 573-378-5900) is owned by the Mennonite Church. Crafts are imported from throughout the world, and you can browse in the thrift shop in the back room for great used stuff as well. Profits from this shop support Mennonite missions all over the world.

In recent years, Versailles has become home to a number of gift and coffee shops, a group of rug weavers, and other arts-oriented businesses. The **Shop at Shady Gables** (300 E. Newton St.) is a favorite place for women to find peace and serenity in a fine cup of tea. This quaint little tearoom is in a Victorian farmhouse in Versailles. Reba Starling-Silvey purchased the big white house and because she loved all things related to tea (her most cherished possession was a white china teapot painted with yellow roses), opening a tearoom came most naturally. It is a favorite spot in town because the menu includes cream teas (tea, scones, clotted cream, and lemon curd before lunch), light afternoon tea (finger sandwiches, sweets, fresh fruit, scones, clotted cream, and lemon curd), and a luncheon tea, which includes a croissant chicken sandwich and miniature quiche in addition to the items in the light afternoon tea. Food is presented on a traditional three-tier tea server with scones on top, sandwiches on the middle shelf, and sweets on the bottom. The scones and sandwiches are all made in the Shady Gables kitchen every morning. Some 40 types of tea are available, but you cannot get so much as a cup of coffee or a soft drink at Shady Gables, because they would overwhelm the delicate scent of tea. Open only Thurs through Sat from 10 a.m. to 5 p.m. Reservations by phone are required; call (573) 378-2740. Many of the Shady Gables recipes are available in Reba's cookbook, *Made in the*

Winter Solace

The Missouri Ozarks are a quiet labyrinth of rugged hills and deep valleys, as famous for the folk culture as the beauty. Our home was perched high above a lake looking down at the very tops of the old oak trees with dozens of dogwoods sprinkled among them. The glass front let us watch the summer people on the lake; the screened porch was a perfect spot for breakfast. A telescope allowed us a view of the other side of the lake, a toll call away by road.

The chimney of the stone fireplace rose to the second-story ceiling; a loft above the one-room living area held our bed. The change of the seasons moved like a kaleidoscope across north window glass; the spring dogwoods and wild pear trees splashed white and pink across the barely budded trees. Bright daffodils popped up in the woods where earlier settlers must have planted them. Summers were intensely green, with ivy taking over the woods around the house. Deer and almost-tame raccoons and foxes shared the woods around the cottage with us. The roar of the boats and shouts of the skiers began early and continued until after sunset.

When the leaves changed in the fall, the quiet made the woods a private place. The color, not so garishly bright as New Hampshire's maples, but a rustic red and gold of Missouri oak, gave the hills a new texture, a different feel. The leaves fell— some years slowly, one by one; other years it seemed, all at once—leaving the view unobstructed and breathtaking when the cool, early-morning lake fog hung over the still-warm water.

The most beautiful spectacle I remember took place deep in winter. One special day the sun was warm, the air crisp and cold. We built a huge fire in the fireplace and grilled steaks and baked potatoes there that evening. In the morning the whisper of snowflakes woke us. The sleeping loft was bathed in the reflected light of a deep snow. The quiet was almost tangible; I could feel it, taste it, touch it. We threw more logs on the smoldering fire and curled up on the couch with the down comforter and a cup of hot coffee. We were treated to the sight of a bald eagle perched on a tree limb outside the window. We watched him dive for fish twice and carry them off to a nearby nest.

Putting the for-sale sign by the roadside of our little wooded acreage was a sad day. But like the seasons, the times of our lives change, and with those changes come new colors and new sights. Our lives move in new directions, just as the winds change from south to north and back again. The memories, though, will be mine forever.

Shade: Simple Recipes for an Elegant Tea Time, available there or at the website shadygables.com.

Emme's Attic (113 W. Jasper; 573-378-5999; emmesattic.net) has become a destination shopping experience with free wine tastings every day so you can browse around the shop and look at bags and jewelry, candles, antiques, and wines. This is a great way to spend a rainy day at the lake, or a day when the guys are going fishing, and just relax in the pleasant atmosphere of this friendly shop. Hours are Mon through Fri from 10 a.m. until 5 p.m. and Sat until 3 p.m.

The *Lake of the Ozarks* area is called the "Land of the Magic Dragon." If you look at the lake on a map and go snake-eyed, it has a dragon shape; hence the name. The Ozark heritage stems from the first immigrants here, who were from Tennessee, Kentucky, and nearby parts of the southern Appalachians. The Upper-South hill-country folks were descended from Scottish-Irish stock.

For many years the Ozark Mountains sheltered these folks, and few outsiders entered the area; you may have heard of the Irish Wilderness. Because of the rough topography, the railroads avoided the area, and this extreme isolation until a little more than 50 years ago created the "Ozark Hillbilly." The values, lifestyle, and beliefs of those first settlers are still much in evidence.

The building of Bagnell Dam to form the Lake of the Ozarks eroded that isolation and turned the area into the Midwest's summer playground. Because it is not a Corps of Engineers lake, homes can be built right on the water's edge; the 1,300 miles of serpentine shore has more shoreline than the state of California!

Miles of lake coves, wooded hills, and steep, dusty roads are still unsettled. Most undeveloped areas have no roads at all leading to them. The east side of the lake, which houses the dam, has become the drop-in tourist side. The track is beaten slick over here. There are restaurants, shopping malls, and water slides galore.

Some of the unique places on the east side deserve a mention before you head to the west side of the lake, where the more fascinating spots hide. If you go to Bagnell Dam from Eldon, watch for wintering eagles—here and at most of the lake crossings. They retreat from the Arctic chill up north, following flocks of migrating geese.

You may not have thought of Missouri as a state for bald eagle watching—and spring through early fall, it's not, though a captive breeding program of the Missouri Department of Conservation has been in effect since 1981 to reestablish a wild breeding population. But come winter, these big birds take up residence wherever they can find open water and plentiful feeding. One recent year, more than 1,400 bald eagles were counted, making this state second only to Washington in the lower 48 states for eagle sightings. At most Missouri lakes, their main diet consists of fish—they have far better luck with fishing than most humans.

Charley's Buffet is a unique spot on this side of the lake, and well worth the drive if you can find it. People come from all around to eat there (and get lost in the process), and because it's only open on Friday and Saturday evenings, folks line up for the delicious Mennonite-cooked and -served food. This restaurant has taken third place in the *Rural Missourian*'s "Best of Missouri" polls in the "Places Worth the Drive" category. They don't advertise and apparently don't need to, based on the size of the crowds there on weekends. Their mailing address is in Lincoln, but begin on Highway 52 between Cole Camp and Versailles and take either Highway B or Highway W. The restaurant is just east on Highway B off of Highway W (in Benton County). If you have a GPS you can cheat and enter 23785 Hwy. B, Lincoln, but that would take away the challenge. They even have a Facebook page. Oh dear, what is the world coming to? In the day, you were lucky to have a number to call, because many Mennonite businesses have neither. Call (660) 668-3806 if you accept the challenge and get lost. When you find it, bon appétit!

Taking the back way around the lake along Highway 52 to Eldon and then US 54 to Bagnell Dam is more interesting than the much-traveled and very crowded Highway 5/US 54 route.

A left turn (north) on Highway 5 puts you in the middle of the Mennonite community. On the roads around Versailles, horse-drawn buggies carry Mennonite citizens on their daily tasks. They are less strict than the Jamesport Amish—the somber black attire is uncommon—and most of the homes have telephones and electricity, though many don't. Old Order Mennonite women wear prayer bonnets but dress in printed fabrics. Some families have cars, but many of the cars are painted black—chrome and all. To get a good tour of the area, begin where Highway 5 splits into Highway 52. Follow 52 to Highway C on the left.

Mennonite Barbara Lehman used to serve people wonderful dinners in her parents' home on Highway C near Versailles. The place was so popular with locals and tourists alike, she outgrew it and moved to a new building on Highway 5 just north of Highway 52 in Versailles, at 15830 Hwy. 5.

The food is still fabulous, with the same wonderful family-style service, home cooked with farm-fresh everything from the garden and barn, prepared daily by Barbara.

The vegetables are fresh by season, this morning's eggs are just in from the barn, and the jam, of course, is homemade. In the winter the vegetables come from the Lehman farm by way of the freezer. Barbara serves two kinds of pie with the meal, and when the season is right, fresh strawberry and peach pie or cobbler. Smoked turkey, ham, beef, or chicken are part of the three-course meal, which includes six salads, two veggies, homemade rolls, and desserts. Call (573) 378-4010 for more information about **Lehman's.** Open Tues through Sat from 6:30 a.m. to 8:30 p.m. They also sell baked goods and homemade jams and jellies.

Follow Highway C about 6 miles to **Pleasant Valley Quilts** in **Barnett.** There is a sign by the road where you can turn and drive about three-quarters of a mile on gravel. The Brubaker family gathers a fine selection of quilts and crafts from Mennonite families in the area. Their daughters, Lydia and Lucille, handle the quilt shop, where quilts of all sizes and colors are hung for display. In fact, quilts will be made to order if you have a particular color or style in mind. Quilts made by local Mennonite ladies join aprons, dolls, and other hand-crafted items for sale here. The store is open from 8 a.m. to 5 p.m. every day but Sun. Call (573) 378-5782 or visit pleasantvalleyquilts.com.

Follow the sign off Highway C down a gravel road to the **Dutch Country Store** (18268 Kelsay Rd., Barnett; 573-378-4395), which carries bulk foods as well as a huge selection of freight-damaged groceries and toiletries. There are usually buggies parked out front along with the automobiles. The store always has a good selection of name-brand cereals and canned goods, shampoo, and dog food—just about anything. The selection is different every week.

Turn north on Highway E, then follow E to Highway K (this sounds harder than it really is), but watch closely for horse-drawn buggies and bicycles on these hilly back roads. Highway K leads east to the tiny, tiny town of *Excelsior* and *Weavers' Market* (113920 Market Rd., Versailles; 573-378-4672), serving this community of about 250 Mennonite families. Weavers' carries fresh-frozen farm produce, frozen homemade pies ready to pop into your oven, an enormous assortment of teas and spices, and other bulk foods, including homemade noodles.

Nearby (follow the signs) is *Excelsior Fabric* (13217 Hopewell Rd.; 573-378-7448), where Anna and Sam Shirk and their family carry an extensive collection of quilting fabrics.

Going along Hopewell Road is an adventure all by itself. You will find the *Excelsior Book Store* (13142 Hopewell Rd.; 573-378-1925) and the *Excelsior Harness Shop* (13142 Hopewell Rd,; 573-378-7218) along there, too, although even though you are off the beaten path, you probably won't need harness repair if you are just a visitor to the area.

If you decide to turn left back at Highway E on some pretty Sunday morning about 10 a.m., you will come to the Clearview Mennonite Church and see dozens of horse-drawn buggies tied up in stables and at hitching posts around the church. It's quite a sight.

The difference between the east and west sides of the lake has been described as like "flipping channels between *Hee Haw* and *Lifestyles of the Rich and Famous.*" Welcome to the St. Louis side, a road more traveled but still lots of fun. The Ozark website has plenty of information about the area: ozarkmissouri.com. The new-ish Community Bridge linking Lake Ozark and Sunrise Beach (the St. Louis side and the Kansas City side) has joined the two and made everything accessible to everyone.

US 54 through *Osage Beach* is, in a word, touristy. The path here is not only beaten, it's six lanes wide and heavy with traffic in the summer— the bumper-to-bumper gridlock type you came here to get away from. The road is filled to overflowing with craft shops, flea markets, bumper cars, and water slides. A new expressway that bypasses Highway 54 is about 12 miles long and helps speed up the trip. There are plenty of good eating places, from fast-food chains to little places tucked in corners. You are on your own here.

If you have taken the route along the west side of the lake, you will begin to see the real Ozarks now. Missouri has surprisingly diverse wildlife, from the blind cave fish to the black bear, which still forages in the heavy woods. The pileated woodpecker (the size of a chicken, no kidding!) will certainly wake you up in the morning if he decides to peck on your shake shingles. The west side of the lake is still undiscovered except by Kansas City people, who have tried to keep it quiet. Here, great eating places abound and small shops hide off the beaten path.

The newest place in town is a favorite with the locals and still somewhat unknown by tourists. **Wok N Roll** (1359B Bagnell Dam Blvd.; 573-365-2029; woknrolllakeozark.com) has Thai and Chinese food by Nok Knernschield (she's called Kok Noi, Thai for "Little Bird"), who was born in rural Thailand, where she learned traditional Thai cooking in her family's restaurant. She went on to cook in some of the best dining establishments in Bangkok. She has lived in this country for the past 25 years and understands American taste as well. She serves dishes that range from Chinese family food to more intense and complex Thai dishes. Of course, all the sauces are made by Kok Noi and I can almost guarantee it will be the best Thai food you have ever had. Open Tues through Sat 11 a.m. to 7 p.m.

The **Savannah Grille** (1622 Horseshoe Bend Pkwy.) in **Lake Ozark** is giving the well-known older restaurants a run for their money. Chef is Robert Sills trained at the Charleston Culinary School and also in Florence, Italy. Rack of lamb, Carolina crab cakes, and—surprise!—rabbit served with sausage and bacon and a curry carrot puree, and most everything coming from nearby farmers. Fabulous food, beautiful view—what could be better? Call (573) 365-1777 for seasonal hours, and take a look at the menu at savannahgrillerestaurant.com.

Highway 5 cuts like a razor slash through the hills between **Gravois Mills** and Laurie. There are some quiet, low-key places not to be missed. Locals recommend a couple in Gravois Mills. Hungry? Look for **JJ's at the Copper Pot** (630 N. Main St., Gravois Mills; 573-374-8077). Prime rib is the specialty of the house, but there are some other interesting things on the menu if you feel adventuresome: chicken tenderloin morel (a local wild mushroom that is the very best, as a life-long morel hunter who suffers ticks and poison ivy every April will tell you). Or perhaps the ultimate comfort food: lobster mac 'n' cheese. Call for reservations (for sure in the summertime). JJ's is open Tues through Sat 4:30 p.m. for cocktails and then 5 p.m. for dining.

The **Olive Branch** in Gravois Mills is in an old church at 26955 Highway 5. The philosophy here is: "Many a new beginning got its start over a good meal, and many a person has felt at peace and in harmony with the world after a time of fellowship and dining. It was for this purpose that the Olive Branch came in being. It is more than a restaurant; it is a gathering place once again just as it was when it was a church." You will be enjoying not only great Italian food, but salmon, grouper, frog legs, shrimp, and fried chicken. There is a full-service bar and, of course, wine—surely something for every taste. Open at 5 p.m. for dinner Thurs through Mon. Call (573) 372-2090, and take a look at the pictures at olivebranchatthelake.com.

A unique idea was born to change the menu with the season—thus the name **Lil's Season's Cafe & Bakery** (248 S. Main, Gravois Mills; 573-207-0331; lilseasonscafe.com) has given this place a new twist. During winter a heartier menu is served, with one specialty being the meat loaf sundae (mashed potatoes take the place of whipped cream on this sundae). The bakery carries all homemade goodies, from melt-in-your-mouth scones to the all-American chocolate chip cookie. Winter hours are Tues through Thurs from 7 a.m. until 2 p.m., Fri until 4 p.m., Sat from 8 a.m. until 2 p.m., and Sun from 10 a.m. until 2 p.m. Summer hours extend to 7 p.m. on Fri and Sat to give everyone more time on the water.

Just outside of **Laurie** on Highway 5 is **St. Patrick's Catholic Church.** Father Fred Barnett is the pastor here. This unique church sits on acres of outdoor gardens that feature waterfalls, fountains, and a shrine dedicated to mothers, the **Shrine of Mary Mother of the Church.** You may add your mother's name to the list to be remembered in ongoing prayers. On summer Sundays, Mass is at 8:30 a.m. at the shrine, and casual dress is in the spirit of a Lake of the Ozarks vacation. The outdoor candlelight procession and Mass on Saturday at 8:30 p.m. at the shrine are beautiful and open to anyone. Times change in winter, so call (573) 374-MARY for a current schedule.

From the town of Laurie you can turn right onto Highway 135, which wanders back to **Stover** and Highway 52, over some genuine roller-coaster dips and beautiful, unpopulated Ozark country.

If you are looking for a bed-and-breakfast instead of a resort on the Lake of the Ozarks, check at **Ozark Mountain Country Bed & Breakfast Service** (417-334-4720 or 800-933-8529). There are listings for cottages on the water in Camdenton, Osage Beach, Sunrise Beach, and other small towns around the lake. For more lake information visit funlake.com.

In the rolling Missouri foothills between Osage Beach and Camdenton lie 160 acres of vineyard. **Seven Springs Winery** (846 Winery Hills Estates,

Linn Creek; 573-317-0100; sevenspringswinery.com) is less than a 10-minute drive from either town. Missouri wines and microbrews are served on the covered porch and patio area. There is a light menu of soups and sandwiches, cheese trays, and dipping oils for bread. The winery is open 11 a.m. to 7 p.m. daily.

Either way you circle the lake, east or west, you will end up in **Camdenton** at the intersection of Highway 5 and US 54. Continue west on US 54 and turn onto Highway D to **Ha Ha Tonka State Park.** High on a bluff overlooking an arm of the Lake of the Ozarks, poised over a cold, aqua-blue spring that bubbles out from under a limestone bluff, are the ruins of a stone "castle" with a story to tell. There is a European feel to the ruins; it's as if you have stumbled onto a Scottish stronghold here in the Missouri woods. The place was conceived in 1900 as a 60-room retreat for prominent Kansas City businessman Robert Snyder. But tragedy struck; Snyder was killed in an automobile accident in 1906 and construction halted. Later, the castlelike mansion was completed by Snyder's son, but in 1942 a fire set by a spark from one of the many stone fireplaces gutted the buildings. All that was left were the stone walls thrust up against the sky. Ha Ha Tonka is now a state park, although the mansion is still a ghostly ruins half hidden in the trees.

The park is a classic example of karst topography, with caves and sinkholes, springs, natural bridges, and underground streams. (This typical southern Missouri geology is responsible for the many caves in the state.) There are 9 nature trails here; explore on your own or check in with the park office (573-751-2479) for a naturalist-guided tour; programs are available year-round.

Missouri places second nationwide for the largest number of caves, but the state beats number-one Tennessee in the number of "show caves" that are developed for touring. The state records more than 5,000 caves. The southern half of Missouri—in the Ozarks region—is where most of the caves are because of the limestone deposits there. The

strangeas itseems

Native Americans valued caves for their shelter and storage capabilities. They would mark the location of caves by creating thong trees— forcing a sapling white oak to a horizontal position using green, forked limbs thrust into the earth. Throughout the Ozarks, these thong trees can still be seen.

complex of caves, underground streams, large springs, sinkholes, and natural bridges at Ha Ha Tonka State Park makes it one of the country's most important geologic sites.

Casa de Loco Winery (442 Riverbird Ln.; 573-317-9695; casadeloco winery.com) in Camdenton is more than a winery, it is also a beautiful inn about 5 miles out of town. It's a favorite place for weddings and reunions around here. The deck hangs over the bluff overlooking the Big Niangua River. You can enjoy float trips, wine, and a great view. Or you can just pop in for lunch or to taste some wine. The winery is open all year 7 days a week: Sun through Thurs 10 a.m. to 6 p.m., Fri and Sat until 8 p.m.

About halfway between Warsaw and Clinton on Highway 7 is the town of *Tightwad* (population 56). There's a UMB Bank in Tightwad, and the branch manager says that people from as far away as Florida have accounts there just to get the checks with "Tightwad" on them.

The city of *Clinton* is every chamber of commerce's dream come true. It has one of the most active squares in the country, filled with more than 150 shops and services, and there is lots of parking. You can't miss the wonderful old courthouse and outdoor pavilion in the center of the square. The town has changed little since 1836, when it began as an outpost in the heart of the Golden Valley.

History buffs will find plenty of research material at the *Henry County Museum* (203 W. Franklin St.; 660-885-8414; henrycountymomuseum.org), just off the northwest corner of the square in Clinton. The building itself was owned by Anheuser-Busch from 1886 until Prohibition. Huge blocks of ice (often cut from the nearby lake) were used to chill the kegs in the cooling room. The second room contains a skylight and double doors leading to the old loading dock and courtyard. Quick dashes in horse-drawn wagons were necessary to transport the beer while still cool to the depot, where there was access to three railroads. The building houses the Courtenay Thomas room, commemorating the Clinton native, who became an international operatic soprano.

Another don't-miss town is *Pleasant Hill,* at the intersection of Highway 7 and US 58. Way back in 1828 David Creek settled a piece of land and became the first recorded non-native settler in Cass County. A town grew here until the Civil War. The "border war" between Kansas and Missouri, which was waged long after the Civil War officially ended, decimated the population. The next big event was the coming of the railroad, when the town began to resurrect itself. Each year the town celebrates Pleasant Hill Railroad Days in September. The town has a cupola-design caboose on display here that was part of the Missouri Pacific Railroad Line. This captivating little town has much to offer. *Neighbor's Cafe* (117 1st St.; 816-987-3723; neighborscafe.net) serves home-cooked meals that will fill you up and make you smile, especially on Sunday when it's all-you-can-eat fried chicken night. Their hours are Sun 7 a.m. to 3 p.m., Mon 6 a.m. to 3 p.m., and Tues through Sat 6 a.m. to 8 p.m. Their interesting and informative menu will give you a "history lesson" about many interesting events in the history of Pleasant Hill.

Mulberry Hill B&B (226 N. Armstrong; 816-540-3457; mulberryhillbandb .com) is a lovingly restored 1900s colonial home. Innkeepers Roy and Pat Keck will welcome you into their lovely home, which has 5 spacious suites. A full breakfast is served with Belgian waffles and all the trimmings. Rates are from $79 to $129 for two. You can just kick back and enjoy the amenities of Mulberry Hill or stroll downtown to hunt antiques. There is also the Pleasant Hill Golf Course and a year-round pool in the town. You might also want to take advantage of the *Big Creek Country Music Show* (110 S. Lake; 816-524-6856 or 816-987-3919 (on Sat); bigcreekcountry.com). Every Saturday night since 1982 Emcee Dennis Dittmore and his wife, Cindy, along with the rest of the cast, have entertained thousands of people. Showtime is 7:30 p.m.

Cheese Country

Large dairy barns and silos built around the turn of the 20th century are still in use, and dairy cattle—Holsteins and Guernseys—graze alongside beef cattle.

The *Bushwhacker Museum* (212 W. Walnut; 417-667-9602) is in the *Nevada* Public Library Facility and is open May 5 to October 31, Tues through Sat from 10 a.m. to 4 p.m. Closed July 4. Groups may call the museum to schedule special tours. Go west on US 54 to *El Dorado Springs* (*Da-RAY-do,* this being a very non–Spanish speaking part of the country) as a shortcut to the Osceola area.

El Dorado Springs, just east of Nevada (pronounced Ne-VAY-da) off US 54, is a pretty little town complete with a nostalgic bandstand in the tree-shaded park at the center of town. It looks like something straight out of *The Music Man*. There's a band here every Friday and Saturday night and Sunday afternoon; a local band has played in the park for more than 100 years. The old spa town was crowded with bathhouses and hotels, but the spa business ended long ago for most towns like this one. El Dorado Springs has done a great job of preserving itself anyway.

Hammons Nut Emporium (2 Public Square; 800-872-6879; hammonsnutemporium.com) in Stockton is the world's largest processor of black walnuts, and its retail store has been moved, enlarged, and improved ("like Starbucks, only better"). Not only can you get walnut brittle or chocolate-covered walnuts for your sweet tooth or a nutty breakfast with black walnut pancake and waffle mix and a bottle of walnut syrup, but you can also have gourmet ice cream, pastries, espresso, or a latte, or buy coffee beans (maybe a walnut-flavored coffee?) as well. The Emporium is open Mon through Thurs from 7 a.m. to 7 p.m., Fri and Sat until 9 p.m., and Sun from 8 a.m. to 6 p.m. Visit the website for recipes using black walnuts in not only cookies, fudge, and muffins, but everything from fish to, well, nuts.

trivia

Ground black walnut shell is a hard, chemically inert, nontoxic, and biodegradable abrasive. It makes up a large percentage of the nut and is a very useful product with a wide range of applications. Hammons began marketing this product more than 50 years ago and is now the world's leading supplier of black-walnut soft-grit abrasives.

If you don't take the shortcut, you will continue down I-71 to **Lamar;** history fans will find **Harry S Truman's Birthplace** here. (No, there is no period after the S, because the president didn't have a middle name—his folks just put an S in there.) It's a long way from this little house at 1009 Truman St. in Lamar to the big white one on Pennsylvania Avenue in our nation's capital. Hours are Mon through Sat 10 a.m. to 4 p.m. and Sun noon to 4 p.m. Call (417) 682-2279 or visit mostateparks.com/trumansite.htm.

In **Golden City** bicyclists know a place called **Cooky's** (529 Main; 417-537-4741), at the junction of Highways 126 and 37 south and east of Lamar. Out of season it's a small-town cafe on the south side of the main drag. During bike-riding season, though, Cooky's is the place to dream about when you are 300 miles out on the trail. Bikecentennial Inc., of Missoula, Montana, put Cooky's on the map—the TransAmerica Trail map, that is—and riders have flocked here ever since for some serious carbohydrate loading. It's not uncommon to watch a rider from Australia chow down on three or four pieces of Jim and Carol Elred's terrific pies; you can be more moderate, if you like. You can get an affordable steak dinner here, too; the home-raised beef will keep you going down the trail whether you come by car or bike. Hours are Mon 6 a.m. until 2 p.m., Tues through Thurs 6 a.m. to 8 p.m., Fri and Sat until 9 p.m., Sun until 8 p.m.

Jerry Overton, president of the Missouri Prairie Foundation, puts in a good word for **Golden Prairie,** designated a National Natural Landmark by the federal Department of the Interior. It's not reclaimed prairie or replanted prairie—this is a virgin remnant of the thousands of acres of grassland that once covered the Midwest, important not only for the historic plants it contains, but also for the varieties of wildlife that inhabit it. Here you can still hear the sound of the prairie chicken. Listen for them exactly 3 miles west of Golden City on Highway 126 and exactly 2 miles south of Highway 26 on the first gravel road.

A roadside park just outside **Osceola** on Highway 82 West will show you what attracted Indians and settlers to the area: the breathtaking view of the white bluffs where the Sac and Osage Rivers meet. Highway 82 also has a Sac River access point and boat ramp if you are hauling a boat to the Truman Reservoir.

Highway 13 bypasses the town square but is home to **Osceola Cheese Shop** and **Ewe's in the Country** (3700 NE Hwy. 13; 417-646-8131; osceo-lacheese.com). Mike and Marcia Bloom own both shops, which share the building. The Blooms buy the cheese in bulk and smoke and flavor it in the former cheese factory; they have been at this same location for more than 50 years. They now offer more than 69 varieties of cheese, mostly from Missouri, with each type cut for sampling. Try jalapeño (extra hot), instant pizza, or chocolate (yes!) cheese. Pick up a catalog; they ship cheese anywhere in the world—except from Apr to Sept, when it might arrive as hot cheese sauce. Hours are variable depending on the season: Mon through Thurs 8 a.m. to 7 p.m., Fri until 8 p.m., and Sat and Sun until 7 p.m.

Places to Stay in Central Missouri

KANSAS CITY

Hotel Phillips
(downtown KC)
106 W. 12th St.
(816) 221-7000
hotelphillips.com
Moderate

InterContinental Hotel
(on the Country Club Plaza)
401 Ward Pkwy.
(866) 856-9717
kansascityic.com
Expensive

Quarterage Hotel at Westport
560 Westport Rd.
(816) 931-0001
Moderate

Raphael Hotel and Restaurant Country Club
Plaza 325 Ward Pkwy.
(816) 756-3800 or
(800) 821-5343
raphaelkc.com
Moderate

INDEPENDENCE

Truman Inn (Best Western)
4048 S. Lynn Ct.
(816) 254-0100 or
(800) 780-7234
Inexpensive

BOONVILLE

Days Inn
2401 Pioneer
(660) 882-8624
daysinn.com
Inexpensive

Holiday Inn
2419 Mid America Industrial Dr.
(660) 882-6882 or
(888) 465-4329
Inexpensive

JEFFERSON CITY

Capitol Plaza Hotel
415 W. McCarty St.
(573) 635-1234
capitolplazajeffersoncity.com
Inexpensive

Holiday Inn
1716 Jefferson St.
(573) 634-4040
Inexpensive

KNOB NOSTER

Whiteman Inn
2340 W. Irish Ln.
(660) 563-3000 or
(800) 563-3321
Inexpensive

SEDALIA

Best Western State Fair Motor Inn
3120 S. Limit 65 Hwy.
(660) 826-6100
Inexpensive

Bothwell Kensington
103 E. 4th St.
(660) 826-5588
Inexpensive

WARRENSBURG

Days Inn
204 E. Cleveland St.
(660) 429-2400
Inexpensive

Holiday Inn
626 E. Russell Ave.
(660) 747-3000
Inexpensive

OSAGE BEACH

Tan-Tar-A Resort and Golf Course
PO Box 188TT
(800) 826-8272
tan-tar-a.com
Moderate

LAKE OZARK

Lodge of the Four Seasons
(spa and golf course)
(888) 265-5500
fourseasons.com
Moderate

WHEATLAND LAKE POMME DE TERRE

Sunflower Resort
(RV sites available)
Route 2, Box 2681
Call for directions; do not rely on GPS
(800) 258-5260
Inexpensive

Places to Eat in Central Missouri

KANSAS CITY

Blue Stem
900 Westport Rd.
(816) 561-1101
bluestemkc.com
Expensive

Savoy Grill (seafood)
219 W. 9th St.
(816) 842-3890
savoygrill.net
Moderate to expensive

LAURIE

Osage River Bar & Grill
247 S. Main
(573) 374-3020
Inexpensive

SUNRISE BEACH

Sunrise Cantina
264 Sunset Hills
(573) 374-8185

Shrimp Daddy's
16218 N. State Hwy. 5
(573) 374-7800

OSAGE BEACH

Buffalo Benny's Bar and Grill
113 N. Main
(573) 373-9900

JEFFERSON CITY

Das Stein Haus
1436 S. Ridge Dr.
(behind the Ramada Inn)
(573) 634-3869
dassteinhaus.com
Inexpensive

Madison's Cafe
216 Madison St.
(across from parking garage)
(573) 634-2988
madisonscafe.com
Inexpensive

BELTON

Oden's Family Barbecue
1302 N. Scott
(816) 322-3072
Inexpensive

GRAVOIS MILLS

Vinny's Cafe and Lounge
751 N. Main (5 Highway)
(573) 374-9982
Inexpensive

Laurie Val's
610 N. Main (5 Highway)
(573) 374-0922
Inexpensive

FINDING HELPFUL VISITOR INFORMATION

Arrow Rock
arrowrock.org
(660) 837-3231

Independence
visitindependence.com
(800) 748-7328 or
(816) 325-7111

Jefferson City
visitjeffersoncity.com
(800) 769-4183 or
(573) 632-2820

Kansas City
visitkc.com
1100 Main St., Suite 2200
(800) 767-7700

Lake of the Ozarks
funlake.com
(573) 348-1599

OSAGE BEACH

The Duck Cafe
HH to Point of Cherokee
Road
(4-mile marker)
(closed winter)
(573) 365-9973
theduckrestaurant.com
Inexpensive

SUNRISE BEACH

Sunrise Cantina
Highway 5 (¼ mile north
of Lake Road 5-35)
(573) 374-8185
sunrisecantina.com
Inexpensive

LAMAR

Lamarti's Truck Stop
54 SE 1 Ln.
(Junction Highways 71
and 160)
(417) 682-6034
Inexpensive

It does get cold in northwest Missouri—make no mistake—especially near the northernmost border, where the plains are chilled by every stiff wind howling down from the frigid north. Alberta Clipper, Siberian Express—whatever you call it, Missouri catches hell in the winter, bringing to mind that old joke: "There's nothing between here and the North Pole but two bobwire (barbed wire) fences, and one o' them's down." In 1989 all records were broken—along with that fence—when the nighttime temperature bottomed out at -23 degrees Fahrenheit (wind chill made that -60 degrees Fahrenheit). It also gets hot in Missouri; August days can soar over the 100-degree mark.

But at its temperate best, Jesse James country is a great place to visit that's filled with great hideouts. (James knew them all. It seems that, like George Washington, Jesse James slept almost everywhere—in northwest Missouri, anyway.)

Not that that's all there is to this section of the state; we'd hate to say we're living in the past on the rather unsavory reputation of our own "Robbing" Hood. There is a national wildlife refuge on the central flyway that is absolutely essential to migrating waterfowl. There is Excelsior

Springs, where folks once came to take the waters and where Harry S Truman heard he had lost the presidential election to Thomas Dewey—at least according to the *Chicago Tribune*.

The Northlands

Just across the Missouri River from the town with a similar name is **North Kansas City.** This is a separate city, with a healthy industrial tax base and a coordinated downtown shopping area complete with plazas, fountains, and wide streets. "Northtown" has its own mayor, its own police department, and its own quirky charm. There are cafes and delis and bakeries; North Kansas Citians know how to eat. Northtown has a website at nkc.org, and the North Kansas City High School Hornets (Go Hornets!) still attract crowds to football games.

As long as you are in Northtown visit **Cheep Antiques** (1228 Burlington; 816-471-0092). The store carries furniture in every price range and features antiques from Belgium, France, Germany, England, and Holland. A specialty is making entertainment centers from old armoires, and restoring other pieces. Hours are 9 a.m. until 3 p.m. Tues through Fri and until 5 p.m. on Sat and Sun.

Tiny **Avondale** is slightly off Highway 210 as you leave North Kansas City. Here you'll discover **Avondale Furniture and Antiques** (2600 N. Bell St.). Hours are catch-as-catch-can; call (816) 452-2690 for an appointment if you prefer. Owner Lillian Waskovsky has an auction service and warehouse and likes to move pieces quickly. This place may not be glitzy, but the prices are very right.

Hayes Hamburgers (2502 NE Vivion Rd.) in suburban Kansas City North (at Antioch Road) serves the kind of hamburgers that you could order before "fast food" was invented. This is the place to go for a hamburger after a North Kansas City High School Hornets football game (Go Hornets!—Are you sensing an alum in here?) or late at night on a date you don't want to end. The hamburgers are small (like sliders) and made of fresh chopped meat rolled into a ball and mashed onto the grill with a handful of onions. The aroma of onions and hamburger grilling together sparks an appetite. People buy them by the bag and have been known to eat a dozen. The chili is all-American good, too. The diner is open all the time—24 hours a day.

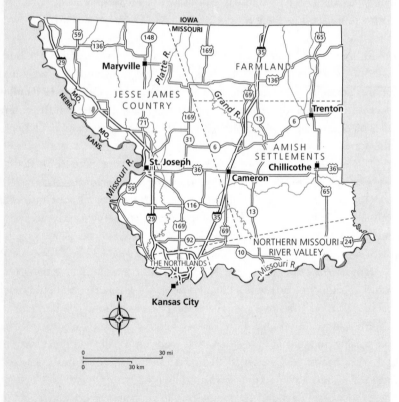

Take the I-435 exit north off I-35 and keep an eye out for Highway 152. A right turn will take you to *Hodge Park,* a fine place to get away from the "two Ps": progress and people.

Those big, hairy critters you spot as you enter the park are American bison; the Kansas City Zoo maintains a small herd here, where once there were thousands. Elk and deer share the enclosure; you may be able to get "up close and personal" with some of the Midwest's largest indigenous animals.

If human history is more your thing, park your car in the lot and keep walking. *Shoal Creek* is a restored frontier town at Hodge Park, full of historic buildings moved here by the Kansas City Parks and Recreation Department. The tiny, two-story jail built of monolithic limestone blocks (how did they lift those things?) came from nearby Missouri City. What a place for a lockup! Local ne'er-do-wells slept off Saturday-night festivities here some 100-plus years ago. Other buildings include square-hewn log cabins, a one-room schoolhouse, a barn, a replica of an old mill complete with mill wheel and race, and some pretty fine houses for the gentry. Stop by during one of their living-history weekends for a re-creation of frontier life; you'll feel as if you've stepped back to the 19th century. Fine nature trails lead into the woods from Shoal Creek.

If you are interested in archaeology and the peoples that inhabited this land before Europeans moved in, get yourself to *Line Creek Park* (5940 NW Waukomis). This is a Hopewell Culture site, where Native Americans

TOP RECOMMENDATIONS IN NORTHWEST MISSOURI

TOP ANNUAL EVENTS IN NORTHWEST MISSOURI

MAY

The Gatsby Festival
Excelsior Springs
Always the weekend after Mother's
Day
(816) 630-0750
epsi.net/gatsby/welcome.htm

Morel Mushroom Festival
Richmond
Parade, food and craft booths,
model train show, carnival
(816) 776-5304 or (816) 776-5306
cofcommerce.home.mchsi.com/festival
.html

SEPTEMBER

Waterfest
Excelsior Springs
Second Sat of Sept
Arts, crafts, and food booths;
games, music, and rides
(816) 630-6161

DECEMBER

Christmas Festival
Jamesport
jamesportmissouri.org

lived and worked from approximately 50 BC to AD 200. The museum houses artifacts found on the spot and in the surrounding areas.

The Kansas City Parks and Recreation Department operates the site, and schoolchildren from grade four up come for mock "digs" (artifacts are salted back into the ground so that the kids have the excitement of discovery). You can take your chances; the museum is usually open Sat and Sun from 11 a.m. to 4 p.m. There's no charge for the museum, but for reservations for group programs, call the above number; there is a small fee for groups.

Do you want to have some real fun now? Well, there is a most unusual place in Kansas City North to do just that if you are up to trying something different. *Jaegers Subsurface Paintball*, deep in the caves at 9300 NE Underground Dr. (816-452-6600; jaegers.com), is the place to find. For $35, manager J. J. Johnson will give you a safety briefing, helmet and goggles, and a semiautomatic weapon with 130 rounds of ammunition—i.e., paintballs.

The caves are spooky—dark stone walls and dirt floors—littered with washing machines, wire spools, and a beat-up delivery van to hide behind or trip over. Old paintball pellets and shards of exploded ones are debris on the floor. Fluorescent lights illuminate parts of the cave; other parts are dark.

The color of your helmet designates the team you belong to. You are the hunter—and the hunted—on a field that consists of the cave's labyrinthine stone passages and lots of sand.

"Paintball . . . may be an inherently dangerous activity that can result in loss of life, eyesight, or hearing," says the waiver you sign before entering the field, and although harmless, those little pellets *hurt* when you are hit. So it is easy to follow the next rule: When hit, you raise your gun above your head and yell "I'm hit!" and run off the field while the referee counts to 10. Aficionados of the game find the rapid-fire shooting under pressure and the thrill of catching the enemy unaware exciting and exhilarating (along with the satisfaction of hitting a moving target). You can spend a lot of money on more advanced equipment (ear-mouth pieces to communicate with your partner or teammates, or an RT Automag semiautomatic airgun for $700) in places such as the Irish Brigade Paintball Proshop and Supplies of Kansas City, or just drop in at Jaegers. Indoor hours are Mon through Thurs, 4 to 10 p.m., Fri until 11 p.m., Sat 9 a.m. to 11 p.m., and Sun 10 a.m. to 8 p.m. Outdoor hours are Thurs 4 to 7 p.m., Sat 10 a.m. till 7 p.m., and Sun until 6 p.m. Jaegers is just off of I-435 near Worlds of Fun. Take I-435 to the Highway 210 exit. Turn right at Randolph Road and go south to Underground Drive.

Northern Missouri River Valley

Head east back on Highway 152 and you'll come to historic **Liberty.** The downtown square has been restored to Civil War–era glory, with authentic paint colors and fancy trim—most of it original.

The restored **Corbin Mill Place** (131 S. Water; corbinmill.com) is now a compendium of 6 specialty shops housed in an old brick mill, among them **Bead Browsery** (816-415-8750), where owner Brenda MacLellan offers classes in the craft of beading. Hours are 10 a.m. to 5 p.m. Mon through Sat. Nearby is **Sandy's Antiques** with a good selection of collectibles and **AMERICAN! Whatever,** open from 10 a.m. until 5 p.m., specializing in traditional hooked rugs, with classes for beginners as well as advanced students. Also there is the **Old Mill Stitchery** (816-792-3670). Behind the mill is **Bratcher Cooperage,** where you can watch the cooper turn out kegs and churns. It is open Mon through Sat from 10 a.m. until 5:30 p.m.

Sandy and Tom Williams opened the mill in 1986 as an outgrowth of their original antiques store a few blocks away, and now they offer a great place to spend an afternoon—it just keeps growing. The mill, with its 24-inch-thick limestone foundation and 18-inch brick walls, is built on an original land grant from President James Monroe for relief from the 1811 New Madrid earthquake (that event had far-reaching consequences!). Corbin Mill Place is open from 10 a.m. to 5 p.m. Mon through Sat.

There are three museums in downtown Liberty, either on the square or within easy walking distance, among them the *Jesse James Bank Museum Historic Site* (816-781-4458) and the *Historic Liberty Jail* (216 N. Main St.; 816-781-3188). The museum provides exhibits, audiovisual presentations, and art to help visitors understand the significant events that took place in the jail. It is sponsored by the Church of Jesus Christ of Latter-Day Saints. Hours are daily from 9 a.m. to 9 p.m.

The town is chock-full of antiques and craft shops, so plan on browsing. You can pick up a map at Corbin Mill or check out the website at ci .liberty.mo.us.

William Jewell College is alma mater of nationally known writer Patti DeLano (having a brother in California, cousins in New York, and friends galore in Florida defines "nationally known" for a writer from Missouri) and the location of one of the most interesting little cemeteries around. The college was founded before the Civil War and used as a military hospital during the war. The cemetery has tombstones dating from the 1800s. Walking around there, you can see the dates of flu epidemics and wars and discover husbands with several wives and those wives buried with their newborns. It is a lesson in history for a sunny afternoon.

howmanytons ofsiltayear?

As the Missouri River cut through mountains and prairie, it gathered huge quantities of silt and sand. It earned its nicknames—the "Muddy Mo" and the "Big Muddy"—because it used to dump about 200 million tons of silt a year into the Mississippi River.

The *Martha Lafite Thompson Nature Sanctuary* (816-781-8598; naturesanctuary.com) offers a wonderful place to watch the wildlife, take a naturalist-guided walk, or enjoy special programs—from making your own bird feeder to learning about the constellations on a night hike. More than 600 species of plants and many fish, reptiles, amphibians, and mammals make their homes here, and more than 160 species of birds have been sighted. Worn out? Take in the lovely new sanctuary building with its displays of indigenous plants, or watch snapping turtles and catfish in the creek-habitat aquarium. Enjoy one of the sanctuary's many programs. Relax on the spacious deck in redwood Adirondack chairs, or buy a book, a bird feeder, or bird call to take home. Watch for the sanctuary sign at 407 N. La Frenz Rd.

N. Water Street is in the Lightburne Historic District and contains a diverse collection of structures built during the late 19th century, such as Lightburne Hall, an elaborate 1852 mansion, and the 1898 Simmons house. These are all private homes.

I-35 South from Liberty will take you to the little town of **Claycomo,** known mostly for the giant Ford Motor Plant that resides there. Of course, if there is a Ford plant in town, then there must be somewhere that serves home cookin' to the people going to or coming off the 24/7 shifts there. That place would be **Nelle Belle's Diner** (150 NE 69 Highway; 816-452-9786). Owner Dixie Edwards knows what to cook for hungry people. Her specials are on the wall, and you can get a really early start there because her hours are from 4 a.m. (yes, you read that right!) to 2 p.m. Mon through Fri and until 1 p.m. on Sat. This is a personal favorite because 4 a.m. isn't early if you have been up all night. It's just very, very late.

Take Highway 210 through the tiny towns of Missouri City, Orrick, Fleming, and Camden, which are dotted along the Missouri River. The views are spectacular, especially from the observation stop just this side of Missouri City. At your back is Nebo Hill, an important site for prehistoric Indians who found this a perfect place for ceremonies and camps; the site was in use for hundreds of years. After a good spring rain, you're liable to see artifact hunters out in the fields nearby.

heatherlywar

The "Heatherly War" of 1836 made it into the history books. Some sources list this as an Indian war; in fact, it was a family of white outlaws who killed their neighbors and laid the blame at the feet of the Iowa Indians. Several companies from Clay and Ray Counties were dispatched to investigate and/or quell a supposed uprising. Ma Heatherly instigated the murders that were carried out by her brood of mixed-blood offspring.

Highway 210 will take you to **Richmond.** Here the **Ray County Museum** occupies a beautiful old brick home on W. Royle Street (816-776-2305). The Y-shaped building is unusual in itself, and the contents will tell you much about this area, from pre–Civil War days to the present. A special natural-history section highlights indigenous wildlife.

To find the museum, go past the four-way stop at the edge of town on Highway 210 to Royle Street, and west to the large brick building atop the hill on the left. The library is open Wed through Sat from 10 a.m. until 4 p.m. If you are here the first weekend in October, you'll find mountain men, trappers, and traders as well as old-time arts and crafts at the Old Trails Festival on the grounds of the museum.

Just 5 miles north of Richmond on Highway 13 is **Die Brot Pann Bakery** (14711 Hwy. 13; 816-776-3275), where you can buy high-quality baked goods as well as bulk foods and cheese. This friendly Mennonite shop is run by Paul and Delores King. It has homemade cookies, pies, and wonderful cinnamon rolls. Doughnuts are fresh every morning. It is open every day but Sun 8 a.m. to 5 p.m.

Amish Settlements

For a visit to a very special small town, spend some time in **Chillicothe;** don't pass it by. (It has a website at chillicothemo.com.)

For sheer indulgence, Francine Davenport can bake some triple chocolate muffins—something so sinful you will repent for days—or you can indulge without the guilt with her low-fat peaches 'n' cream muffins. Whatever you choose, **Francine's Pastry Parlor,** tucked away inside a plain white storefront at 1007 Bryan St., is the place to go if you are looking for some warm, fresh-from-the-oven treats. Hours are 6:30 a.m. to 1:30 p.m. Tues through Fri. The just-like-mama-made apple and cherry pies are the favorites, but how about a "Cow Pattie" for breakfast? It's a delightful Danish sweet roll, albeit a yucky name. All the cookies are from scratch; the soybean cookie is her own recipe and has won awards at the state fair, as has her Blue Ribbon Carrot Cake. Call Francine at (660) 646-3333.

North on US 65 is the town of **Trenton.** Don't mistake Trenton Cemetery Prairie for a neglected eyesore, with its rough grasses obscuring some of the old tombstones. Established in 1830, its protected status as a cemetery happily resulted in one of the few precious parcels of native prairie remaining in the state. Today it is maintained by the Missouri Conservation Department. Preservation is especially crucial; prairie north of the Missouri River is scarce. These patchwork remnants produce the seeds adapted to the northern Missouri climate that are essential to reestablishing prairie ecosystems.

This is an area of oddities; what you see may not be what you get. *Riverside Country Club* (660-359-6004), Trenton's golf course, has tree stumps carved into life-size animals around the fairways. (If you hit a birdie or an eagle around here, it may be a wooden one.) Former greenskeeper Don McNabb was an artist with a chainsaw and has salted the 9-hole course with bears and other critters. The club is open for golf to anyone for the cost of a greens fee (and cart rental, if you wish), but nongolfers are welcome to check out the carvings.

"Real World" Experience

It was a warm and wet November day, the color gray and dismal. Yellow leaves had begun to stick to the raindrops and fall with them, cluttering the streets with mats of browning vegetation. We were looking for a day trip from Kansas City and chose Jamesport. Saturday is a busy day in this Amish community. Local residents were hurrying by in their horse-drawn carriages—wooden boxes with tiny windows in the back—headed for the nearby bulk food stores.

Books give only the minimum information about the Amish, the strictest branch of the Mennonite Church. The founder, Jacob Amman, was a Swiss religious reformer who laid the foundation for the difficult lives the Amish lead. It is strange to see the farmhouses sitting unattached to the life-giving power poles we are so accustomed to seeing in neat rows down the roadway. Forbidden modern conveniences, the Amish live in a sunrise-to-sunset world. The absence of television antennae or satellite dishes transports the little farms' appearances back to simpler times. The people shun vanity. Their clothes are black and fastened with straight pins—they are forbidden the vainglory of buttons—and their hair is hidden under bonnets and hats. They will not allow themselves to be photographed.

We bought handmade quilts and hand-loomed rugs. We drove away in our fast car, back to our modern lives, stocked with every possible convenience, from zippers to microwave ovens. So why do the women of the Amish community have the time to quilt by the light of a kerosene lamp while we are so busy we barely have time to sew on a lost button? Ah, vanity. It is such a time-consuming sin.

Jamesport is a different world. It is the largest Mennonite settlement in Missouri and home to the most orthodox "horse-and-buggy" Mennonites. Here the Amish wear black, fasten clothes with pins, and allow no electricity in their homes. Don't ask the Amish to pose for pictures, though; it's against their beliefs.

There are lots of shops in the area so you can, and should, pick up a map of Jamesport. Now, with map in hand, let's tour Jamesport. Remember, just about everything in town is closed on Thurs and Sun. You can begin and end where Highway 6 meets Highway F and leads into the western part of downtown. *Anna's Bake Shop* (660-684-6810) off of Highway F in Jamesport would be a good place to start, with fresh-baked doughnuts, pies, breads, or cinnamon rolls. It opens at 8 a.m. so you can get an early start. It stays open until 6 p.m. (closed from Christmas until Feb).

Still in the city square just past the four-way stop at 115 E. Aulbury Grove is *Downhome Oak* (660-684-6526; jamesportmo.com), specializing in oak furniture and woodcraft. It's open 9 a.m. until 5 p.m. Mon through Sat.

The Mennonite-owned *Gingerich Dutch Pantry and Bakery* (660-684-6212; gingerichdutchpantry.com) is right at the four-way in Jamesport and has real Amish-style meals with lots of wonderful homemade food and baked goods. It is open Mon through Sat from 6 a.m. until 9 p.m.

Now let's get out of town a bit. The roads here are described as "gravel roads," but gravel would be a big improvement. You won't need an all-terrain vehicle to find them, but driving slowly is definitely in order unless you want to disappear into a pothole, never to be seen again. The horse-and-buggies pack down a couple of very strong little paths in the center of the roads, but the rest of the road is pretty much shot. It makes passing another car going the other way a bit of an adventure, and the buggies, understandably, won't leave the path under any circumstances. But aside from a bit of horse poop on your tires, you will emerge undamaged if you go slowly. Remember most of these shops are closed on Thurs and Sun and have no telephones or electric lights.

Kerosene lamps light the *H & M Country Store* (660-684-6108) just south of Jamesport. It's a good place to stock your kitchen. You'll find bulk groceries at great prices (wonderful high-gluten flour for your bread machine), dried fruit, beans, homemade mixes for just about anything you want (biscuits, pancakes, muffins), and spices and herbs by the wall-full.

You want noodles? Every kind you can imagine is here. You can buy fresh produce and brown eggs here, too.

To find a nice selection of hand-quilted pieces, venture out of town east on Highway F and 1 mile south on Highway U for **Sherwood Quilts and Crafts,** which has a large selection of handmade quilts, rugs, and baskets. It has a bed piled high with beautiful quilts; dig through until you find the one you can't live without. It is open from 8 a.m. until 5 p.m.

South of town on Highway 190 is the **Rolling Hills Store,** offering sturdy dry goods at excellent prices and lots of natural-fiber fabrics, plus boots and shoes.

You can stay at the **Country Colonial Bed and Breakfast** (106 E. Main; 660-684-6711 or 800-579-9248) and allow hosts Myrick and Nina den Hartog to tell you a little bit about the area. After shopping, you can return to this early 1900s home and enjoy playing the baby grand piano, and when night falls again snuggle back into the featherbed. You will awaken to the aroma of a large country breakfast being prepared, and if the weather is fine, it will be served in the flower garden. Ladies, you can have a free facial, sigh, and you can even take a sunset or moonlight carriage ride for $25 and see Jamesport Amish-style. Rooms are $75 to $95.

So many places to see, so little time! If you leave town the way you came in, you can stop at the **Country Cupboard Restaurant,** in downtown Jamesport (1011 Old Highway 6; 660-684-6597), open Tues through Sun from 6:30 a.m. until 9 p.m. They always have a daily special and homemade pies and breads, well, actually, everything is homemade, hometown cooking.

There are easier ways to do this: **Amish Country Tours** (660-684-6711 or 800-490-6606) has car (the guide directs you in your vehicle), van, or coach tour buses starting at only $40 per car or van up to 10 people. After spending a day wandering around Jamesport's Amish community, you might want to stay at the **Jamesport Inn** (305 W. Auberry Grove; 800-884-5946; jamesportinn.com). The rooms are $59 and $69 a night with free Wi-Fi and coffee in the lobby. The general store has food and beverages items, too. Just so you won't miss anything, go to the Jamesport website, jamesport-mo .com, or call (800) 490-6606.

The Mormons settled in western Daviess County in the 1830s. Just north and west of Gallatin (take Highway 13 north and turn west onto Highway

P) is the historic **Adam-Ondi-Ahman Shrine,** believed by Mormons to be the place where Christ will return. Northwest Missouri is important historically to the Mormon people; there were once thousands of them here. The majority were forced out during the Mormon Wars, when the state militia was ordered to drive them out of Missouri. The town of **Far West,** now no more than a historical marker, comprised 5,000 souls, all exterminated or driven from their homes. Many died during a forced march in this land of religious freedom. The marker is off Highway 13, west on Highway HH and north on Highway D, near Shoal Creek (just northwest of Kingston).

Ever wonder where retail giant J.C. Penney got his start? No, not New York, or even Chicago. It was right here in **Hamilton** in 1895 that he got his first job at Hale's Department Store. By the time he returned to Hamilton to buy his old employer's place of business in 1924, it was number 500 in his chain of stores. His company motto was: "Honor, confidence, service, and cooperation"—no wonder he did so well.

The **J.C. Penney Memorial Library and Museum** (816-583-2168), uptown on Davis Street in Hamilton, is open Tues through Sat from 10 a.m. to 5 p.m. You'll love the displays of early merchandise—makes you wonder who wore the stuff. The Penney farm cottage has also been restored.

Even cattlemen like this area's history. J.C. Penney once raised great herds of Angus, and at the Penney farm there is a monument—a big monument—to Penney's prize bull.

Jesse James Country

Take the Business 69 exit to **Excelsior Springs.** Once a magnet for people who wished to "take the waters," this old spa has enough moxie to try for a comeback. The health-spa ship was scuttled in the 1950s when an article in the *Saturday Evening Post* declared mineral waters an ineffective form of treatment; the demise was clinched when Missouri passed a bill prohibiting advertising by doctors. So now we enjoy the waters—and the baths and massages—for the lovely, hedonistic fun of it. The town was founded in 1880 for the waters. Even the Native Americans living here valued the healing properties.

Visit the **Hall of Waters** (201 E. Broadway, Excelsior Springs; 816-630-0750; exsmo.com), the world's longest mineral-water bar, and sample some of the waters that attracted thousands near the turn of the 20th century. There are more naturally occurring types of mineral waters here than anyplace else on earth except the German city of Baden-Baden, which ties Excelsior Springs.

The lovely art deco–style building, built in 1937 as "the finest and most complete health resort structure in the US," is a fine example of a WPA project begun during the Great Depression. Moreover, how many towns have city offices that have a 25-meter indoor pool?

The **Paradise Playhouse** (101 Spring St.; 816-630-3333; paradiseplay house.org) is a dinner theater done in a Hawaiian theme. It's right across from the Hall of Waters. The buffet is cooked right there in the shiny, cutting-edge kitchen. Tables are tiered for the best view of the stage, and the plays are very well done.

Slightly Off Broadway at 114 Marietta St. (slightly off Broadway, look at the street signs) in the old Methodist church is the home of the community theater here, too. Who would have thought a smallish town like this would have two theater groups? For ticket information call 816-637-ESCT (3728).

trivia

Frank and Jesse James's dad was a preacher at the Pisgah Baptist Church in Excelsior Springs. They moved to the farm in 1843.

Theaters remind one of popcorn, no? Nearby, actually ON Broadway, is **BobKorn** (246 E. Broadway), a kettle corn shop. More than 10 flavors are available at any given time, including customized treats like chocolate drizzle. Oh my. And try the Lemon Shaker to quench your hot summer thirst. These treats make fine gifts, too, and you can order them at (816) 900-1138.

Since you went off your diet for BobKorn, might as well check out **Oooey Gooey Chocolates by Lane** (113 W. Broadway; 816-630-9255). It is just what the name implies: candy, cakes, whatever. Go for it.

If you like old-fashioned burgers, don't miss **Ray's Lunch** (231 E. Broadway; 816-637-3432). The hash browns are killer good, and the secret chili recipe is a favorite with locals. It's the kind of small-town diner where men hang out for coffee every morning to straighten out the world situation.

The **Old Bank Museum** (101 E. Broadway; 816-630-3712), in a former bank building, circa 1906 and itself an interesting architectural achievement, preserves spa-town history. (Check out the dentist's office, and thank your lucky stars this is the present.) Look up to find a pair of murals; they're wonderful copies of Jean-François Millet's *The Gleaners* and *The Angelus,* painted by an itinerant artist with more talent than fame. You can buy postcards, homemade lye soap, or a museum membership; you may find the Women's Auxiliary of the museum quilting or weaving rag rugs when you visit on a Wednesday. The chamber of commerce also is here. The **Olde Towne Mall** (1225 N. Jesse James Rd.; 816-630-5174) has antiques galore.

Hometown Notes

From a childhood in Kansas City's North End, an inner-city Italian neighborhood, to my years at North Kansas City High School (Go Hornets!), I am a Missouri girl born and reared. I call Excelsior Springs my hometown because of the many years I lived there. I have always been very active in the community, beginning with a few years as PTA president when my children were young. To say I was active in the community is probably an understatement, but I loved it. I was on the Planning and Zoning Commission, the Road and Bridge Commission, and the Beautification Committee. I was on the board of directors of the Good Samaritan Society, a local charitable organization that ran a food pantry, among other things. Then I ran for and was elected to the City Council. I ultimately became the mayor. While on the council, I was elected to the board of directors of the Missouri Municipal League and so traveled around the state and met people from other small cities who were working through the same problems our city was facing.

For three years I wrote a weekly humor column for the *Daily Standard,* the local newspaper. I then went back to school at William Jewell College in Liberty and earned my B.A. in communication. I worked for the college as a recruiter for the re-entry program, to encourage older people to go back to school, and wrote a weekly humor column called "A Different View" (looking at college life from the perspective of a 42-year-old wife and mother) for the school paper. I was even a DJ at the radio station with my own late-night jazz program. I am proud to say that I was the oldest graduating senior, and on the dean's list. I gave those college-age kids a run for their money and had great fun doing it. My home became the home-away-from-home for all of the Japanese exchange students at the college who had nowhere to go over the holidays when the dorms closed. We even had a full-time exchange student from Japan from our own high school living with us. Excelsior Springs will always be my hometown though I am now very far away.

It's a huge space filled with lots of stuff. This "Olde Towne" area is bursting with shops, and it is a fine place to walk on a Saturday afternoon. Hours are Mon through Sat from 10 a.m. until 5 p.m., and Sun 1 to 5 p.m.

An old-fashioned hardware store has withstood the test of time—the newest generation of *Brunke's Supply* (423 Thompson; 816-637-3155) is exactly like the old one: Row upon row, deep into the bowels of the store, lined up in some kind of order only John Brunke knows, are thousands and thousands of things. Stuff. Gadgets. Cast-iron pots. Aluminum pans. Screws. Bolts. Signs. Anything. Everything. A real if-we-don't-have-it-you-probably-don't-need-it kind of place. You're gonna love it. Open Mon through Fri from 8 a.m. until 5 p.m. and on Sat until 4 p.m.

What do Harry S Truman, Al Capone, and Franklin D. Roosevelt have in common? They all stayed at the *Elms Hotel* at Elms Boulevard and Regent Street in Excelsior Springs (800-843-3567; elmsresort.com). You can, too. The elegant old hotel—built originally in 1888—and the beautiful grounds around it underwent a complete renovation The hotel has been a resting place for the famous and the infamous, from Presidents Franklin Roosevelt and Harry Truman to Al Capone, who hosted all-night drinking and gambling parties here during Prohibition. The look celebrates the time of that bygone era. In fact, the workers in the renovation process claimed to have seen the ghost of someone who looked a lot like Al Capone drifting down the hall of the fourth floor.

Look for the 1948 Chevrolet Stylemaster out front of the hotel. President Truman arrived in just such a car on election night in 1948. He came to avoid the press on a night when everyone thought he would be defeated by Thomas Dewey. He went to bed thinking he had lost the election and was awakened at 3 a.m. to learn that he had been reelected. The famous photo of him gleefully holding an early copy of the *Chicago Daily Tribune* carrying the blatant headline Dewey Defeats Truman was taken in front of the Elms Hotel.

The original tile floor and the huge "walk-in" fireplace in the lobby, as well as the art deco designs and stained glass in the Monarch Room, make this magnificent hotel worth a visit. It is, of course, on the National Register of Historic Places.

The Elms offers 153 guest rooms and suites, and the feeling of Truman's genteel time is augmented with such modern amenities as a communications

strangeas itsounds

Mormon travelers on the old trails left legends and stories. There is still a site inside the Excelsior Springs city limits that is visited by pilgrims. Mormons were being chased from the country and took refuge in an old church; such a storm came up that it spooked their pursuers' horses, the river rose, and the pursuers gave up and went home, leading the Mormons to believe they had been delivered by a miracle.

system with voice mail, dataport, and cordless phones. There is 24-hour room service and concierge service. A gourmet shop features coffees, espresso, cappuccino, entrees, and homemade ice creams. A beauty salon for hair and scalp treatments, facials, manicures, pedicures, and makeup is also available.

Boxer Jack Dempsey used the hotel as a training center. Now a complete fitness center on the grounds has tennis courts, riding stables, jogging trail, mountain biking, and, of course, an outdoor pool. Indoors there is a European swim track and banked jogging track. This indoor pool is shaped like a paper clip, with two sides extending the length of the room, and then curling back through two short rounded ends so that you can swim laps without having to turn around. The small islands in the middle of the pool are set with brightly painted giant flowers and playing-card symbols—hearts, spades, clubs, and diamonds—and bright bursts of color hang above the pool.

Various golf, spa, and honeymoon packages are also offered.

The beautiful little stone church across the street from the Elms, at the corner of Regent and Kansas City Avenues, is the ***Church of St. Luke, the Beloved Physician.*** The Episcopal congregation began having services in Excelsior Springs as far back as 1905, but it was 1933 when the church was built on property donated by Major W. A. J. Bell of Blechingly, England. The church is built in the English style, similar to the Church of St. Mary the Virgin of AD 1090 in Bell's home parish. It is built of stones quarried on Major Bell's property nearby. The inside of this remarkable church is so lovely that it is often requested for weddings. Guests at the Elms are frequently visitors on Sunday mornings. You will be most welcome, so sign the guest book and plan to stay for coffee and refreshments in the undercroft. Be sure to visit the quiet and beautiful little memorial garden out back.

Across the street is a little B&B called ***Bishop's House B&B*** in a 1917 stone house that matches the Elms and St. Luke's. It was built as the rectory for the former St. Ann's Catholic church next door. Members have moved on to a much bigger church on the edge of town, so the old rectory offers guests a quiet spot to rest and good food for breakfast in the dining room. Go to the website at bishopshousebb.com for reservations. Rooms are $70 and $80 a night.

Right down Kansas City Avenue at Chillicothe Street—beside the Elms Hotel—is an old depot where trains brought guests from Chicago and Kansas City to the hotel. Now it is the ***Wabash Barbecue*** (646 S. Kansas City Ave.; 816-630-7700; wabashbbq.com). The meats smoked in the old brick garage out back are very good and so is the secret barbecue sauce. Jim McCullough and his wife, Cheri, have restored the building to its 1925 charm. After its days as a depot, which ended in 1933, new owners converted it into a dairy, delivering milk to the residents of Excelsior Springs. The dairy sold milk shakes and burgers, too, and Jim—whose family goes back six generations in town—remembers hanging out here in the 1960s. He

Taking the Waters

Excelsior Springs has long been famous for its waters. Native Americans were aware of the benefits of the springs, but the settlers called them poison (or "PIE-zen," as they pronounced it). The medicinal uses of the waters were responsible for the founding of the town in 1880. There are five categories of mineral water, and each has a medicinal purpose. Excelsior Springs is one of only six cities in the world to have all of them—one of two in the US—and you can still experience most of them at the Hall of Waters there. First is iron manganese, which as the name suggests is a source of iron; then there's sulfo-saline, which is a very, very strong laxative (given a 2-ounce cup, people were told not to drink it in the elevator but to wait until they got to their rooms. This was no joke!). The next is soda bicarbonate, which was naturally carbonated and was used to settle a queasy stomach. The fourth category used to be the last—the neutral waters, which could be drunk in unlimited amounts—until it was discovered that they had very different compositions and served different purposes. These were calcium and lithium waters. The lithium water had properties that soothed depression (the most famous and best-tasting water in the world was Blue Rock Lithia) and of course the calcium water, which is the only water still bottled today in Excelsior Springs, is an excellent no-calorie source of calcium.

and Cheri looked at the walk-in coolers that once held cans of fresh milk and knew they would be perfect for slabs of meat, the big garage fine for smoking. On summer weekends you can enjoy music out on the patio. This is where the young crowd hangs out. Call for carryout, too.

There are plenty of artists in this little town. Some of the galleries are worth a visit. *Molly Roberts' Studio* (100 E. Broadway; 816-900-1028; mollyrobertsstudio.com) has so much fun art to touch and hold. Molly is fun to talk to, too. She has classes to help you unleash your inner artist if you are staying in town awhile.

The Artisan Gallery (451 S. Thompson Ave.; 816-637-2111; artisan-graphix.carbonmade.com) shows the work of local artists like Cathy Johnson, who is known nationally for her art and books.

As far as shops go, there are plenty of those, too: *Blue Raddish Studios* (108 E. Broadway; / 816-506-8129; blueraddishstudios.com) is one you might like. There are all kinds of interesting goodies to enjoy.

Downtown the old *Mill Inn Restaurant* (415 St. Louis Ave.; 816-637-8008) looks vaguely south-of-the-border. Inside you'll find wonderful cinnamon rolls (if you can beat the local farmers to them!), peanut butter pie, and on Wed and Sat only, homemade bread pudding.

Edward and Irene Heege are the innkeepers at the *Inn on Crescent Lake* (1261 St. Louis Ave.; 816-630-6745; crescentlake.com). It is a three-story Georgia colonial mansion on 22 acres. The home was built in 1915, and the crescent-shaped moat for which it was named still encircles the estate.

The guest rooms all have private baths (some have whirlpool tubs) and individual temperature control and cable television. Edward and Irene shared a dream of having the perfect country inn where people could unwind. This is a good place to do it. The swimming pool is a fine spot for cooling off, and the ponds are great for fishing. Paddleboats are available for tooling around the little lakes. There is even a fishing boat to use. Breakfast may be served in the dining room, living room, or in the sun-filled solarium.

Excelsior Springs also has one of the most beautiful old golf courses in the Kansas City area in *Excelsior Springs Municipal Golf Course,* and since it is a municipal course, it's affordable. Rolling hills, big trees, and surrounding woodlands make it challenging; watered fairways and paved cart paths make it pleasant year-round. It is an "English-type" course, unique because it has no sand traps or bunkers, which keeps play moving smoothly (so leave your sand wedge in the car). If you go into the snack bar for a cold drink, don't miss the tiny log cabin tucked inside the clubhouse. It's one of the original structures in this old town and lets you see how Missouri settlers once lived. The Battle of Fredericksburg, a Civil War skirmish, was fought along the southwest sector of the course, and a monument commemorating the event stands near the 15th tee. At the bottom of Golf Hill Drive in East Valley Park, you can stop and take a walk along the Fishing River path to see a new view of this old town—here you'll find one of the original mineral-water wells towering over the park. Visit the website at exsmo.com. From Excelsior Springs go east on Missouri 10, turn left on Highway M, then right onto Highway U, then right onto Crowley Street/Highway C (still with me?). Follow Highway C and what a surprise to find, just east of Excelsior Springs in the tiny town of **Rayville,** a winery and really good pizza. At **Van Till's Winery** (13986 Hwy. C; 816-776-2720; vantillfrms.com) they do wood-fired pizza in a semi-outdoor oven. There's a tasting room and wine shop (Tues through Thurs 11 a.m. to 5 p.m., Fri and Sat to 9 p.m.). Friday night is pizza night from 5 to 9 p.m. and Sat noon to 9 p.m. They boast of farm-to-table goodness from their own huge garden near the heated patio in the peaceful countryside. It's worth the trip just to see the oven and greenhouses. This is a great spot for private parties, too.

Just south of Excelsior Springs about 10 miles is the little town of **Orrick,** and there, in my humble opinion, you can find Missouri's greatest tenderloin sandwich. This sleepy little town used to raise lots of potatoes. That business has moved on, but this is delta land from the Big Muddy Missouri. The place to find that tenderloin is **Fubbler's Cove** (109 Front St.; 816-770-3878). Owners Tim and Cheri Heady work hard to make you a memorable meal in this old storefront. They feature a walleye dinner on Friday. Top off your meal with homemade blackberry or peach cobbler. Their breakfast menu features the Farmer's Special—enough food to keep any farmer going all day for the reasonable price of $5.45.

Or from Excelsior Springs, follow the signs to the **Watkins Woolen Mill State Historic Site** west off US 69 onto Highway 92 near Lawson and get ready to walk back in time. The visitor center is open from April 15 through October 15. The decades fall away like leaves as you wander down the footpath from the parking area. You pass deep Missouri woods, then a tiny stone-walled cemetery where the gravestones are encrusted with lichen. Farther along the path a brick giant rises to your right, and a graceful mansion crowns the hill to your left. A young belle could make quite an entrance down the lovely curved walnut staircase in the entryway—and probably did, more than once.

Waltus Watkins built his empire here around 1850, in the years before the Civil War. Quite an empire it was: The three-story brick mill employed dozens, providing woolen fabrics to the area. The milling machinery, from washing vats to looms, is still intact, providing pristine examples of early industrial ingenuity. The house and its outbuildings reflect a gracious life— the reward for hard work and hardheaded business sense.

Before it became a state park, the mill seemed destined for destruction. The family was selling it after more than a century of occupancy, and the place was on the auction block. Representatives from the Smithsonian were on hand to bid on rare equipment—but the day was saved, along with the integrity of the mill complex, when private individuals bought the site lock, stock, and barrel (and there were a few of those about). Eventually they were able to pass the mill complex along to the State of Missouri, and now you can tour the mill and the elegant home on the hill, participate in living-history weekends (try not to miss the Victorian Christmas), or watch an ongoing archaeological dig intended to discover still more about day-to-day life in the 19th century. Tours are given Mon through Sat from 10 a.m. to 4 p.m. and Sun from 11 a.m. to 4 p.m. Winter hours are from 11 a.m. to 4 p.m. Special events are usually free. An interpretive center acts as museum and buffer between now and the 19th century. Call (816) 580-3387 for more information.

A brick church and an octagonal schoolhouse are nearby, both restored to their original condition. The Watkins children and those of mill workers and local farmers attended to their readin', 'ritin', and 'rithmetic here. See the schoolhouse when it's open, if you can; call (816) 296-3357. The ventilation system of windows high in the octagonal clerestory turret is ingenious. Sunlight reflects softly around the white-painted walls inside; not much artificial light would have been necessary, with the tall windows on every side.

The park also has a 5-mile bike path through the woods as well as a sandy beach for swimming in the lake. Riding trails for horses are also a feature of the park. There are 98 campsites with hookups. Check mostateparks

.com/wwmill/camp.htm for special events held during the spring, summer, and fall months.

Going to **Lawson**? Look for the **Candyman** at 202 W. 6th St. (816-296-7231; candymancorp.com). The store carries just about every kind of candy you can imagine. It's a kiddie's dream come true. Chocolate. Jelly beans. It's all here but what is most important is that it's your center for home-making candy. You can buy coatings, molds, recipes, and tools you will need. Call or order online.

History buffs should look for the **Jesse James Farm Historic Site** (816-628-6065; jessejames.org) just off Highway 92 on Jesse James Drive, between Excelsior Springs and **Kearney** (watch for signs). The white house with its gingerbread trim and cedar roof sits just over a rise, a little ways back from the road; the new asphalt drive and path make the place wheelchair accessible. The original part of the house is a log cabin, which was rescued from a precarious slide into decay. The cabin contains, among other things, the remains of Jesse's original coffin, which was exhumed when the body was moved to nearby Kearney (pronounce CAR-ney); the family originally buried him in the yard to keep the body from being disturbed by those bent on revenge or looking for souvenirs. The coffin is odd by today's standards; there was a glass window at face level—presumably for viewing the body, not for providing a window on eternity for the deceased!

The newer section of the house was a Sears & Roebuck mail order. Mrs. James decided that the old place was getting too run-down—not to mention crowded—and she sent for the two-room addition, assembled on the spot. It still sports the original wallpaper.

This is the famous outlaw's birthplace, the place where his father was hanged and his mother's arm was lost to a Pinkerton's bomb. Enjoy the on-site museum, which includes a gift shop full of James memorabilia, books, and local crafts, or stick around in August and September for the play *The Life and Times of Jesse James*. Brother Frank was there, too. Oh, you want to know about the DNA test, do you? It was Jesse, all right.

Admission to the museum and home is $7.50 for adults, $6.50 for seniors, and $4 for children ages 8 to 15. The hours are from 9 a.m. to 4 p.m. 6 days a week, Sun from noon to 4 p.m.

July 17, 1995, was a big day in Kearney. The body buried in Jesse's grave was exhumed for DNA testing to finally settle the debate about who exactly was buried in the James family plot. Jesse's descendants offered DNA samples, and another man who claims that his grandfather is buried in Jesse's grave also offered his DNA for testing. People who believe that James died in 1950 at a very old age as well as people who believe it is Jesse's body in Mt. Olivet Cemetery brought folding chairs that morning to watch. "You goin' to the digging?" was the question asked at the local cafe when it opened early that morning. By closing time, lots of people were wearing "We Dig Jesse" T-shirts.

Slivinskis' Bakery (196 W. SR 92; 816-903-2245) is where Doug Slivinski bakes scrumptious muffins and other decadent delights. Get there very early if you want to try the white chocolate raspberry muffin and a cup of great coffee. Early means 5 a.m. Tues through Fri. You can sleep in on Sat and Sun, when Doug doesn't open until 6 a.m. Everything is gone by 1 p.m. all week, which is when he closes. You can call manager Terry Kinney and have a few saved for you.

And if you've ever wanted to lay a flower on the outlaw's grave, it's located in *Mt. Olivet Cemetery* on Highway 92, a half mile east of I-35 in Kearney. Look for it near the cedar trees at the west end of the cemetery, which is open during daylight hours year-round.

Legend has it that Jesse, Frank James, and/or Cole Younger visited darn near every fallen-down log cabin in this part of Missouri—not to mention the surrounding states. The James gang would have had to be in three places at once, the way their exploits were reported, but no matter. That's the fun thing about legends: They're much more elastic than the truth.

On the same path, but in the historic downtown area, is *Trash & Treasure* (109 E. Washington; 816-628-6119), where new and used clothing, toys, office supplies, tools, whatever! can be found. You can also visit Jeanette Montgomery's shop online at stores.ebay.com/trashandtreasure, too. Store hours are Tues through Thurs from 10 a.m. to 6 p.m., Fri from noon to 6 p.m., and Sat from 10 a.m. until 3 p.m.

Speaking of treasure, mosey on over to *Gracie's Chocolate* (101 W. Washington St; 816-903 9001) from 11 a.m. until 5:30 p.m. Tues through Sat. Locals in Kearney keep this specialty shop so busy the owner doesn't even have time to brag about all the yummy chocolate treasures she has in the shop. But to this outside observer, the strawberries dipped in chocolate are at the top of the healthy list as chocolate goes. The pecan and peanut clusters would bring in a tight second to a grown-up eye, but the chocolate chip cookies fly off the shelves, so there must be some youngsters voting, too.

Now you and your chocolates can slip into **Mojo's to Go** (100 E. 6th St.; 816-902-6656), which according to locals is the best little coffee shop in town. Great coffee, and great people who, a recent visitor said, make you feel so welcome you feel like a native—a chocolate-filled native, at that. It's open Mon through Fri from 6 a.m. to 6 p.m.

Gino's Italian Cuisine (123 E. Washington; 816-903-4466; ginosinkearney.com) has the old-world charm and ambience of Italy. It is located in downtown Kearney in an old storefront that has been beautifully restored. They feature authentic Sicilian and northern Italian cuisine. Gino's is family owned by George (Gino) and Julie Disciacca. Gino has more than 30 years of restaurant experience, and his entrees are influenced by his mother's Sicilian recipes and the tutelage of one of the premier Italian chefs in the area, Sam Gianini, who specialized in northern Italian cuisine. You can start with homemade mozzarella sticks and one of Gino's signature entrees, Pasta Gino (penne pasta, meat sauce, one meatball, and one Italian sausage topped off with mozzarella cheese and then baked in the oven). Their steaks are superb and can be cut with a fork. One of my favorites is the Steak Mediterranean—a 5-ounce filet topped with a red cream sauce, shrimp, and crabmeat. The luncheon menu features daily specials and is very reasonable. Gino's also specializes in Italian desserts. They range from tiramisu, Italian almond cream cake, spumoni amaretto cheese cake, and Gino's premier dessert, which he calls Xanadu: a flour tortilla with cream cheese filling, fried and topped with cherry, chocolate, and amaretto, and covered with whipped cream and fresh bananas. Your meal will be accompanied by lovely romantic music, and you can enjoy their full wine list. If you are really lucky, Gino will serenade you himself. Hours are Mon through Thurs 11 a.m. to 9 p.m. and Fri and Sat 11 a.m. to 10 p.m.; closed Sun.

Are you ready for breakfast? Fast-growing Kearney still hangs on to small-town charm. In any small town there is always a place that is the "heartbeat of the community." Here in Jesse James's hometown is an old restored farmhouse called **At Sarah's Table.** At the intersection of Highways 92 and 33, go north 1 block to 405 S. Jefferson St. (816-903-6627). Owners Carl and Sarah Moore, together with Tammy Grosserode, serve up the best breakfast in town. The parking lot begins to fill up at about 5:30 a.m. with the locals, as well as travelers on I-35 who are lucky enough to take the Highway 92 exit east through town. There is always a daily breakfast and luncheon special. Fresh tenderloins and chicken-fried steak are specialties, and the home-cooked meals will fill you right up. Dinner selections range from walleye to steaks. The Sunday lunch special is fried chicken with all the trimmings. One of the restaurant's philosophies is "Life is short; eat dessert first." Good advice when you see the array of homemade pies and cobblers. The waitresses are great here and always greet you with a smile and a hot cup of coffee. Hours are Mon through Wed and Sat 5:30 a.m. to 4 p.m., Thurs and Fri 5:30 a.m. to 8 p.m., and Sun 7 a.m. to 1 p.m.

Kearney may be a small town but it does not lack diversity. If really good Mexican food is what you desire, ***LaFuente Mexican Restaurant*** (105 S. Jefferson, in the Old Church Plaza Shopping Center; 816-903-9922; lafuentemexrest.com) serves authentic specialties. Try chilaquiles Mexicanos with green tomatillo sauce or the chile rellenos with a cold Dos Equis. The service and food are both excellent, and they are open 7 days a week for lunch and dinner. Hours are Sun through Thurs 11 a.m. to 10 p.m. and Fri and Sat until 10:30 p.m.

Rock Inn Cafe & Fourth Street Deli (400 S. Jefferson St.; 816-903-4010) gets big votes from the lunch crowd. Homemade soups as well as comfort foods like stuffed green peppers and mashed potatoes and gravy are on the Wednesday lunch buffet (only $7.99).

Western Way Bed & Breakfast at Over the Hill Ranch (13606 Henson Rd., Holt) is a unique B&B. Over the Hill Ranch, 4.5 miles north and west of Kearney, has been Connie and Bill Green's home for more than 30 years. Not only do they take care of people in a wonderful way, but they will also board horses overnight. That is one reason their first year in the B&B business was such a raging success. The production company filming the movie *Ride with the Devil* in the Kansas City area spent time here with their steeds, and Connie and Bill make appearances in the movie as wagon drivers. Country singer Shania Twain is one of the bed-and-breakfast's most famous guests. The singer spent three days at the ranch with her horse while appearing in Kansas City. The Greens have a draft horse now, too, so carriage rides are available for guests. The guesthouse offers all the privacy you could want. A suite with a king-size bed and double Jacuzzi goes for

$125 a night. The other room has a smaller Jacuzzi tub and rents for $110. A room in the main house is $120. Horses stay for $25 a night per stall (two or more for $20). Call for information and directions (the driveway is a half mile long and in the woods) or visit bbonline.com/united-states/missouri/kearney/westernway.html.

Highway 9 will lead you to the charming little college town of **Parkville,** just 20 minutes from Kansas City. This is a bustling yet pedestrian-friendly crafts and antiques center that moves at a leisurely pace with longtime shops interwoven with new establishments. Wear comfy shoes and a warm coat in cool weather and enjoy the brisk walk between shops. Stop to rest at the **Cafe Cedar at the Skillet** (2 E. 2nd St.; 816-505-2233; cafecedar.com), next to the post office; it serves Mediterranean cuisine. It is not only luscious food but healthy as well. Owners Osama Aburas and Jahad Saleh are rightly proud of their creations. They offer plenty of vegetarian dishes and any kind of kebab—lamb, chicken, shrimp, beef—you could want. The entrees cover a range from rack of lamb to baked salmon or stuffed Cornish hen. Nothing is fried; everything is baked or broiled. There are 6 kinds of salads, lots of sandwiches, and appetizers. Entertainment is offered some nights, too—light jazz. The **Missouri River Museum** is in the Cafe Cedar, as well. Hours are Mon through Sat 11 a.m. to 10 p.m. and Sun noon to 9 p.m. The Skillet is in the same place and owned and operated by the same people. It serves good old-fashioned American comfort food, such as fried chicken and mashed potatoes.

Just past the shopping complex is quiet English Landing Park on the banks of the Missouri. Look for the historic Waddell "A" truss bridge, built in 1898, one of only two left in the country. It was salvaged and moved to its present location. Now it's the focal point of the park, providing a walkway across a small feeder creek leading to the big river.

Peddler's Wagon, a quilt shop at 115 Main St. in downtown Parkville (816-741-0225), sells anything a quilter may need as well as some country gifts. There are also classes in quilting and silk embroidery. Hours are Tues through Sat from 10 a.m. until 4 p.m. year-round.

At **River's Bend Gallery** (102 E. Main St.; 816-587-8070) you will find a collection of fine arts and crafts, delicate mobiles, and other beautiful things. Hours are Tues through Thurs 10 a.m. to 5 p.m., Fri and Sat until 6 p.m., and Sun from noon to 5 p.m.

Downtown Parkville is loaded with places to shop, so it is a fine day trip from Kansas City. You can taste wine at **Wines by Jennifer** (405 Main St.; 816-505 9463; winesbyjennifer.com), which gives lots of choices when it comes to wine, mostly from small boutique wineries around the world. Sample wines in the tasting room Tues through Sat from noon to 8 p.m. There are cheeses from Osceola Cheese Company, local fresh breads, fruit, meats, crackers, and other foods that complement wine. Do a little shopping, too, for wine racks, decanters, and openers as well as cheese plates and more. Then scout out new kitchen gadgets at **Now You're Cookin'** (111 Main St.; 816-505-2338). Just pick up a little map of downtown at any shop and spend the day.

When lunchtime comes you have multinational choices downtown: **J. Yoshiko** (160 English Landing Dr.; 816-741-9966), a Japanese steak house and sushi bar; **Piropos Grille** (1 W. 1st St.; 816-741-3600; piroposgrille .com), an Argentinean restaurant in the more expensive range; **Blue Agave** (100 S. Main St.; 816-587-0060), for Mexican food; and **Cafe des Amis** (112 Main St.; 816-741-5387; cafedesamiskc.com), for a French bistro. But let's head for **Stone Canyon Pizza** (15 Main St.; 816-746-8686; stonecanyon-pizza.com). A personal favorite here is the Verdura pizza: fresh mushrooms, artichoke hearts, sun-dried tomato, sweet roasted red peppers, mozzarella, and fresh basil. This is not just a pizzeria, though; it has plenty of other choices as well. The tequila-lime chicken comes to mind. It is a cozy, rustic place with lots of small-town friendliness. Hours are Mon through Fri from 11 a.m. to 9 p.m. and on weekends from 11 a.m. to 10 p.m. (until 11 p.m. on weekends in the summertime).

Here's an interesting place to stop just for the heck of it: **H.M.S. Beagle** (180 English Landing Dr.; 816-587-9998; hms-beagle.com), a shop that makes science fun for both kids and grown-ups. A real live scientist is on duty every day to help you conjure up your own perfume recipe of essential oils and all other kinds of fun scientific stuff.

Take Mill Street to NW River Road out of town and onto I-435 and head north. Then merge onto I-29 (exit 31) and follow it to **Platte City**.

A former millionaire's estate on 73 acres is now the **Basswood Resort** at 15880 Interurban Rd. (816-858-5556 or 800-242-2775; basswoodresort .com), **Platte City.** This 1935 lakeside home has 6 suites—each with 2 bedrooms and a mini or full kitchen, some with fireplaces, and all in country

French decor. Besides the lodge itself, there are cabins, RV sites, and campgrounds.

Just off Highway 45, **Weston** is a beautiful town tucked between rounded hills, its past shaped as much by the nearby Missouri River and its thread of commerce as by the orchards, vineyards, distilleries, and good tobacco-growing soils here. After the signing of the 1837 Platte Purchase, it attracted settlers who recognized its rich soil—and appreciated the low prices.

Historic preservation in Weston has been a high priority for many years; the place exudes charm as a flower exudes scent. A beautiful old Catholic church overlooks the town, and tobacco and apple barns stand tall on many of the surrounding hills. It has a foursquare flavor that just feels historic—and in fact, Weston bills itself as the Midwest's most historic town. There are more than 100 historically significant homes and businesses from before the Civil War alone. Book a tour of the homes (advance reservations are required for the tour; call 816-640-2650 and ask to arrange a mini-tour for groups of 15 or more of two of the homes), or visit the **Weston Historical Museum** (601 Main St.; 816-386-2977; westonhistoricalmuseum.org). Hollywood has discovered Weston, and it's not unknown for movie cameras to roll on Main Street. Life in Platte County goes way back, long before these neat homes were built or the first still was cranked up; the museum will take you from prehistoric times through World War II. Hours are Tues through Sat from 1 to 4 p.m., and Sun from 1:30 to 5 p.m. (Closed Jan and Feb.) This one is a bargain; admission is free, and it's a day trip all by itself.

Weston's **McCormick Distilling Company** (816-640-2276) is a rare treat, 1¼ miles south of town on Highway JJ. They say this is the oldest continuously active distillery in the country—or at least west of the Hudson River. It was founded in 1856 by stagecoach and Pony Express king Ben Holladay.

You can't tour the distillery anymore, but be sure to visit the **McCormick Country Store** (420 Main St.; 816-640-3149; mccormickdistilling.com) in Weston, where Terri French handles all McCormick goods. You can find mugs, T-shirts, and other gift items as well as a fine line of cigars. There's a tasting room in which you can taste the products of the distillery for 25 cents.

Pirtle's Weston Vineyards Winery (502 Spring St.; 816-640-5728; pirtlewinery.com) is one of Missouri's most interesting wineries, located in the former German Lutheran Evangelical Church. Jesus made wine, so why not Pirtle's? Owner Elbert Pirtle's striking stained-glass windows depict the winery's logo and a wild rose—the math professor from the University of Missouri–Kansas City is quite the Renaissance man.

Northern Platte County soil is conducive to some fine viticulture; taste the products of these rolling hills Mon through Sat from 10 a.m. to 6 p.m. and Sun from 11 a.m. to 6 p.m. The Pirtles love to talk wine and vines. Schedule a wine-tasting party here, and don't forget to try the mead, a honey-based beverage once thought to be a "love potion." (So what have you got to lose?) It's sweet and smoky—and so it should be, because it's aged in McCormick Distillery oak barrels. Newest in the mead line are sparkling and raspberry mead. Great stuff and just as romantic as the original. They say that originally the church was upstairs and a cooperage was in the basement, where barrels were made to serve northwest Missouri. The winery now has a wine garden where you can take a basket of cheese, sausage, and bread to enjoy with your wine.

Across the street you'll find **The Vineyards** (505 Spring St.; 816-640-5588; thevineyardsrestaurant.com). The restaurant features country Continental cuisine and is considered one of the finest places to eat in the Kansas City area. With that reputation, you'd best call for reservations; the place is charming but small, seating only 36 . . . well, 42 in a pinch, if they push the tables together. It's an intimate cottage with white tablecloths and silver. (Romantic spot to propose, no?) The kitchen is tucked into every nook and cranny in the basement. Duck, lamb, salmon, and white perch are just some of the featured items on the menu. Appetizers of baked Brie with roasted garlic and fresh fruit give you some idea of the restaurant's Continental style. Patio dining during fine weather is a treat. There's a nice mix of art and music in the tiny 1845 Rumpel House. Lunch is served Wed through Sat from 11 a.m. until 2:30 p.m. Dinner is from 6 until 9 p.m. Owner Cheryl Hartell says reservations are a must on weekends. There is a Sunday dinner, too, from 4 to 7 p.m.

Just around the corner northwest from The Vineyards is the **American Bowman Restaurant** ("where the Past is Present"), at 500 Welt Street, the oldest continuously operating pub in Weston at 150-plus rollicking years old. Owners Mike Caokley and Corey Weinfurt offer Irish-style food and entertainment, pewter mugs, and kerosene lamps on the tables. There's

O'Malley's 1842 Pub, the Post Ordinary, the Heritage Theater, and malt and hops cellars in the same building. There's an actual brewery here! They call it "your trip to Ireland without the airfare," and that it is, laddie.

At Christmas try the Dickens Dinner; during other seasons, 1837 Dinners, Civil War Dinners, and 19th-Century Irish Banquets are yours for the ordering. For reservations call (816) 640-5235. Visit their website at westonirish.com. Hours are Mon through Sun 11:30 a.m. to 9 p.m. Pub hours are Friday 4 p.m. to 1:30 a.m. with live music from 8 p. m. to midnight, and Sun from 3 to 9 p.m.

You can choose a B&B or the renovated 1845 **St. George Hotel** (500 Main St.; 816-640-9902; thesaintgeorgehotel.com), which has 26 guest rooms that have seen steamboat captains and traveling salesmen from long ago. The hotel bar features Weston-made beer, wine, and whiskey as well as coffee and soft drinks. The rates are reasonable, beginning at a modest $89 and going to $239 for the largest room on a Saturday night, when Weston is lively.

If you prefer a B&B, "steamboat gothic" describes the circa 1898 **Benner House Bed and Breakfast** (645 Main St.; 816-640-2616; bennerhouse .com). With its double-deck, wraparound porch and gingerbread trim, the jaunty, turn-of-the-20th-century mansion looks as if it could steam away like the nearby riverboats. Brass beds and baths with pull-chain water closets are mixed with Jacuzzi tubs to add to the interior decor and to your mood. There is a private bath for each room. The view from the second-floor rooms is spectacular. You can see the wide Missouri across the floodplain. The candlelit breakfasts star delightful little pastries and secret-recipe muffins. A new hot tub has been added that guests may use. Visit the website to see pictures of everything.

The **Missouri Bluffs Boutique** (512 Main St.; 816-640-2770; missouribluffs.com) is full of quirky, unique clothes, jewelry, and handmade purses. It's like a maze, with rooms opening off rooms, but the clothing is delightful and the art is worth the search. The owner obviously enjoys shopping to stock the boutique. Hours are Mon through Sat 10 a.m. to 5 p.m. and on Sun noon to 5 p.m.

If you're in the mood for something a bit more upscale, the **Avalon** (circa 1847), across the street from the museum at 608 Main St. (816-640-2835; avaloncafeweston.com), offers an excellent beef tenderloin with a bourbon sauce—kind of a salute to Weston's distillery history, but as tender and flavorful as it's possible to be. A little bar area opens onto a charming outdoor courtyard. Owner-chefs Kelly Cogan and David Scott grill a fine salmon and offer an entire wild-game section on the menu. There are pasta dishes, salads, and sandwiches for the lunchtime crowd, too. Hours are Tues through Sat for lunch or dinner and Sunday brunch from 10 a.m. till 2 p.m.

Take a short jaunt west of Weston back on Highway 45 to see a view worth going way out of your way for. **Weston Bend State Park** is one of Missouri's newest, and the scenic overlook that spreads a panorama of the Missouri River and rolling fields, wooded loess hills, and Leavenworth clear across the river in Kansas is simply not to be missed. There's also camping, picnicking, hiking, and bicycling, if that's your pleasure. Call (816) 640-5443 for more information.

Snow Creek Ski Area (816-640-2200; skisnowcreek.com), just north of Weston, is open 7 days a week through the cold months. There's plenty of man-made snow (up to 4 feet), lifts, a ski rental, and a cozy lodge for après-ski. Normal costs include a snow pass (a lift ticket), plus rental equipment if needed. (Yes, there is downhill skiing in Missouri; the big hills near the Missouri River are satisfyingly steep, if not long. You can still break a leg if you're so inclined.) Snow passes are sold 30 minutes before each session. Beginning in early January every year, there is a special midnight-madness ski on Fri and Sat from 10 p.m. to 3 a.m. The regular rates vary so much that calling (816) 640-2200 and listening to the recording is a good idea. Snowboards are available, too. To reach Snow Creek from the north, take I-29 south to exit 20 (Weston), then go to Highway 273 and drive about 5 miles. When you reach a flashing red light at Highways 273 and 45, turn right onto Highway 45 and go 8 miles north. Snow Creek is on the right. There is a restaurant and bar, so you can stay for dinner. Lessons are available, too.

Iatan Marsh near the water treatment plant is the place to be in winter if you're a birder. The warmer waters here attract flocks of migrant waterfowl; who knows what you might spot. Nearby Bean Lake and Little Bean Marsh catch the birds—and birders—year-round. You may see rails and bitterns, yellow-headed blackbirds, green herons, and egrets along with the ducks and geese. An observation tower makes sighting easier; Little Bean Marsh is the largest remaining natural marsh in Missouri, a remnant of our wetlands heritage.

If you've read Lewis and Clark's journals, you'll remember the description of an oxbow they dubbed "Gosling Lake." This is now thought to be Sugar Lake in *Lewis and Clark State Park* (816-579-5564; mostateparks .com), just off US 59. There's a huge fish hatchery here; you can see anything from fry to fingerlings to lunkers.

St. Joseph ("Where the West Officially Started Getting Wild") is a river town that lost the race to Kansas City when KC was first to bridge the Muddy Mo with the Hannibal Bridge. Still a big and bustling town, it has plenty for the day-tripper to do and see. Consider this: St. Joe has eight (count 'em!) museums. The *Albrecht-Kemper Art Museum* (2818 Frederick; 816-233-7003 or 888-254-2787; albrecht-kemper.org) has a collection of some of the finest American art in the country, including works by Mary Cassatt, William Merritt Chase, George Catlin, and Missouri's own Thomas Hart Benton. Traveling shows are often exhibited at the Albrecht, including an excellent George Catlin exhibit. Remember Catlin? He's the artist who gave up virtually everything to record the Indian tribes in the early 1800s. It's the best record we have. Housed in an old Georgian manse, the museum has been in operation since 1966. Hours are Tues through Fri from 10 a.m. to 4 p.m., Sat and Sun from 1 to 4 p.m. Entry fees are $5 for adults, $2 for seniors, and $1 for students with any type of ID. Children younger than age 6 get in free. Then of course there's the 1858 Patee House at 12th and Penn, St. Joseph's only National Historic Landmark. The magnificent old hotel was the original headquarters for the Pony Express. It houses a tiny village inside a downstairs room, plus a steam engine that almost pulls into the rebuilt "station." Admission is $5. Also at 12th and Penn is the *Jesse James Museum* (816-232-8206), and the *Robidoux Row Museum* is at 3rd and Poulin. Admission to each is $2. The *Pony Express Museum* at 914 Penn St. chronicles the history of these early mail runs. Admission is $3, and it is open March through Oct from 9 a.m. to 5 p.m. Mon through Sat and 11 a.m. to 4 p.m. on Sun. In the winter the hours are a bit shorter; the museum closes at 4 p.m. on weekdays.

There's a morbid fascination to this next one, the *Glore Psychiatric Museum,* at 3408 Frederick Ave., 1 mile west of I-29 exit 47 (816-364-1209 or 800-530-8866; gloremuseum.org). The museum is housed in an old, rather forbidding wing on the hospital grounds. If you get a little shaky mentally, consider yourself fortunate; the museum features 20 display rooms of arcane treatments for psychiatric disorders, from prehistoric times to the recent past. (What did cavemen do, you ask? Knocked a hole in your skull to let out the evil spirits. Some patients even lived!) The museum is wheelchair accessible, and admission is free.

Missing a museum? It's the **Sally Rand Museum** (1716 Francis St.; 816-671-0670; missouribeautiful.com). Now for you young'uns who don't remember Miss Sally Rand, well, what can I say? She had a career in, um, the performing arts that spanned 50 years. She starred in silent films, but she was most celebrated for her creation called the Fan Dance. (Ah, now you remember hearing of her.) The museum is located inside the historic Barnard House (1877) and is open May through Sept, Tues through Thurs and the first Sat and Sun of those months (except holiday weekends).

As long as we are on the subject of museums, here's a bizarre one that might interest you: The **Heaton-Bowman-Smith & Sidenfaden Funeral Museum** (3609 Frederick Blvd.; 816-232-3355 or 816-232-4428) in St. Joseph displays the state's oldest funeral home, circa 1842, belonging to the state's first licensed funeral director. The museum is full of creepy things like old coffins, the small basket Jesse James's body was carried to the undertaker in, old cooling boards (yuck, don't even think about it!), as well as lots of photos and newspaper clippings. Please remember that this is a working funeral parlor, so be respectful of the families there. It is free, but you have to call first.

Did we neglect dinner? Oh dear! Find the **Bad Art Bistro** for some "gourmet food in a quirky atmosphere." What does that mean? Go downtown among the old brick buildings and freight houses to 707 Edmond and find out, or I guess you could call them at (816) 749-4433 and ask about the menu. Better yet, let's go there: okay, cheeseburgers (with gruyère; this is a *French* restaurant where you get haricots verts, not green beans) and instead of fries, how about some plantain fritters. Really good scallops considering this is the Midwest, braised lamb, quail, duck tamales (!), and desserts like crème brûlée and Vacheron Glace, plus a good wine list. What more could you ask? The food is so good you won't care about the funky, even kitschy, bad art. Even though it is in the somewhat depressed downtown area, you'd better make reservations because it tends to fill up quickly. For some good Cajun cuisine also in a historic brick building downtown, find **Boudreaux's Louisiana Seafood & Steaks** (224 N. 4th St.; 816-387-9911) and *Laissez les bon temps roulez.*

Stay at **Whiskey Mansion** (1723 Francis St.; 816-676-1529; whiskey-mansion1885.com), a historic 1885 mansion that has been restored in Saint Joseph's historic center. The rooms are quiet and full of antiques, and they are reasonably priced between $79 (for the maid's room) to $129. Or move from whiskey to beer and step into the wealthy world of the **Shakespeare Chateau Inn & Gardens Bed & Breakfast** (809 Hall St.; 303-232-2667; shakespearechateau.com). This incredible old mansion has to be seen to be believed. It is in the Hall Street Historic District downtown. This spooky-looking old mansion is perfect setting for murder mystery dinners, which are always fun, but the home isn't spooky at all. It is a luxury bed-and-breakfast furnished with pricy antiques. There are beautiful gardens for weddings, and gourmet breakfast. The rooms each have Wi-Fi, Jacuzzi tubs, private baths, and a plasma big-screen HDTV.

Visit stjomo.com for a complete listing of everything going on in town.

For sheer spectacle visit **Squaw Creek National Wildlife Refuge, Mound City** (660-442-3187; fws.gov/midwest/squawcreek), during the fall migration. You may see up to 350,000 snow geese fill the air like clouds. These clouds, though, are full of thunder; the sound of that many wings is deafening. Snow, blue, and Canada geese, migrating ducks, and attendant bald eagles (as many as 150 representatives of our national symbol), plus coyote, beaver, muskrat, and deer, make this a wildlife lover's paradise. At least 268 species of birds have been recorded on the refuge. It's an essential stop on the flyway for migratory waterfowl, as it has been for centuries; this area was described in the journals of Lewis and Clark. There are now 7,193 acres on the refuge just off Highway 159; watch for signs. Unusual loess hills that look like great dunes, reddish and fantastically eroded, are threaded with hiking trails.

Now let's head to **Maryville.** Go east on US 159, then north on US 59 to Hwy. 113. Follow it east to Hwy. 46 and east into Maryville. Maryville is home to **5 Mile Corner Antique Mall** (30622 US 71 South; 660-562-2294). Hours are 10 a.m. to 5 p.m. Mon through Sat. Gailen and Twilla Hager have 5,000 square feet of antiques for you to peruse. There's more to do here than just shop, of course. For instance, you can visit the Mary Linn Performing Arts Theater to hear a concert or watch a play performed by the Missouri Repertory Company.

If all this antiques hunting has you ready for a bit of quiet, retreat from the world at **Conception Abbey** at the junction of US 136 and Highway VV in **Conception Junction.** Benedictine monks run the Printery House (660-944-2218; conceptionabbey.org), where they make greeting cards and colorful notes (ask for their catalog) when they are not going about their real work. Benedictines consider their true work to be prayer—but the work of their hands is prayer, too. Stay over at the 1,000-acre retreat, 900 of which is productive farmland; visit with "the weather monk," or learn along with the seminarians. The Romanesque Basilica of the Immaculate Conception (1891) adjoining the monastery has examples of Beuronese art. Tours can be arranged by calling the guest center (660-944-2809) to make a reservation.

A little southwest of Plattsburg on US 169 and Highway Z is the town of **Edgerton.** Here **Harmer's Cafe** (501 Frank St.; 816-790-3621) has long specialized in old-fashioned favorites, such as pan-fried chicken, mashed potatoes, and cobbler. Karen Belt, who took over the restaurant from her mother, hasn't changed it much. You don't mess with success. The green beans are done in the traditional Midwestern way with bacon, brown sugar, and onions and slow cooked for hours. They alone are worth the trip. Hours are Mon and Tues 6:30 a.m. to 2 p.m., Wed through Sat to 6:30 p.m., and Sun 8:30 a.m. to 2 p.m.

Smithville is near the intersection of US 169 and Highway 92, and if all you know about the place is that it used to flood, you're in for a nice

President for (Less than) a Day

The Greenlawn Cemetery in Plattsburg is the final resting place of a man who served as president of the US for one day—Sunday, March 4, 1849. Outgoing Vice President George M. Dallas had already resigned from office the Friday before. The term of President James K. Polk expired at noon on the fourth. The incoming Zachary Taylor refused to take his oath on the Sabbath, waiting until 11:30 Monday morning. For that 23½–hour period, the nation had no elected chief executive. The Succession Law of 1792 stated that the head of the Senate automatically became president should the top two offices be vacant. David Rice Atchison was that man. They say the president slept through much of his term of office. There is no presidential library here, but there is a statue of Atchison at the entrance of the Clinton County courthouse in Plattsburg.

surprise. *Justus Drugstore* (106 W. Main St.; 816-532-2300) is the place to stop and order the grilled Berkshire port rib eye and smoked crispy shoulder on chestnut risotto. What! In a drugstore? It's been reviewed in the *KC Star, Bon Appetit Magazine,* and *Time* magazine in the past few years. So trust me on this or check it out yourself at drugstorerestaurant.com. Dining hours are Wed through Thurs 5:30 to 10 p.m., Fri and Sat 5:30 to 11 p.m., Sun 5:30 to 9 p.m.

The town is close by *Smithville Lake* for summer fun, and there are plenty of shops to browse in. Smithville Lake is a fairly recent addition to Missouri's array of man-made lakes. Constructed by the US Army Corps of Engineers to control the flooding that Smithville residents have lived with since there was a Smithville, the lake is also a magnet for water-lovers. Turn north off Highway 92 (between Kearney and the town of Smithville) for sailing, fishing, boating, or just messing around.

Also at the lake is Missouri's own *Woodhenge,* a re-creation of a Woodland Indian site that may have been used as an astronomical observatory around 5,000 years ago. The original location of Woodhenge was uncovered during the building of the lake, and dredging was halted until archaeologists could study the area. It was important enough that the present site was reconstructed as an aid to further study; scientists from Woods Hole, Massachusetts, have come here to observe the solstice and equinox.

Near the dam at Smithville Lake, one of the largest glacial erratics in the area squats like a patient dinosaur under an accretion of graffiti. A large, pink Sioux-quartzite stone, this elephant-size monster was brought here by the last glacier some 15,000 years ago. It may have been an important landmark for the Paleo-Indians who lived in the area.

At the *Jerry Litton Visitors' Center* (816-532-0174; nwk.usace.army .mil), also near the dam, you can find out about these earliest inhabitants, about visits by Lewis and Clark as they came through on the nearby Missouri River, about the pioneer settlers, and about the birds and animals that make this area home. Admission is free. Stop for lunch at the *Brick House Cafe and Pub* (111 N. Bridge St.; 816-532-8865) for a grown-up grilled cheese made with fresh mozzarella, basil, and tomato on ciabatta bread.

Places to Stay in Northwest Missouri

KANSAS CITY
Holiday Inn
11130 Ambassador Dr.
(airport)
(816) 891-9111
Inexpensive

NORTH KANSAS CITY
Marriott at the Airport
775 Brasallia Ave.
(816) 464-2200
Moderate

LIBERTY
Days Inn
209 N. 291 Hwy.
(816) 781-8770
Inexpensive

Fairfield Inn
8101 N. Church
(816) 792-4000
Inexpensive

GALLATIN
Sandman Motel
512 S. Main
(660) 663-2191
sandmanhotels.ca
Inexpensive

EXCELSIOR SPRINGS
Monterey Motel
217 Veterans' Memorial
Dr.
(816) 637-3171
Inexpensive

Places to Eat in Northwest Missouri

KANSAS CITY
Cascone's Italian Restaurant and Lounge
3733 N. Oak Trafficway
(816) 454-7977
Moderate

Majestic Steakhouse
931 Broadway
(downtown)
(816) 471-8484
majestickc.com
Expensive

Stroud's
5410 NE Oak Ridge Dr.
(816) 454-9600
stroudsrestaurant.com/
north.html
Moderate

AVONDALE
The Depot Saloon & BBQ
2702 N. Bell
(816) 452-2100
Inexpensive

LAWSON
Catrick's Cafe
410 N. Pennsylvania Ave.
(816) 580-4177
Inexpensive

RIVERSIDE
Corner Cafe
4541 NW Gateway Dr.
(816) 741-2570
thecornercafe.com
Inexpensive

WESTON
Weston Red Barn Farm
16300 Wilkerson Rd.
(816) 386-5437
westonredbarnfarm.com
Inexpensive

FINDING HELPFUL VISITOR INFORMATION

Excelsior Springs
exspgschamber.com
(816) 630-6161

NORTHEAST MISSOURI

North of St. Louis the land changes. Hills are gentler; they are the legacy of a wall of glacial ice that smoothed rough edges and brought with it tons of rich, deep soil some 15,000 years ago. Thanks to that gift, quintessentially Mid-American towns are dotted with the docile shapes of cows; barns are large and prosperous-looking; fence rows blossom with wildflowers; and bluebirds and meadowlarks sing.

Northeast Missouri is rich in history as well. That consummate storyteller Mark Twain was born here; he has endowed us with more colorful quotations than any writer before or since. You've heard of Mark Twain Cave and his boyhood home in Hannibal, but did you know that near Florida, Missouri, you can explore Samuel Clemens's birthplace? General Omar Bradley's birthplace is in this area, too, along with General John J. Pershing's boyhood home and a monument to General Sterling Price. (Generally speaking, it seems to be a great place for great men.)

The Civil War raged from St. Louis to the Iowa border, where the Battle of Athens took place. Tiny Palmyra was the site of an atrocity that Presidents Abraham Lincoln and Jefferson Davis called the worst of war crimes.

NORTHEAST MISSOURI

0 ____ 40 mi
0 ____ 40 km

IOWA
MO.

136

136

Kahoka

61

Kirksville

MARK
TWAIN'S
RIVER

GLACIATED

63

PLAINS

36

Macon

36

Hannibal

ILL.

MO.

24

61

Mississippi R.

Moberly

Mark Twain
Lake

BLUFFS
OF THE
MIGHTY MO

Mexico

54

ANTIQUES
AND
ANTIQUITY

MISSOURI'S
MONARCHY

Columbia

Troy

70

St. Peters

63

54

Fulton

Missouri R.

Lake St. Louis

NORTHERN
WINERIES

All along the Missouri River valley are tiny, picturesque towns, many with a German heritage, and many with wineries where you can taste the best the US has to offer. (Mount Pleasant's port won the gold in international competition.) Lewis and Clark passed by these town sites on their way to the Northwest Passage and remarked on them in their journals.

The mighty Mississippi is busy with commerce, as it has been for more than 200 years. Barges churn by, and the power of that mile-wide channel vibrates under you as you stand on a riverboat deck. The Great River Road, which runs along the Mississippi from New Orleans to its source, is so picturesque that plans are afoot to make it a National Scenic Byway.

Bald eagles feed along both rivers in winter, drawn by open water and good fishing below the locks and dams. Amish communities, college towns, museums, eateries, petroglyphs, wildlife refuges—whatever your interest, you'll find it satisfied in northeast Missouri, where literally everything is off the beaten path.

missouriborders

Missouri borders eight states. Only Tennessee touches as many neighbors.

Antiques & Antiquity

Just north of St. Louis is **St. Charles.** The first capitol of Missouri is located at 208–216 S. Main St. (636-940-3320); legislators met here until October 1826, when the abandoned buildings began to settle slowly into decay. In 1961 the State of Missouri began a 10-year restoration project that sparked the revitalization of St. Charles. Shops, restaurants, and delightful little surprises abound. Take a walking tour of history; the St. Charles Convention and Visitors' Bureau (636-946-7776; historicstcharles.com) can get you started.

Boone's Lick Trail Inn (1000 S. Main St.; 636-947-7000; booneslick .com) is an 1840 federal-style home on the Boone's Lick Trail, right where the trail has crossed Main Street for more than 155 years. Seven guest rooms are decorated in regional antiques, and there are 2 gathering rooms. It is close to the airport, the **KATY Trail,** and the casino.

The city is the state's largest National Register Historic District, with 10 blocks of mid-1800s buildings authentically restored. Stroll along cobblestone streets, watch the river flow by, and enjoy fine dining, antiquing, and history.

Both of our big rivers have claimed more than their share of casualties. Steamboats sank with dismal regularity, and to this day—locks and dams notwithstanding—riverboat captains watch their charts and take their soundings much as Samuel Clemens did when he sang out, "Mark Twain." The channels of both the Missouri and the Mississippi are graveyards for boats, from tugs to stern-wheelers; the rivers are not to be taken lightly. Our Lady of the Rivers Shrine, a lighthouse-like monument at Portage de Sioux, is a reminder that brave travelers needed all the help they could get. That said, it's time to board at the ***Ameristar Casino St. Charles*** (1260 S. Main; 636-940-4300; ameristar.com). The station is off I-70 just 10 minutes west of Lambert Airport and gives you two action-packed casinos. The casino on the boat is open from 8 a.m. until 5 a.m. during the week and 24 hours Fri, Sat, and holidays. Take the 6th Street exit (229a) just across the bridge.

trivia

The Missouri River flows north—the wrong way and against all natural order—along St. Charles County. It flows north for several miles, then turns east to join the Mississippi River. This is one of the few places in the Western Hemisphere where a major river flows north.

If you enjoy a little wine tasting, try the ***Little Hills Winery & Restaurant*** (427 S. Main St.; 636-946-9339; littlehillswinery.com) and have the Shrimp Davila (rolled in breadcrumbs and butter fried with lemon garlic sauce) or the lobster ravioli. If beer is more to your liking, head over to Trailhead Brewing Company, at the corner of Main Street and Boonslick (636-946-2739; trailheadbrewing .com) in historic downtown St. Charles. Trailhead crafts its own beer and carries a variety of other brands. It's a good place to find a sandwich, salad, or burger, too. Hours are 11 a.m. to 10 p.m. Sun through Thurs; Fri and Sat until 11 p.m. with a special late-night menu from 11 p.m. till midnight.

People who like to have just a salad or soup for lunch so that they can justify indulging in dessert will love Miss Aimee B's Tea Room (837 First Capitol Dr.; 636-946-4202; missaimeeb.com). Hours are 9 a.m. to 3 p.m. Tues through Sat. If you're there in the spring or summer, be sure to try a seasonal dessert, such as the chocolate-strawberry pie.

TOP RECOMMENDATIONS IN NORTHEAST MISSOURI

The **Mother-in-Law House** (500 S. Main St.; 636-946-9444; motherin lawhouse.com) must first have its name explained. In 1866 a French bride so missed her mother that her understanding husband built her a home with a dividing wall down the center so his mother-in-law could come to America and move in with them. Donna Hafer found the redbrick beauty on Main Street in the historic district of St. Charles and gave it the TLC it needed to become the gracious, antiques-filled restaurant it is today. The dining room has the original oil lamps. Glittering prisms pour a soft glow on the antique furnishings. Fresh flowers adorn each table and the staff wears dainty pinafores. The recipes have been in Donna's family for more than a century and make the salad bar a delight. Her coconut cream pie is renowned in the area.

The restaurant is open for lunch Mon through Sat 11 a.m. to 2 p.m. and for dinner Tues through Sat 5:30 to 9 p.m. Reservations are recommended.

This is an area with more than 100 quaint shops and restaurants plus many art, crafts, and historical festivals offered throughout the year. Be prepared to spend at least a day here. St. Charles is also right on the KATY Trail. If you didn't bring your bike, you can rent one at the **Touring Cyclist** (11816 Saint Charles Rock Rd.; 314-739-5183; touringcyclist.com) in **Bridge-ton.** They will provide bikes, tours, transportation or anything a cyclist needs to do the KATY Trail. Carol Bodeker and Don Humphries have been doing this since 1971, so they know the answers to all your questions about the trail.

Winfield, Clarksville, Louisiana—the names are strung like beads along the Great River Road (now scenic Highway 79) between St. Louis and Hannibal. These little towns harbor more antiques shops than you will know what to do with. There are so many, in fact, that we have room to include only those towns that have additional attractions. Don't let that stop you, though; Missouri is a mecca for affordable goodies. If you can't find what you're looking for, you just haven't found the magic spot yet, and isn't the search as much fun as the finding?

Age-old traditions of quilting, stained glass, blacksmithing, and furniture making are found in Clarksville. Much of the town is on the National Register of Historic Places, and it has a good museum.

snakingfrolics

Clarksville was called Appletown by river men because of the huge quantity of apples it shipped on the river each fall. But "Snakeville" would have been more accurate, because the really big feature of the town was its rattlesnake population. During its early years Clarksville was a choice place for a popular sport called "snaking frolics." The record was set by the town constable, who along with others in town killed 9,000 rattlers on one of the town's annual spring hunts.

Little **Eolia** has **St. John's Episcopal Church** and cemetery, the oldest Episcopal church west of the Mississippi.

Bowling Green features antiques shops along Business US 61. **Honeyshuck** is the restored front-gable-and-wing frame home of House Speaker James Beauchamp "Champ" Clark, who was elected to the US House of Representatives in 1892 and went on to become Minority Leader in 1909. Clark was a frontrunner for the Democratic nomination for president but lost it to New Jersey Governor Woodrow Wilson on the 46th ballot. The house got its name from the yard's honey locusts, whose shucks fall to the ground. Several miles outside Bowling Green on Highways Y and M is a thriving Amish community. It is filled with talented craftspeople who carry on the traditions passed down to them by their parents. Several families make and sell handmade crafts and bakery goods. A woodworking shop creates beautiful handmade furniture and cabinets. You can arrange for a tour of the area by calling the Bowling Green Chamber of Commerce at (573) 324-6800.

TOP ANNUAL EVENTS IN NORTHEAST MISSOURI

JULY

National Tom Sawyer Days
(and National Fence Painting Contest)
Hannibal
(573) 221-2477
toll free at 1-TOMANDHUCK

Annual Demolition Derby
Macon
maconmochamber.com

SEPTEMBER

Annual Buzzard Run Antique Car Show
Macon

NOVEMBER

Fall Craft Show
Columbia
Missouri's largest indoor craft show,
Hearnes Center
600 Stadium Blvd.
(573) 874-1132
Columbia Chamber

FEBRUARY

True/False Film Festival
(documentary films)
Bands play at screening and directors
chat with audiences
Buy a weekend pass, $60
(573) 442-8783

If your sweet tooth needs satisfying while you're in Bowling Green, be sure to visit **Bankhead Chocolates** (810 N. Business US 61; 573-324-2312; bankheadchocolate.com). They've been making hand-dipped chocolates since 1919, and experience does make a difference! Four generations are involved and owner Laura Portwood says most people tell her that candy is an impulse item, not a destination—"Not with us!" she says with a laugh. The candy is still prepared in large copper kettles and poured onto a marble table and cut and hand-dipped. But that's not all! This is also the home of an old fashioned ice-cream soda fountain and a bistro, as well. Ah, the bistro—home of the Bistro Salad with candied pecans, strawberries, and bacon. Perfect with a hot smoked-turkey melt or the quiche of the day. The bistro is open for lunch Wed, Thurs, and Fri from 11 a.m. till 2 p.m. Bankhead Chocolates, the coffee bar, and ice cream parlor are open all day from 9 a.m. to 5 p.m. Mon through Fri and 9 a.m. to 5 p.m. Sat. Chocolates can be ordered online but will not be mailed in the summertime, when they would melt. Oh yes, and grab a bag of the white-chocolate-covered popcorn to take with you. It's addictive.

Lock and Dam No. 25 on the Mississippi is a fine place to watch the eagles feed in the winter. Or take the old Winfield Ferry across the river to Calhoun County, Illinois. (Don't worry, you can come right back if you're not through antiques hunting.)

If you fancy a bit of wilderness about now, a short detour west on Highway 47 will take you to spectacular *Cuivre River State Park* (636-528-7247; mostateparks.com). More than 31 miles of trails will let you discover one of the state's most rustic parks. The rough terrain is more like the Ozarks than the rest of glacier-smoothed northern Missouri, and like the Ozarks, it encourages many plants found only farther south, such as flowering dogwood, Missouri orange coneflower, and dittany. Frenchman's Bluff overlooks the Cuivre River Valley. The Lincoln Hills region, where Cuivre River State Park is found, formed millions of years ago when intense pressures caused the earth to buckle. Erosion cut even deeper; the resulting springs, sinkholes, and rocky cliffs make this an outdoors-lover's paradise. Archaeologists speculate that the region was home to prehistoric humans as early as 12,000 years ago; a 1937 dig unearthed a stone chamber containing a skeleton and pieces of a clay pot.

Clarksville is finding its way back—but back toward the past. With about the same population that it had in 1860, this spic-and-span town has new life in its old veins. A historic preservation effort mounted in 1987 has saved many of the delightful buildings in record time. There are also some antiques and gift shops to explore.

The town commands an 800-square-mile view of the valley of the Big Muddy from an aerie on the highest point overlooking the Mississippi. Surprisingly, barge traffic on the river below is constant—you don't expect to see so much action. See ice-formed drumlins (those are hills) in this panoramic view.

Clarksville is a great place to observe wintering eagles; the Missouri Department of Conservation's Eagle Days, held here the last weekend of January, can swell the town's normal population of 500 to more than 5,000. Is it worth it? You bet it is. Even the *New York Times* visited to check out the bald eagles, which can number from the hundreds to the thousands, depending on the weather. (The colder the winter has been, the more eagles gather here.) The *Clarksville Eagle Center* offers information, a museum, and spanking-clean restrooms. Call (573) 242-3132 or check out seatriverroad.com/hannibal/hanevents/eagledays.htm.

Erin Garrison and her husband, Bud, retired to Clarksville a few years ago and now spend their time at the potter's wheel. This quaint Mississippi River town is dedicated to preserving the past while offering artists the opportunity to work in the restored buildings. They are at the highest point on the Little Dixie Highway (dubbed that when it was the only road heading south) along the river's banks. She and her husband established the **Great River Road Pottery Shop** (107 S. 1st St.; 573-242-3000), where Erin creates unique stoneware pottery. Her signature pieces have original wildflower design brushwork on an eggshell-colored clay body. There is oven- and tableware, oil lamps, and many things for the garden, including flowerpots, planters, and bird feeders. Each piece is wheel thrown or hand built by Erin. This high-fire stoneware is oven, microwave, and dishwasher safe, and the glazes are lead free. Erin's working studio and gallery overlook the river in downtown Clarksville. Shop hours are 10 a.m. to 5 p.m. Wed through Sat, 11 a.m. to 5 p.m. on Sun, and by appointment Mon and Tues. Plan to visit the many artists' studios and antiques shops while in historic Clarksville: **Simpatico** is an art gallery co-op open on weekends, Sat 10 a.m. to 5 p.m. and Sun from 11 a.m. to 5 p.m. **Bee Naturals** (573-242-3475; beenaturals .com) has bath and body supplies, the **Clarksville Glassworks** (clarksville-glassworks.com) offers hand-blown and kiln-formed art glass, and the **Bent Tree Gallery** (573-242-3200; thebenttree.com) sells bent-willow furniture, baskets, and fiber art. This is just a sampling of what's in Clarksville. Visit clarksvillemo.us for more information.

The entire business district of downtown **Louisiana** is on the National Register of Historic Places and is well known for its antiques shops along Georgia and Main Streets. There are two museums: the **Louisiana Historical Museum** and the **Phillips Museum.** But most interesting is the fact that it has the most intact Victorian streetscape in the state. Dozens of historic homes line Georgia and Main Streets and it still, of course, has a town square. Also worth a visit, perhaps, is the old **Gates of Peace Jewish Cemetery** off US 54. There are also many antebellum homes in this old river town.

There is some good antiquing in Louisiana. Right down the street at 515 Georgia St. is **Kate's Attic Antiques and Mini Mall** (573-754-4544), with 40 booths to browse through. Hours are 10 a.m. to 4:30 p.m. every day except Sun, when hours are 11 a.m. to 4 p.m.

There's a newer place to stay in town, too. ***Eagle's Nest Winery, Inn, and Bistro*** has it all (221 Georgia St.; 573-754-9888; theeaglesnest-louisiana .com).The bistro can begin your day with omelets made to order, waffles, homemade biscuits and sausage gravy, or jumbo cinnamon rolls. Special breakfasts like the Eggs Ranchero (English muffin topped with shaved ham, pico de gallo, poached eggs, and hollandaise) are served from 7 to 10:30 a.m. Mon through Fri and 8 to 10:30 a.m. Sat and Sun, and brunch is from 9 to 11 a.m. and lunch from 11 a.m. to 2 p.m.

From 11 a.m. to 4 p.m. Tues through Sat and from 11 a.m. to 2 p.m. Mon, you can try the Eagle (hickory-smoked turkey breast, smoked bacon, baby swiss cheese, red leaf lettuce, tomato, and basil mayo on focaccia bread) or the chicken Caesar wrap (grilled chicken in a herb and garlic wrap with Caesar dressing, grated Parmesan, romaine, and red onion) or the daily pizza specials.

Dinner is prepared between 3:30 and 5 p.m., but coffee and other beverages, soup and house salad, and items from the bakery are available in the bistro during that time, so all is not lost. The bakery prepares all the baked goods at the Eagle's Nest. Jumbo cinnamon rolls, apple strudel, cherry turnovers, muffins, cookies, elephant ears, orange–golden raisin scones, breads, cranberry walnut bread pudding, and specialty cakes and pies are warm from the oven.

The winery is a destination by itself. The wines are very Missouri: Pikers Blush is made from Catawba grape; Mississippi River Rouge is Chambourcin grape with some Cabernet and other red grapes; Red Bud is Catauba and various French and American hybrid red and white grapes; Rivera de Sel is made with Seyval, Vidal, and Vignoles grapes; and the Sweet Louisiana Basye is from the Vida and Muscat grapes. Buffalo Fort Norton is made from Missouri's own Norton grape and then aged in oak barrels. If wine is an important part of your dinner, you will enjoy the Thursday Nights After Glow from 4 to 7 p.m. to taste some of these unusual wines with snacks of the specialty foods from the bistro. The patio is open Apr through Oct. The garden is tucked in by the four Eagle's Nest buildings and a hundred-year-old 10-foot stone wall, providing protection from brisk winds on cool days and a cooler environment on hot days.

If you want to take a bit of Missouri home, the Winery Shop has gifts—a custom gift basket can be filled with gourmet foods, wine accessories, little gift items for the home, coffees, teas, and of course, any of the wines.

Rooms at the inn begin at $95 and go up to $125 for the suite, and include full breakfast in the Bistro.

Due to the historical nature and furnishings, children younger than 15 years of age are not accepted. Everything except the wine garden is nonsmoking.

Mark Twain's River

For tourists, **Hannibal** is not exactly "off the beaten path." Half a million people annually come through this picturesque little town. Everybody knows about the Mark Twain Boyhood Home. Everybody's seen that fence—or at least pictures of it—where Tom Sawyer tricked his buddies into doing his work for him. (The original fence was 9 feet tall and a lot longer than the one that stands here now—no wonder the kid didn't want to paint it by himself.) You may even know about Margaret Tobin Brown's home (remember the Unsinkable Molly Brown?) and the fine dinner cruise on the Mississippi riverboat the *Mark Twain*. So we'll let you find them on your own—it's easy.

But did you know that right across the street, at 211 Hill St., is the ***"Becky Thatcher" House***? Actually Becky was Laura Hawkins, who lived here in the 1840s and attended school with young Sam Clemens. She was his childhood sweetheart, immortalized in print as Tom Sawyer's Becky Thatcher. The upstairs parlor and bedroom of the home are restored and are open to the public at no charge. The main floor features a bookshop carrying the largest selection anywhere of books by or about Mark Twain. First editions and out-of-print books are sometimes available. This is owned by the Mark Twain Museum (573-221-9010; marktwainmuseum.org).

Stop at ***Becky's Old Fashioned Ice Cream Parlor & Emporium*** (318 N. Main; 573-221-0822; beckythatcher.com), which is right around the corner from the Mark Twain Boyhood Home, for a cool ice-cream treat. The back third of the shop has a collection of Mark Twain books and other children's classics as well.

While you're in the historic district, look for ***Ayers Pottery.*** Steve Ayers does beautiful work, using primarily Missouri clays, and the shop is set up to encourage your involvement. There's a hall around three sides of the work-shop, so you can see every step in the process. He also stocks a selection of beautiful kites, porcelain jewelry, baskets, and hand-forged things—goodies he picks up while on the craft-show circuit.

Even when Steve's out of town, the shop is open at 308 N. 3rd, 7 a.m. to 3:30 p.m. Mon through Fri (573-221-6960 or 800-227-6960; ayerspottery.com). It's only half a block from the Mark Twain Museum. Steve has opened another shop, aptly named *Java Jive Coffee House,* at 211 N. Main St. in Hannibal (573-221-1017), where, along with pottery, Steve also carries coffee beans in many flavors. If you want to try some of them, there is a delightful cappuccino bar in the back of the store. Hours are Mon through Thurs 7:30 a.m. to 10 p.m., Fri and Sat to 10:30 p.m., and Sun 10 a.m. to 6 p.m. Steve is involved in a project to list all of the artists living along the river route. While you sip your espresso, he can give you directions to many other craftspeople to visit along the way. Steve also owns *Fresh Ayers* (209 N. Main), where he has a fine collection of primitives and furniture.

trivia

The word *twain* means "two" when used as a mark or measurement of the depth of the water. *Mark twain,* therefore, means two fathoms.

If elegant Victoriana is your weakness, stay in gingerbread heaven at the *Garth Woodside Mansion* (11069 New London Rd., Hannibal; 573-221-2789 or 888-427-8409; garthmansion.com). This one's on the National Register, and it deserves to be. Mark Twain was often a guest of the Garths. Built in 1871, this stunning Victorian summer mansion is on 39 acres of gardens and woodlands.

You won't believe the three-story flying staircase with no visible means of support; you might not trust it, either, though they say it's quite safe. Enter the walnut-lined library through 9-foot doors, or check out the extra-wide hostess's seat in the dining room. (No, the hostess wasn't that wide; it accommodated the voluminous petticoats of the era.) The 8 bedrooms still have the discreet opulence of Twain's era. The aroma of freshly baked pastries and muffins draws you to the dining room, where the eight-leaf walnut table is just as it was then. You can spend the day rocking on the veranda or watching deer or fox from the library window, and spend the evenings leisurely near a fire. Christmas is an especially fine time to visit, when the mansion becomes a fairyland of authentic Victorian decorations. Rates are from $175 to $395. Innkeepers Julie and John Rolsen say that the new featherbeds make people sleep later. Julie serves hot chocolate-chip cookies every day at 4 o'clock. Not only do the guests congregate for this, even the UPS delivery person and the mail carrier show up. The mansion is in a beautiful setting—39 acres of meadows and woodlands that retain the feel of early Hannibal countryside.

Don't miss the mansion where Mr. Clemens addressed the cream of Hannibal society on his last visit here in 1902. It's **Rockcliffe Mansion** (1000 Bird St.; 573-221-4140; rockcliffemansion.com), a wonderfully quirky place full of art nouveau decor, which was a breakaway style from the established Victorian. It, too, is on the National Register of Historic Places. There are guided tours daily year-round, 10 a.m. to 4 p.m., and from Dec through Feb, noon to 3 p.m. There's a small admission charge.

Mrs. Clemens Antique Mall (305 N. Main St., Hannibal; 573-221-6427) is one of the largest antiques malls in the area. More than 40 booths offer a great selection of glassware, dolls, primitives, and all manner of collectibles.

Pudd 'N' Heads (115 Bird St.; 573-248-1018) is open 8 days a week. No, just kidding. Owner Vicki Lewis says that and means it. She'd do it if she could. This shop has hand-crafted items made by local artists and craftsmen. There are also stuffed animals, antique glass wear, quilts, and collectibles of all sorts, and the shop is open year-round.

If you're at all Irish (and who isn't, at least one day of the year?), don't miss **St. Patrick,** the only town in the world (with a post office) named for everybody's patron saint. If you like, send a package of mail containing stamped, addressed envelopes to Postmaster, St. Patrick, MO 63466, to get the special St. Paddy's Day cancellation.

It's more fun to visit the post office, though. The letter boxes are antique, and the hospitality is the old-fashioned kind you'd expect in a town of 14 souls. Hours are 9:30 a.m. to 5 p.m. every day of summer, but Tues through Sat 10 a.m. to 4 p.m. the rest of the year.

The **Shrine of St. Patrick** is fashioned after the Church of Four Masters in Donegal, Ireland; the style is ancient Celtic. There's a round bell tower with a circular staircase of the kind used on the Auld Sod. Dublin-made stained-glass windows are patterned after the famous illuminated manuscript, the Book of Kells; the most unusual has St. Patrick surrounded by the symbols of Ireland's four provinces: Ulster, Leinster, Munster, and Connaught. Perhaps you are beginning to catch the flavor of the place.

Oh, yes, there's another unusual attraction: geodes. What's a geode, you may ask? You must not be a rock hound, if you are wondering. A geode is a rather undistinguished blob that looks like a rounded river rock. But inside—ah, inside—there is magic. Beautiful crystal formations fill the hollow center of a geode like a Fabergé egg; they're considered gemstones.

Some of the world's finest geodes are found in this small area. You can buy one at Buschling Place, 3 miles north of Dempsey; the Buschlings specialize in country crafts, turquoise, and of course, geodes. Or you can find your own at **Sheffler Rock Shop and Geode Mine** (located 2 miles south of Wayland on US 27; 660-754-1134). A new highway has gone in here and the old rock shop has been demolished. The new one is a little harder to find but follow me: Go to the intersection of Highways 27 and 61 then get on the access road going north, stay on it for about 6 blocks and the rock shop will be on the west side of the road. This is the only geode mine in the US that is registered with the Federal Bureau of Mines. Watch for the round rock building made entirely of 60 tons of mineral specimens. This shop is open year-round and has been selling minerals, agates, and jewelry-making supplies for more than 30 years. If you come to dig your own geode, bring a rock hammer and a bit of muscle; these treasures don't come without sweat equity. The mine is usually open in the winter from 9 a.m. to 5 p.m., but all manner of conditions affect a mine—cold temperatures, rain-induced flooding—so best to call Tim Sheffler and see what's going on when you plan to visit. He will be there to help you. He has expanded the shop and added a huge collection of fossils.

Bethel is the kind of place you dream about when you're feeling nostalgic for the "good old days," when things were simpler and the world was more easily understood, when people could meet one another's eyes directly and a handshake meant everything. Bethel old-timers say, "When you get it right, why change?" And here, they've pulled it off.

It's not all old-time ambience and down-home goodies. Bethel has a thriving art colony. The town plays host to frequent festivals, workshops, and seminars celebrating its agricultural, cultural, and social heritage throughout the year. Thousands of people flock here for the World Sheep and Wool Festival (ouch! a pun!). Other festivals throughout the year draw folks for antiques, fiddlers, music, and Christmas in Bethel. If you see a line on the sidewalk downtown, likely it's for the family storefront bakery that opens only during festivals. Breads, cinnamon rolls—they've got it. Get in line!

Founded as a utopian religious colony in 1844, the whole town is listed on the National Register of Historic Places. The museum can fill you in on the details; it's open daily.

Bethel is friendly; you're family as soon as you arrive. And it's best to arrive hungry. The *Fest Hall Restaurant* on Highway 15 in Bethel (660-284-6493) serves "good food and plenty of it," the folks say, at reasonable family prices. They also serve homemade pies 7 days a week that make it worth jettisoning a diet. Hours are from 6 a.m. until about 4 p.m.

If you want to stay overnight, the *Bethel German Colony Bed and Breakfast* (same telephone number as Fest Hall) welcomes visitors to 4 rooms furnished in a simple country style above the Colony Restaurant. Incredibly affordable rates include a country breakfast blessed with home-baked bread and the Fest Hall's own apple butter. (Close your eyes. Imagine the rich, sweet aroma of bubbling apples and spices in an old copper kettle. That's what goes on your breakfast muffins.) For a full list of accommodations and places to eat in Bethel, look at the website bethel.macaa.net.

Northern Wineries

Take a different loop to see the Missouri River and the little wineries that sprout like vines along its banks. There's a lot of history along the Missouri; whatever your interest, you'll find plenty to see and do.

Take Highway 94, for example. It's for people who don't like their roads straight and flat: mile after mile of two-lane blacktop that curves and winds from St. Charles to Jefferson City. It is one of the most beautiful and exhilarating drives in the state and is a practical route to mid-Missouri for those of us who don't enjoy the mind-numbing 70 mph of the interstate. Since you have this book with you, the assumption can be made that you like to drive, so Highway 94 is a "must-do" trip. Cross US 40 outside St. Charles, go a mile, and turn into the *August A. Busch Memorial Wildlife Area.* This 7,000-acre preserve has nature trails, hunting areas, shooting ranges, and 32 lakes for fishing. It features a self-guided tour of native prairie, pine plantation, and farming practices that benefit wildlife. In the spring and fall, thousands of migrating birds can be seen at the shorebird and waterfowl preserve.

Missouri Vintners—1800s and Beyond

Winemaking isn't new to the state. The first designated wine district in the country was actually here in Missouri—not California! In the 1800s the wine business thrived here and the wines were internationally acclaimed. By the late 19th century, the entire nation's wine manufacturing and distribution was centered in St. Louis, and Missouri was producing 2 million gallons a year. It was second only to California in wine production. Then Prohibition shut down the wineries, and the state's wine industry all but disappeared for more than four decades. Only one winery continued to operate during the 1920s: St. Stanislaus Winery, located at a seminary, made sacramental wine for religious orders.

Missouri River State Trail, Missouri's part of the KATY Trail following the old MKT Railroad right-of-way, meanders through here, and on weekends large crowds of bikers and hikers wander along the 26 miles of trail from US 40 at Weldon Springs to Marthasville. If you have a bike on the roof, there is convenient parking all along the trail. There are plenty of places to get a meal or rent bikes if you didn't bring your own. There's even a bed-and-breakfast and a winery for a picnic lunch along the trail.

There's a spectacular view of the river beyond the outskirts of St. Louis on I-70. There are so many good destinations along this route that you don't have to tell anyone that you are on it because you like to hug the corners and push the federally mandated speed limit to its max. This road will challenge the best Grand Prix wannabe with its collection of diamond-shaped signs warning of another set of sharp curves. But slow down and watch for wild turkey and deer. Enjoy the tidy farmhouses and pretty churches as you aim for towns such as Augusta, Dutzow, and Hermann that wait along the route.

You will enjoy *Defiance's* little shops and taverns and be amazed to learn that this whole town was under water during the Great Flood of 1993. History buffs will want to take a 6-mile detour from Highway 94 down Highway F to the Daniel Boone home. You could also stop in for a visit to the *Sugar Creek Vineyards & Winery* (125 Boone Country Ln.; 636-987-2400; sugarcreekwines.com) to taste some of Missouri's wine. Becky and Ken Miller will show you around. Take Highway 40-61 and turn south onto Highway 94, travel 12 miles along the Lewis and Clark Trail and watch for the sign. It's the first winery on the Weinstrasse overlooking the Missouri River valley and the KATY Trail. Hours are Mon through Sat, 10 a.m. to 5:30 p.m.; Fri in June, July, and Aug only, 10 a.m. till dusk, Sun noon to 5:30 p.m. All of the wineries are closed Thanksgiving, Christmas, and New Year's Day.

Somehow you would imagine a log cabin—or a sod hut, maybe—to have housed Daniel Boone. This beautiful stone house with ivy clinging to its double chimneys, crisply painted shutters, and ample back porch is not what you'd expect at all. Built in 1803, *Daniel Boone's Home* (1868 Highway F, Defiance; 636-798-2005; lindenwood.edu/boone) is ruggedly elegant and comfortable. Add a DVD player and a microwave, and you could move in tomorrow. Boone lived to a ripe old age. The naturalist John James Audubon described him as a "stout, hale, hearty man." He died here in 1820 at age 86.

trivia

Defiance is so named because the local townsfolk were so defiant in gaining a stop for their community when the railroad was being built through the area.

Here are Daniel's powder horn and his long rifles, his writing desk, and the very bed where his long career on the American frontier ended. It's a small bedchamber; the four-poster bed looks as if it were just made up with fresh sheets and a clean white counterpane, ready for the man himself to come in from a hard day of hunting, settling the frontier, and making history. Daniel kept a coffin he had made for himself under the bed and periodically tried it out. Alas, he grew too big for it and had to give it away!

The kitchen is cozy, with low beams and a huge fireplace. Mrs. Boone's butter churn sits nearby, and you can almost see the family gathered here, waiting expectantly for that rich, yellow butter to spread on hearth-baked bread. Your tour guide will point out where the whole foundation of the house moved thanks to an earthquake. A chapel, summer kitchen, and spool house have been added on the grounds, and down in a little valley are a number of historic structures that have been moved to the property. A small chapel done in blue and white still hosts weddings set to its 1860 organ music.

Tours are given daily during the winter from 9 a.m. to 4 p.m. Mon through Sat and Sun from noon to 4 p.m. Spring/summer hours are Mon through Sat 9 a.m. to 6 p.m. and Sun noon to 6 p.m.

Leaving Defiance, you'll enter the Missouri River valley wine region. There are more wineries along Highway 94 than anywhere else in the state. There is a wide choice of places to sample wine and have a meal. You can visit *Montelle Winery* at *Osage Ridge,* 201 Montelle Drive, a half mile east of Augusta on Highway 94. The tasting room is open daily at 10 a.m., Sun at 11 a.m., and closes at 5:30 p.m. during the week and later on weekends. If you know you are going to be there at dinnertime, you can enjoy a sunset dinner if you call (636) 228-4464 or (888) 595-WINE or visit montelle.com to make a reservation. Dinner is served at 7 p.m.—gourmet meals on linens and china. Very nice. The Klondike Cafe offers wonderful lunches to enjoy with the wine. All of the wineries along the river offer wine tasting and sales as well as great spots to enjoy a bottle of wine with a picnic lunch.

Just down the road a piece from Dan'l's house you'll find the little German wine-producing town of *Augusta.* More than 150 years ago it was a self-sufficient town with a cooperage works, stores, and a German school. Before Prohibition, when Missouri was the second-largest wine-producing state in the nation, there were 13 wineries located in Augusta's valley, beyond the bluffs above the southernmost bend of the river. Deep, well-drained soil and freedom from spring frosts were perfect for viticulture. This is recognized as America's first official wine district and the first in the New World to bear an official "Appellation Control" designation.

Augusta still deserves its reputation. *Mount Pleasant Estates* (5634 High St.; 800-467-WINE; mountpleasant.com), at I-44 at the Highway UU exit, 2 miles east of Cuba, was purchased in 1966 by Lucian and Eva Dressel (it's now owned by MPW Inc.). A short 20 years later, the Dressels' 1986 Vintage Port took top port honors in the International Wine and Spirit Competition in London, England, making theirs the first Missouri winery since Prohibition to win an international gold medal, from a field of 1,175 wines and more than 20 countries.

Mount Pleasant's 1987 Jour de la Victoire Ice Wine also won a silver

trivia

Mount Pleasant's sparkling wine Genesis was used to christen the aircraft carrier USS *Harry Truman* in 1996. At first the shipbuilders sent the bottles back because they wouldn't break, so the people at Mount Pleasant just rebottled the wine in cheaper, thinner bottles for the occasion.

medal, the highest award given to an American ice wine. The *Cheese Wedge,* on-site at the winery, features products made in Missouri. You can buy cheese from Emma (that's a town), sausage from Washington, and mustard from Wolf Island, Missouri. There is cider and grape juice and fresh area fruits in season, along with the Missouri cheeses and sausage for a picnic in the grape-entwined patio. Hours are noon to 5 p.m. Mount Pleasant even delivers!

Augusta Winery (636-228-4301, 888-MOR-WINE; augustawinery.com) has a wine and beer garden to bring picnic baskets to and is open Mon through Fri from 10 a.m. until 5:30 p.m. and on Sat and Sun until 6 p.m.

If you appreciate lovely wooden sculpture and vessels with an elegant, contemporary feel, you'd hardly expect to find them in the backcountry. But at *Michael Bauermeister Studio,* craftsman Michael Bauermeister is full of surprises. He works with Missouri woods to create delicate, finely designed pieces that would grace the best of homes.

Michael's shop is in an old-fashioned store building in Nona, which isn't a town anymore. It's just Michael's house and shop and a few other buildings. Follow High Street west, which turns into Augusta Bottom Road, 3 miles to the shop on the left side of the road. Shop hours are unpredictable because special orders and commissions keep the craftsman hopping. Call (636) 228-4663 to make sure your trip won't be for nothing. Visit the website at michaelbauermeister.com. He prefers e-mail to make an appointment to visit his studio: michael@bauermeister.com.

Augusta is a town worth the visit. Go to augusta-missouri.com to get the grand tour. There you will find a link to *Augusta Wood Ltd.* (5558 Walnut; 636-228-4406 or 800-748-7638; augustawoodltd.com), which was established in 1979. Framed artwork by well-known artists such as Thomas Kinkade and Jesse Barnes, as well as many local artists, are on display. Beautifully hand-carved early American furniture can also be viewed. New artists are added all the time. Hours are 10 a.m. to 5 p.m. Mon through Sat.

There are several bed-and-breakfasts in Augusta. The most luxurious is the *H.S. Clay House* (219 Public St.; 888-309-7334; hsclayhouse.com). Leigh and Alan Buehre give 100 percent to making guests feel like royalty, including a gourmet breakfast. They serve not just homemade cookies but appetizers and wine at 5 p.m., and a glass of port appears in your room with the turndown service. Visit the website for more about the Buehres and their beautiful home surrounded with 1,600 feet of deck. Rooms range from $150 to $264.

A one-lane bridge followed by a 90-degree turn leads you to **Dutzow.** (If you found Augusta charming, Dutzow is downright quaint.) This historic Dutch town, founded in 1832 by Baron Von Bock, was the first German settlement in the Missouri River valley. In the mid-19th century "Missouri's Rhineland" attracted immigrants who were inspired by enthusiastic accounts of natural beauty and bounty; among the most convincing was Gottfried Duden's *Report on a Journey to the Western States of North America,* published in 1829, which contributed to the settlement of these lovely little enclaves all up and down the Missouri River. The town offers several antiques shops.

The severe floods of 1993 and 1995 were setbacks for **KATY Trail State Park,** which runs along the river for more than 200 miles. This long, skinny state park snakes along connecting towns from the St. Louis area to Clinton. The finely crushed gravel trail allows biking or hiking for 45 miles, from St. Charles west to Treloar. You cross bottomland forests filled with migratory birds, wetlands, fields of wildflowers, and dolomite bluffs. The small towns along the way welcome trail users. You can stop for wine tastings at Defiance and Marthasville and lunch at Augusta.

Blumenhof Vineyards and Winery in Dutzow (636-433-2245; blumenhof.com) takes its name from the Blumenberg family's ancestral farm in the Harz Mountains of Germany; *blumenhof* translates as "court of flowers."

Enjoy the winery's Teutonic decor and the welcome invitation to stop and smell the flowers—along with the bouquet of the wine. Blumenhof produces wines from the finest American and European varietal grapes. There's a full range of wines, but dry table wines are a tour de force. (The Vidal Blanc won a gold medal in international competition.) Visit any day except Easter, Thanksgiving, Christmas, or New Year's, 10:30 a.m. to 5:30 p.m. Mon through Sat and noon to 5:30 p.m. on Sun. Fri it is open until 8 p.m. and often has live classic-rock music.

Marthasville celebrates Deutsch Country Days every October—rain or shine—a German living-history festival on the Luxenhaus Farm, 3 miles northeast of town on Highway O. Everything from homemade jellies and apple butter to crafts and lace is there. There's a covered bridge that takes you to a time when life was simpler. The sweet aromas of sorghum and grilled wurst and *aptel nachtisch* (apple cake) fill the air. Crafters in 19th-century costumes make the weekend educational and fun. Watch a lantern being made in a tin shop or see gourd crafters at work. Drink ice-cold home-made root beer while you watch gunsmithing and listen to period music, whistling steam engines, and the ring of the blacksmith's anvil. Tickets are higher at the gate, so call ahead. For more information call (636) 433-5669 or visit the website at deutschcountrydays.org.

The **Concord Hill Bed and Breakfast** (473 Concord Hill Rd., Marthasville; 636-782-2042; concord-hill.com) offers city-weary guests 2 large bedrooms and a huge loft that comfortably sleeps 5 adults. Add a hot tub and full kitchen, and it's an ideal weekend retreat for groups of up to 11. Try the Carriage House Room, complete with an antique claw-foot bath, an antique iron bed, and a lovely view. A full breakfast is provided, and anything from elegant candlelight dinners to lunches can be prearranged; now that's a getaway. This 19th-century farmhouse is in the tiny agricultural town of Concord Hill, population 40; this is definitely off the beaten path! Call hosts Maggie Fendelman and George McVicker for more information. Rooms are moderately priced.

When you are ready for dinner, find **Twin Gables** (101 W. Hwy. 47; 636-433-5048) in Marthasville, and let owner and cook Linda Murphy fix you some real down-home food. You are especially lucky if you happen to be there on a Friday or Saturday night, when she's out back fixing her famous barbecued pork. Your nose will lead you to the building with the four gables. It is a "family tavern," as locals describe it, a very casual place with a full bar ("John the Bartender" handles orders here), where children are welcome. From the trailhead the cross street is One Street, go south on One about 0.3 miles to Highway 47/94. It's only ³⁄₁₀ mile. Hours are daily 6 a.m. to 11 p.m., Fri and Sat until 1:30 a.m.

Bluffs of the Mighty Mo

Highway 94 winds over steep hills set with ponds and quiet, picturesque farms. Small and almost picture-postcard pretty buildings nestled in the trees are clearly visible in winter and half-hidden in summer; you'll have to look sharply. The highway follows the river through a series of tiny towns that give you a taste of Missouri past. Rhineland, Bluffton, Steedman,

Mokane—each is as inviting as the last. Heads up: You may find a great little cafe here or a hidden mine of antiques.

Plan to stay awhile in **Columbia.** It's a great base camp for some far-flung exploring—that is, once you can tear yourself away from the town itself.

Columbia is home to the **University of Missouri,** which has a beautiful campus that houses a number of disciplines. If you have an interest in antiquities, don't miss the **Museum of Art and Archaeology,** boasting a collection from six continents and five millennia. The museum, in Pickard Hall at the corner of University Avenue and 9th Street, is on the historic Francis Quadrangle. Built in 1894, it's on the National Register of Historic Places. You'll find artwork by Lyonel Feininger, Lakshmi, Francken the Younger, and many well-known classical and contemporary American artists. The museum is open 9 a.m. to 5 p.m. Tues through Fri and noon to 5 p.m. on weekends.

Archaeology has long been a strong field of study at the university, which offers bachelor's, master's, and doctoral degrees as well as courses in museum studies. The museum's collections reflect almost a century of work by students and faculty in places as diverse as Africa, Egypt, South Asia, Greece, and the American Southwest. Pre-Columbian and Oceanic works round out the collection.

futureanchors—takenote!

The University of Missouri–Columbia was the first state university west of the Mississippi. The first school of journalism was founded and the first degree in journalism in the world was awarded at the University of Missouri–Columbia in 1908.

The museum is wheelchair accessible; there are tours for the visually impaired available without prior notice. Other guided tours can be arranged by calling (573) 882-3591 (at least two weeks in advance for groups). See the website at maa.missouri.edu for more information.

The **Museum of Anthropology** (573-882-3764 or 573-882-3573) was extensively renovated and now has displays of Native America that are most interesting. Included in the displays are an Arctic fishing village and a pre-pioneer Midwest settlement—a one-room prairie cabin and a fur trader's canoe filled with beaver pelts and ropes of tobacco.

While the museums are easy to find, a well-guarded secret on the university campus is ***Buck's Ice Cream,*** in Eckles Hall, at the corner of Rollins and College Streets (573-882-1088; bucks.missouri.edu), part of the food and nutrition service. Ice cream and frozen yogurt are made here daily, and it is wonderful stuff. Try their own special Tiger Stripe ice cream. (Just because the nutrition service makes this wonderfully sinful treat doesn't mean it isn't high in butterfat. It is. But what the heck, it is sooooo good.) Hours are noon to 5 p.m. Mon through Fri and on Sat during warm weather. (Buck's is closed between semesters.)

The ***Flat Branch Pub and Brewery,*** downtown at 115 S. 5th St. (573-499-0400; flatbranch.com), needless to say, is very popular with students here. (They love the homemade root beer and ginger ale.) You can tour the brewing area or have lunch in the pub. Hours are 11 a.m. to 1 p.m. Mon through Sat and 11 a.m. to midnight Sun.

Columbia has an active and varied crafts community. ***Bluestem Missouri Crafts*** (573-442-0211; bluestemcrafts.com) showcases the work of more than 80 Missouri artists and craftspeople. Whatever your particular weakness, from wrought iron to weaving, from folk-art whirligigs to fine jewelry, you'll find it at Bluestem (named after the native prairie grass); the shop is located at 13 S. 9th St. Shop 10 a.m. until 6 p.m. Mon through Sat (until 8 p.m. on Fri), noon until 5 p.m. on Sun.

Another source for handmade and unusual items in Columbia is ***Poppy*** (920 E. Broadway; 573-442-3223 or 866-92-POPPY; poppyarts.com).

A Place to Call Home

The Devil's Icebox is a unique sinkhole in Rock Bridge Memorial State Park near Columbia. It is the only habitat worldwide for a small flatworm called the pink planarian. This park is known for its many sinkholes, caves, underground streams, and small springs. These are all characteristic of a topography known as "karst." Devil's Icebox Boardwalk leads visitors over the rock bridge to Devil's Icebox, by a sinkhole, past Connor's Spring, and back through the 125-foot-long natural tunnel. The icebox is pretty cool, and that's literal because cooler air flows through along the underground stream. Devil's Icebox Cave, upstream, is closed except to those who register in advance for day-long wild cave tours, which is worth doing.

Whether you are looking for a gift or just browsing around, this is a place with personality, upbeat and colorful. Barbara McCormic and Jennifer Perlow work directly with the artisans who do what they do for a living—professionals—as you can tell from the high quality of their work. The store features hand-blown glass, pieces shaped in clay or created from fiber, and a line of exquisite—and expensive—jewelry. Although there is some two-dimensional art, it is mostly a gallery of fine crafts. The shop is open 7 days a week: Mon through Sat from 10 a.m. to 6 p.m., Thurs to 8 p.m., and Sun from noon to 5 p.m.

One more gustatory note—okay, two: truffles and chocolate pizza. You'll find these and too many other rich temptations to mention at the **Candy Factory** (701 E. Cherry St.; thecandyfactory.biz). These folks call themselves "your hometown candy makers," but the good news is that even if Columbia isn't your hometown, they'll be glad to ship anything you want, nationwide. Use the special order number: (573) 443-8222. You can even buy sugar-free chocolates for those people on restricted diets who still need a treat. Prices seem moderate enough; a holiday gift basket ranges from $12 to $52. Hours are 9:30 a.m. to 5:30 p.m. weekdays and 10 a.m. to 5 p.m. on Sat with extended hours in Dec.

Carol Leigh Brack-Kaiser is the talent behind two businesses: **Carol Leigh's Specialties** and **Hillcreek Fiber Studio.** Carol Leigh's Specialties was created to market products made by Carol's own hands: handspun yarns and fabrics colored with natural dyes, woven shawls, blankets, and wall hangings. Hillcreek Fiber Studio is for teaching. It all began with a spinning class at the nearby university. Spinning led to weaving and then to dyeing, which led to advanced studies in fiber arts. Carol began to take her work to living-history events and rendezvous, where people appreciated the labor and old-world methods of her handmade textiles. Now she sits by her adjustable, triangular loom, which she and her son, Carl Spriggs, patented and now manufacture at her home at 7001 Hillcreek Rd., just outside Columbia. Today she has several classes in spinning special fibers, floor loom, and in the ancient methods of inkle and tablet weaving. She also conducts classes in Navajo-style weaving and a designer's yarn class. Standing over a simmering vat of wool dye, she produces vibrant colors from indigo; Osage orange (also called hedge apple), which gives vibrant yellows and golds; brazilwood for red, purple, plum, maroon, and burgundy; logwood for lavender and black; cochineal, a bug from Central and South America, for bright reds; madder root for orange-red; and other natural dyes. Carol Leigh asks that you call before you visit (573-874-2233 or 800-TRI-WEAV (874-9328). The shop is open Tuesday through Saturday from 9 a.m. to 5 p.m. The website is HillcreekFiberStudio.com.

Formosa Restaurant is upstairs over 913 E. Broadway (573-449-3339; formosa.i8.com) and serves 7 styles of Chinese cooking. While this little spot is sort of hidden away, plenty of people know about it. Open Mon through Sat 10 a.m. to 10 p.m. and Sun noon to 9 p.m. (dinner only). There is full bar service.

Missouri's answer to the Hard Rock Cafe—**63 Diner**—is just outside Columbia at 5801 N. New Highway (573-443-2331; 63dinercolumbia.com). Black, white, and chrome decor, dozens of photos of rock 'n' roll favorites and old movie stars, waitresses in saddle shoes and circle skirts, and the end of that big red '59 Cadillac sticking out of the front wall make the place loaded with atmosphere. The food's every bit as good as you remember, too. Hours are 11 a.m. to 9 p.m. Tues through Fri and 6:30 to 9 a.m. Sat for breakfast.

Swing by **Artichoke Annie's** (1781 Lindberg Dr.; 573-474-2056; artichokeannies.com/artichoke) to prowl around about 90 antiques dealers with furniture and tchotchkes from the 1800s to the 1960s. Owner Louann Riggs says it feels like the hours are 8 to 8, 8 days a week. She got the hours right.

Rocheport is a good spot to sample the KATY Trail through Missouri's middle; it is among the longest of the nation's growing network of rail-trails and stretches more than 200 miles from Machens just north of St. Louis to Clinton 75 miles southeast of Kansas City. The KATY Trail follows the old Missouri-Kansas-Texas Railroad bed that curves along the north bank of the Missouri River, and one of the most scenic parts of the trail rolls from Rocheport southeast to Jefferson City along a wooded band between the river and the cliffs—sheer limestone walls rising 100 feet above the Muddy Mo. The compacted rock pathway is easy riding even for thin racing tires, the canopy of oak and sycamore trees offers brilliant color in the fall, and the trail is flowered with dogwood and redbud in the spring. Summertime rides lead through kaleidoscopic colors of wildflowers and trumpet vine blossoms fluttering with hummingbirds.

Rocheport and many other small mid-Missouri river towns invite modern-day explorers to follow in the footsteps of Lewis and Clark. In the middle of Rocheport is a popular trailhead for the KATY Trail State Park, so whether you choose to follow Lewis and Clark's journey by river, by bike, by foot, or by car, Rocheport is a good place to begin. Missouri's ***KATY Trail State Park*** is the longest nonmotorized public portion of the entire Lewis and Clark Trail. The trail travels along the Missouri River for much of its 238-mile distance across the state. The scenery is beautiful, and it is the perfect place to find solitude with Mother Nature along the Mighty Mo. For more information about the KATY Trail, contact the Department of Natural Resources at (800) 334-6946 and order your free color brochure. For general trip planning call the Missouri Division of Tourism at (800) 877-1234 or visit visitmo.com.

Rocheport is an interesting hamlet; it is so historic that the whole town was placed on the National Register of Historic Places. Its website is rocheport.com. It basks in the sun on the banks of the wide Missouri River and still has dirt streets, which is fine with the bicyclists who flock there to ride the KATY Trail. But there are outstanding antiques shops, such as ***Richard Saunders Antiques*** (201 Columbia St.; 573-698-3765) in the historic Wilcox House. Here you will find not just antiques, but home accents, jewelry, and uncommon items from all over the world.

You can rent bikes from the ***Trailside Cafe & Bike Rental*** (700 1st St.; 573-698-2702; trailsidecafebike.com) is open Sun, Thurs, and Fri from 9 a.m. to 7 p.m., on Sat from 8 a.m. and on Mon and Tues from 9 a.m. to 6 p.m.; closed Wed. The cafe and patio are good places to eat breakfast before you take off on the trail or to grab a burger or tenderloin (and maybe some fried pickles or okra) if you are en route.

When you've biked up an appetite, stop for pasta at ***Abigail's*** (573-698-3000; abigails-restaurant.com), a family-owned restaurant located in an old church at 206 Central St. Open Wed through Sun for lunch, 11 a.m. to 2 p.m., and dinner starting at 5 p.m. The menu changes daily.

More unusual than just your average antiques shop is the art and antiques and blacksmith shop at 3rd and Pike Streets, also known as Christina Riesberg Robb's ***Under the Oak Tree Studio*** and George Robb's ***Red Dog Forge and Blacksmith Shop.*** Here, along with fine art and antiques (estate jewelry, silver, Oriental carpets, and china) is a working blacksmith shop where you can watch demonstrations on weekends. Hours are 11 a.m. to 4 p.m. Wed through Sun or by appointment. Call (573) 698-3111 or visit artandantiquesrocheport.com.

If you are on the KATY Trail, then you must be a cyclist or hiker. Look for ***KATY Trail Bed & Bikefest*** (101 Lewis St.; 573-698-BIKE (2453); katytrailbb.com) in Rocheport. This historic Adirondack-style carriage house is on the KATY Trail and has 4 guest rooms. It would be fine for a group doing the trail. There is even an outdoor hot tub, and you will be sent off with a fine breakfast.

Okay, you want to get totally off the beaten path? Hit the water. Find ***Mighty Mo Canoe Rentals*** (205 Central St.; 573-698-3903; mightymo.com) and paddle the Mighty Mo with a local naturalist and river historian as your guide. Saturday excursions of up to 10 canoes and kayaks depart from the Pebble Publishing Bookstore. Ride a shuttle or bike back from Huntsdale on the KATY Trail. Reservations required.

If it's not telling tales out of school, you may want to enroll for a term at the ***School House Bed and Breakfast*** (504 3rd St., Rocheport; 573-698-2022; schoolhouseBB.com). Innkeepers Mike and Lisa Friedemann run this big foursquare edifice at 3rd and Clark Streets and made it more inviting than any school we've seen. The three-story school was built in 1914 and served as the area's cultural center for more than 60 years.

There are now 10 guest rooms, each with its own style; there are antique bathtubs, sinks, and toilets. The Teacher's Pet Suite contains a two-person Jacuzzi. The garden courtyard invites relaxation. Room rates are from $159 to $209 per night and include a hearty country breakfast.

The family-owned winery ***Les Bourgeois Vineyards*** (573-698-3401; missouriwine.com) welcomes visitors. It is located south of Rocheport on Highway BB, 1 mile north of I-70. Admire a spectacular view of the Missouri River and watch the barges float by as you sample Bordeaux-style wines—plus a generous basket of Missouri sausage, cheese, and fresh fruit. The sunsets are divine here. Wine garden hours are noon to sunset, but the winery and sales room are open every day of the year from 11 a.m. to 6 p.m. Now food is served daily except Wed in the Bluff Bistro. Call the bistro (573) 698-2300 for seasonal hours.

All this driving makes a body thirsty, but by now you've had enough wine; how about an old-fashioned cherry phosphate? Or maybe a thick, rich malt made with hand-dipped ice cream? Stop by tiny *Glasgow,* where you'll find *Henderson's* (523 1st St.; 660-338-2125), a fifth-generation drugstore on the main drag. They'll fix you the fantasy float of your dreams. Hours are Mon through Fri from 7 a.m. until 4:15 p.m., Sat until 11 a.m.

Glasgow's narrow, two-story city hall has a surprised expression; the round-topped windows look like raised eyebrows. But there's nothing too shocking in this historic little town unless you discover that the old bridge on Highway 240 is the world's first all-steel bridge, built in 1878. Eight hundred tons of steel were used in construction at a cost of $500,000; it costs more than that to salt the wintry streets of a small city today.

Near Fayette is the only spot in the entire Western Hemisphere—that's hemisphere, folks—where you'll find inland salt grass. *Moniteau Lick,* near the more familiar Boone's Lick, is the place. This area was once important for naturally occurring salt; there are more than 80 place names in Missouri containing the words "salt" or "saline."

Glaciated Plains

Civil War buffs will discover the General Sterling Price Monument by the highway at *Keytesville.* This is the heart of Little Dixie, the part of the state with its roots firmly in the South. The original courthouse, circa 1834, was burned by Bushwackers—bands of Confederate renegades who spent their time burning farms and killing Union sympathizers—in 1864. George Todd and John Thralkill, with 130 men, surrounded a Union garrison of 35 men stationed in the fortified courthouse. When they surrendered, it was torched.

Sterling Price came to Missouri from his native Virginia in 1831. His father, mother, sisters, and brothers, who were all adults, came by ox wagon with their household goods. Slaves drove the livestock. He married and raised seven children at Val Verde, his family home. He became Missouri's 11th governor in 1853 and served two terms. But with the threat of war he felt compelled to cast his lot with the Confederacy, although he favored the Union. He became a Confederate general in April 1862 and participated in several battles for the state—at Lexington, Pea Ridge, Poison Springs, Helena, Wilsons Creek, and West Port—but was forced to retreat south.

At the close of the war, General Price went to Cordova, Mexico, where he was granted a tract of land by Emperor Maxmillian to establish a colony for former Confederate soldiers. That failed with the fall of Maxmillian's government. Price returned to Missouri in 1867 and died in St. Louis that year. The **General Sterling Price Museum** (412 Bridge St., Keytesville; 660-288-3204) is in the Masonic Lodge Building. It has an 1860s parlor with a square grand piano. Price Museum is open from May 15 to October 15, Mon through Fri, 2 to 5 p.m. There is a General Sterling Price Monument, too.

This fine bronze statue was dedicated to his memory by the State of Missouri and the people of Chariton County in 1915. It stands in Price Park, which also includes a classic bandstand, to remind you of summer concerts and ice cream socials.

The magnificent, three-story **Hill Homestead,** also in Keytesville, is open for tours during the summer months. It was built by William Redding in 1832. He was killed there by Union soldiers. It is Georgian architecture, and is listed on the National Register of Historic Places. The original east section dates from 1832. His daughter Elizabeth married William E. Hill and this union saw additions of a large parlor, hall, and front porch in 1866. Finally, in 1870, the upper-story balconies, captain's walk, and tower were added. Embellishments of filigreed wrought iron and wooden gingerbread unite the additions.

Farther north you'll pass through a real Mickey Mouse town (**Marceline** is where Walt Disney grew up) on your way to Brookfield. Every Labor Day hot-air balloon races are held nearby. There's a sustained *swooooosh* as the balloons lift off; it sounds like the sharp intake of the watching crowd's breath, but it's the hot breath of the craft themselves, rising in the morning air. More than 50 balloons join in the fun, filling the sky with crayon-box colors.

From here, a short jaunt north and west will take you to **Laclede** and the **General John J. Pershing Boyhood Home.** The rural gothic building is a National Historic Landmark and is as ramrod straight as the old man himself, softened with just a bit of gingerbread. The museum highlights Pershing's long career. Only 3 miles away is **Pershing State Park** (mostateparks .com/pershingsite.htm), with the largest remaining wet prairie in Missouri, Late Woodland Indian mounds, and the War Mothers Statue. Also, Locust Creek Covered Bridge State Historic Site is just north of Pershing's home.

You are now in what is known as the Glaciated Plains. A good example of the huge Laurentide ice-sheet movement is the **Bairdstown Church**

Erratic, a huge, pink, lichen-covered granite boulder that stands 10 feet high, 20 feet wide, and 24 feet long and is estimated to weigh the same as a Boeing 747 (768,000 pounds). It sits in the middle of a pasture on the Dunlop family farm near Milan. Over the years these huge gifts from the north have been cut by pioneers for millstones or converted to monuments. This one remains untouched. It came to the state when the glacier pushed its way from Canada 175,000 years ago. It is obviously a very strange visitor to this flatland.

Open farmland dominates Highway 5 North; the rolling hills recall the prairie that covered much of presettlement Missouri. East of Milan on Highway 6, discover busy ***Kirksville*** and environs. There's a lot happening in Kirksville, as always in a college town. This is the home of Truman University and the ***Kirksville College of Osteopathic Medicine*** (atsu.edu/kcom)—lots of lively young things running around here, having fun, eating out, and just generally being college kids.

Is your family doctor an MD or a DO? If he is a Doctor of Osteopathy (DO), his profession got its start right here in Kirksville when Andrew Taylor Still established the first school of the osteopathic profession in 1892, in a one-room schoolhouse. The college has grown; today there are 15 buildings (including 2 hospitals) on a 50-acre campus, and the student body numbers more than 500. Former US Surgeon General C. Everett Koop delivered the 1988 commencement address.

Visit the ***Andrew Taylor Still National Osteopathic Museum*** (311 S. 4th St.) in Kirksville, weekdays from 10 a.m. to 4 p.m., Sat from noon to 4 p.m. It's a three-building complex that includes the log cabin birthplace of Dr. Still, the tiny white clapboard cabin that served as the school, and the museum itself, with its impressive collection of osteopathic paraphernalia. Admission is free.

Buildings of many architectural styles, from Romanesque and Renaissance revival to Italianate and Victorian, from art deco and art nouveau to beaux arts and prairie, strut their stuff on the walking tour of Old Towne Kirksville. Begin the grand tour at Old Towne Park (Elson and Washington Streets) and follow the signs, or pick up a map at any of the businesses marked with a red flag. It's only 1.5 miles by foot—but well over 100 years if you're traveling in time.

When the nightlife gets too much for you in hoppin' Kirksville, head out of town to ***Thousand Hills State Park.*** This part of Missouri was sculpted by glaciers; rich, glacial soil is the norm, not the exception, and the streams and rivers that cut through this deep soil formed the "thousand hills."

The park straddles the Grand Divide. Like the Continental Divide, this geologic landform is an area where high ground determines the direction of surface water drainage. It always seems as if you should feel the difference as you cross, but you don't. This mini-mountain ridge runs along US 63 from the Iowa-Missouri border to just south of Moberly; western streams and rivers flow into the Missouri River, eastern waters into the Mississippi.

Much of the park is remnant prairie—look for big bluestem, rattlesnake master, blazing star, and Indian grass, which are maintained by periodic burning. Because of the cooler climate here, you'll find plants not found in other parts of the state, such as the lovely interrupted fern in the deep ravines in the park. There is a natural grove of large-toothed aspen, a tree common to northern states but quite rare in Missouri. In Thousand Hills State Park, you can find our grand-champion aspen.

If prehistory interests you more than natural history, don't miss the petroglyphs near camping area no. 3. Archaeologists believe these crosses, thunderbirds, sunbursts, and arrows were scratched into the sandstone by peoples who inhabited the site between AD 1000 and 1600. They may have been reminders of the order of the ceremonial rituals passed along by the Middle Mississippi culture, which were in use for a long period of time. Many glyphs appear to have been carved by hunters of the Late Woodland culture between AD 400 and 900. The site is listed on the National Register of Historic Places; it's nice to know this list contains more than the usual antebellum mansions and federal-style courthouses we seem to expect.

Take the highway south to *Ethel*—that is, if you love hand-thrown pottery. This little town is the home of *Clay Images* (23067 Hwy. 149; 660-486-3471; clayimages.com). Jim and Melissa Hogenson are well-known artists who work in clay; you may have seen their whimsies—dragons and wizards—at Renaissance festivals around the country. Don't miss this little gold mine (all right, clay mine). Visit in person by appointment only.

It seems that everyone in this town of barely a hundred people must own a little business of some kind. The *Ethel Museum* is at 211 W. Main St. The next stop, for lunch, is the *Santa Fe Restaurant* (101 N. Main St.; 660-486-3334). Owners Ray and Velma Mager will tempt your palate with steaks, chicken, and pork chop specialties. Homemade breads and desserts will top off your meal. Hours are Thurs and Fri from 5 a.m. to 8:30 p.m., Sat from 7 a.m. to 8:30 p.m., and Sun from 11 a.m. to 2 p.m. (closed in Jan).

Visit **Weathervane Antiques,** owned by Paul and Phyllis Tate, at 2214 US 63 in **Macon** (660-385-2941), for a walk down memory lane. It's open 7 days a week from 10 a.m. to 5 p.m. If you are just in the mood for a sweet treat, there is a soda fountain in **Miller's Rexall Drug Store** (115 Vine St.; 660-385-2147), where you can sip a cherry phosphate or have a vanilla Coke. And here is a bit of a surprise . . . Macon's **Royal Theatre** (660-385-2924; maplesrep.com) is 4 blocks west of Highway 63 (called Missouri Street in the city) on the corner of Vine and Rubey Streets. It's a grand old building built in 1889. It has gone through many names and venues, from vaudeville to movies. There are 400 seats on the gently sloping floor and it's all air conditioned and modern and yet still in touch with its origins. It is the home of the Maples Repertory Theatre and one of the latest seasons of theater included the musicals *Honky Tonk Angels* and *Best Little Whorehouse in Texas.* Call or visit the website to see about getting tickets to the current season.

There are several B&Bs in Macon, too, so if you relax and enjoy the nearby golf course and antiques shops in town, and shop till you drop, you can choose where to drop. One of them is the **Phillips Place Bed & Breakfast** (705 Jackson St.; 660-385-3535; phillipsplacebandb.com) in Macon, owned by Carol and Scott Phillips. It is a yellow-brick house surrounded by a black iron fence. Built in 1899, it boasts a big, comfortable front porch with a swing. There are 4 suites, a day spa, hot tub, sauna, and even a lap pool. There is also a massage room with a massage therapist to make this the most relaxing of stays. Rooms are from $99 to $159 with breakfast.

Tiny **Ten Mile** just north of Macon doesn't even show on the map; it's an Amish community near Ethel. Watch for little yard signs; many of these places have tiny shops on the farmstead where baked goods, yard goods, homemade candy, and baskets or quilts are sold.

Moberly is made up of farms in the Amish countryside, which begins at the end of Urbandale Drive and goes all the way to the town of Clark. **Beaner's Bar and Grill** (104 W. Wightman St.; 660-263-7744) in Moberly has great burgers and fries and hand-cut and pounded tenderloins (pan fried, not deep fried). Nothing is frozen. It's sandwiches and appetizers and a fully stocked bar. Hours for the grill are Mon through Sat from 4:30 to 9:30 p.m. but the bar is open until 1:30 a.m.

Take the grand tour through **Paris** (no, not the long way around; this is Paris, Missouri). Tiny **Florida** is the closest town to the **Mark Twain Birthplace State Historic Site** (573-565-3449) and **Mark Twain State Park,** which offers camping, swimming, and river recreation. Visit mostate-parks/twainpark.htm. The two-room cabin where Samuel Clemens came into the world reminds you of something; it could have come straight from one of his books. A bit of Twain was Tom Sawyer and Huck Finn (you remember Huck, that red-haired scamp who lived life to the hilt, devil-take-the-hindmost). If you've read *The Adventures of Huckleberry Finn,* this won't come as a big surprise.

What is a surprise is that the two-room cabin is totally enclosed in an ultramodern museum, which houses first editions of Clemens's works, including the handwritten version of *Tom Sawyer* done for British publication. Sit in the public reading room to conduct personal research—or just to get in touch with the old wag. For example, Twain once wrote, "Recently someone in Missouri has sent me a picture of the house I was born in. Heretofore I always stated that it was a palace but I shall be more guarded now." There is an admission charge. Hours are 10 a.m. to 4:30 p.m. 7 days a week; in winter (Nov to Apr), closed Mon and Tues.

ancienttrees

If you are interested in antique trees, look at the bicentennial tree at 710 Cleveland. This oak tree is more than 300 years old. There is a California redwood tree at 406 W. Monroe that was brought by covered wagon from California in 1832. I hope they are still alive when you decide to search them out!

On the second full weekend of August each year, the US Army Corps of Engineers, the Missouri Department of Natural Resources, and the Friends of Florida sponsor the Salt River Folklife Festival in the tiny town of Florida.

Although this is not Madison County, 5 miles west of Paris and 3 miles south on County Road C, you'll find a different kind of nostalgic symbol, the **Union Covered Bridge.** It is the only Burr-arch covered bridge left in the state. Named for the Union Church, which once stood nearby, this 125-foot-long, 17½-foot-wide bridge was built in 1871.

You can almost hear the clatter of horses' hooves and the rumble of wagon wheels through the old wooden tunnel. (You'll have to use your imagination; the recently restored bridge is open to foot traffic only—it's blocked to vehicles.) A set of interpretive displays at the unmanned site fills you in on covered-bridge history in Missouri. Call the Mark Twain Birthplace at (573) 565-3449 for information and directions to the bridge.

After a picnic at the covered bridge, continue west on US 24 to Highway 151. (Pay attention, now.) Go south to Highway M. After a few miles you will come to Highway Y. A drive south on Y will take you through another Amish community. There are no retail shops along the route except Sam's Store, which has no sign out front—you have to ask for directions—but there are signs in the yards offering a variety of handmade goods, including homemade candy, quilts, and furniture. Fresh garden produce, eggs, and honey are also sold. You can get off the highway and take many small buggy roads to explore the community. Small schools, like the one named Plain View, dot the landscape, and buggies leave dust trails on the roads. This is Middle America in its simplest form.

There are some pretty exotic destinations around here, aren't there? Milan, Paris—and now *Mexico,* south of "gay Paree." Mexico is called "Little Dixie," because of its strong Southern sympathies during the Civil War; now you can visit the Little Dixie Wildlife Area nearby.

In Mexico is the *Graceland House Museum* (501 S. Muldrow; 573-581-3910; audrain.org), a stately antebellum mansion housing the Audrain County Historical Society. It is located in the 11-acre Robert S. Green Park,

Where to Winter If You're a Canada Goose

Southeast from Chillicothe (take US 65 to Hwy. H) is a "birders" detour not to be missed. Swan Lake National Wildlife Refuge (fws.gov/refuge/swan_lake) is the wintering grounds for one of the largest concentrations of Canada geese in North America. This 10,670-acre refuge also attracts more than 100 bald eagles each winter. The main entrance is 1 mile south of Sumner on County Road RA. Photography and bird watching are permitted, and there is a ¾-mile habitat trail and observation tower.

which has a playground, picnic area, and gracious lawn. It is one of the oldest homes in the county, built in 1857. This Greek revival home is listed on the National Register of Historic Places. You can experience the lifestyle of the era with wedding dresses, an extensive doll collection, china, silver, and antique furniture as well as antique tools. Hours are from 1 to 4 p.m. Tues through Sat and from 2 to 5 p.m. Sun. Admission is $3 for adults and $1 for children.

American Saddlebred Horse Museum is also at 501 S. Muldrow. Here is a fine-art exhibit including works by artists George Ford Morris, Gladys Brown, and B. Beaumont, and Saddlebred primitives by Audrain McDonough from the 1920s. Many famous horses are featured in the photographs and paintings. This museum is the oldest saddlebred museum in the nation, established to complement Graceland while commemorating Mexico's longtime renown as the Saddle Horse Capital of the World. There is an extensive collection of saddlehorse memorabilia. Hours and admission are the same as for Graceland.

The *Audrain Country School,* also part of this complex, was constructed in 1903 and is furnished with authentic items used in country schools—slate blackboards, desks, games, and other memorabilia saved from rural schools in the county. An outhouse behind the school adds to the authenticity of the setting. Call (573) 581-3910 for information on all three places. The complex is closed from December 22 to February 1. Visit their website at audrain.org.

Notice all the redbrick buildings in the Mexico/Vandalia area? The land is underlaid with a type of refractory clay that makes great bricks; there are still four brick plants in Audrain County.

A 14-mile jog back east from Mexico will take you to *Centralia.* Don't miss it if you enjoy "kinder, gentler" countryside. *Chance Gardens* includes a turn-of-the-20th-century mansion, home of the late A. Bishop Chance. Built in 1904, its onion-domed turret, gracious porticoes, and ornate woodwork invite visitors with an eye for elegance. A gift to the public from the A. B. Chance Company (the town's largest industry), it's been Centralia's showplace for years.

The gardens that surround the home say something about the kind of luxury money can't buy. It takes time to plan those masses of color that bloom continuously through the seasons and lead the eye from one brilliant display to another—time to plan and time to maintain. That's a luxury most of us don't have.

While you are there, you will want to visit the ***Centralia Historical Society Museum*** (319 E. Sneed St.; 573-682-5711; centralia.missouri.org/history.shtml), in a house built in 1904 and dedicated to preserving and exhibiting artifacts that document the history of the area. In the fall the museum is host to a quilt show, and hundreds have been showcased here. Hours are from 2 to 4 p.m. Wed and Sun, May through Nov.

Tiny ***Clark,*** a hoot and a holler from Centralia, is the birthplace of General Omar Bradley. There's an active Amish community in the Clark area; watch for those horses and buggies. Some sport bumper stickers, much easier to read at this speed than on the interstates. I'M NOT DEAF, I'M IGNORING YOU and I MAY BE SLOW, BUT I'M AHEAD OF YOU seem to be local favorites. You'll want to slow down yourself to admire the clean, white homes and commodious barns of the Amish.

Missouri's Monarchy

Winston Churchill journeyed to ***Fulton*** to address Westminster College in 1946 just after he had been defeated for reelection as England's prime minister. Churchill delivered the most famous speech of his life, the "Iron Curtain" speech. "From Stettin in the Baltic to Trieste in the Adriatic, an iron curtain has descended across the Continent. Behind that line lie all the capitals of the ancient states of Central and Eastern Europe. . . . "

The invitation to speak at Westminster College had a handwritten note at the bottom in a familiar scrawl: "This is a wonderful school in my home state. Hope you can do it. I'll introduce you. Best regards, Harry Truman." The president and his respected friend arrived in Fulton on March 5, 1946. The Cold War is over now and the iron curtain lowered, but the ties between the college, the town, and Great Britain remain unbroken. In the 1960s Westminster president R. L. D. Davidson wanted to honor those ties. The resulting plan was bold and perfect—if not as well-publicized as the move of the London Bridge to Arizona. The college acquired the centuries-old Church of St. Mary the Virgin from Aldermanbury, England, and dismantled it stone by stone. The edifice was shipped across the Atlantic and cross-country to Fulton, where it was reconstructed on the Westminster

Biscuits and Gravy—the Ultimate Test

I have been writing since 1985, and as I read my notes and journals, it seems that most of my memories revolve around food. So it doesn't surprise me that I gain weight with each book I write. I have photos to remind me of the Eiffel Tower, but when someone asks, "Best meal of your life?" my memory of sweetbreads in champagne sauce take me back to Paris, the world's most beautiful city.

And so it is with Missouri. I remember strolling along Washington's Front Street and watching the river amble by, hearing the trains approaching along the track that parallels the river, but if someone asks, "Best biscuits and gravy?" I remember a little diner in town. The waitress heard me say I had never had biscuits and gravy. So she gave me no other breakfast option. I would have biscuits and gravy. They were wonderful: soft, flaky biscuits covered with thick, sausage-filled gravy. Since that fateful day I have ordered B&G at hundreds of restaurants, and it has never been the same. Hockey pucks covered with Elmer's glue—bland, dry, tasteless attempts at a meal fit for the gods. It is my ultimate test of an eating establishment that claims to serve breakfast.

Fried chicken—now there's another test. The best pan-fried chicken in the state is at Stroud's in Kansas City. Serving family style on big platters with green beans and mashed potatoes covered with pan gravy, it is an all-you-can-eat-and-take-the-rest-home heaven. Oh my, is it any wonder you have to get there before they open to line up for a seat?

When I wrote about Arkansas, it was fried catfish and hamburgers (in honor of President William Jefferson Clinton) I searched out, but none of the hamburgers matched the tiny burgers at Hayes Hamburgers in suburban Kansas City.

In Kansas it was fried chicken and muffins (it seems that most of the B&Bs in Kansas make delightful muffins that are soft and warm and huge) that drew my attention. And while Missouri is famous for its steak and barbecue, there was a cold smoked-trout dish at the Blue Heron in Osage Beach that has lingered in my memory for years.

Say what you will about scenic highways, back-road museums, and shopping; what is really important is the answer to the age-old question: "Where should we eat?"

campus (Harry Truman himself turned the first spade of earth in 1964), and rededicated in 1969. It now houses the **Winston Churchill Memorial and Library** (501 Westminster Ave., Fulton; 573-592-5369; churchillmemorial .org), currently the only center in the US dedicated to the study of the man and his works. Churchill's original oil paintings (the very public man had a private side, and enjoyed relaxing with his paints), letters, manuscripts, family mementos, and other memorabilia are on display, in addition to the fire-scarred communion plate rescued from the ruins of the church after World War II.

The church itself is deeply historical; built in 12th-century London, it was redesigned in 1677 by Sir Christopher Wren, one of the finest architects of the period. Damage caused by German bombs seemed to signal its end until Westminster College stepped in to rescue the building. It is open from 10 a.m. to 4:30 p.m. 7 days a week. Tours are available.

The Berlin Wall fell in 1989, and a piece of it, marked with angry graffiti of the past, was made into a sculpture by Churchill's granddaughter, Edwina Sandys. She cut out simple but powerful shapes of a man and a woman as openings in the wall and called it *Breakthrough*. That piece now stands on campus. In 1992 Mikhail Gorbachev spoke at Westminster, further symbolizing the end of the Cold War.

The ***Auto World Museum*** (200 Peacock Dr., Fulton; 573-642-2080; autoworldmuseum.com) has rare cars (among them the shiny black 1931 Marmon, a 16-cylinder car gangsters made infamous), vintage fire trucks (including a 1922 Ahrens Fox Pumper), tractors, and buggies. Open daily Apr through Dec from 9 a.m. to 5 p.m. it is the dream come true of Bill Backer. Bill has been collecting and restoring old cars for more than 50 years. When the local Kmart left town, Bill had the opportunity to grab 37,000 square feet of work space. When he moved in he thought he would open a museum for a month or so to show off his cars. It became so popular that he decided to divide the area and use the front as a museum and the back as a workroom. The rare cars were a hit—cars such as a Stanley Steamer, a DeLorean, and a 1986 Pulse (not old, but only 60 of these motorcycles-become-cars were made). They are right there with the Edsel and Studebaker as unique collectibles. He also has an 1875 Haynes, the only one in the US in private hands (there is one in the Smithsonian in Washington, DC). If you want to see a great collection of more than 100 vehicles, from horseless carriages to solar cars, this is the place. There is also a gift shop with local artisans contributing military memorabilia, railroad collectibles, fine china and crystal, and a little bit of flea market. In addition there's a large display of Kennedy memorabilia. You can make an appointment for a tour in the winter, too.

The **Loganberry Inn,** a turn-of-the-20th-century Victorian home, offers guests bed-and-breakfast accommodations at 310 W. 7th St., Fulton (573-642-9229 or 888-866-6661; loganberryinn.com), only a block from Westminster College. This inviting 1899 Victorian home welcomed Margaret Thatcher in 1996. Hosts Carl and Cathy McGeorge bake fresh cookies for your arrival and serve a gourmet breakfast on fine china each morning. It is walking distance from the Churchill Memorial Museum and the Rare Car Museum downtown. The Loganberry Inn offers many creative packages to suit the traveler. One of the most popular is the Fireplace Dinner for two, for those weary travelers who arrive late on Friday and wish for a private, intimate repast in their room by the fire. Then there is the Pedal & Picnic package (in season), where a pair of bicycles are provided and a gourmet picnic lunch in a secluded park is found along a 6-mile loop. How about the KATY Trail for two? Bicycles and a bike rack are furnished in case you didn't bring your own. Other popular escapes are golf packages, Girl Friend Get-Aways, and a Wine Country Weekend. Rooms (and a suite) are $119 to $189.

Beks Restaurant (511 Court St., Fulton; 573-592-7117) offers upscale dining for medium prices. This charming eatery is housed in a circa 1880 building and serves imported beer, steaks (no, not just steaks, but filet with bleu cheese crumbles), and seafood. Try the salmon or shrimp Alfredo or some of the other specialties, such as pepper-crusted elk rib loin. See the complete menu at beksshop.com. There is live jazz music every Sat from 6:30 to 9:30 p.m. Restaurant hours are Mon through Wed 7:30 to 9 p.m., Thurs and Fri 7:30 to 10 p.m., and Sat 8:30 to 10 p.m.

Fulton was also the home of Henry Bellamann, author of *King's Row*. Set in Fulton, the novel was made into a movie in the 1940s starring none

strange as it sounds

If you can, find Founder's Cemetery on the north edge of Paris. It is listed in *Ripley's Believe It or Not* because it is the home of possibly the only tombstone in the world to list three wives of one husband.

As long as you are searching out cemeteries, find the Walnut Grove Cemetery and take a good look at the caretaker's building. Its architecture is Little Dixie Victorian, and it was constructed around 1870. The round turret originally enclosed a water tower for water storage.

other than Missourian Bob Cummings and a prepresidential Ronald Reagan. ***Kingdom of Callaway Chamber of Commerce and Visitor's Center*** (409 Court St.; 573-642-3055 or 800-257-3554; callawaychamber.com) displays memorabilia from the movie and offers a walking tour of the *King's Row* setting. Hours are Mon through Fri 8 a.m. to 5 p.m.

thekingdom
ofcallaway

Callaway County in effect seceded from both North and South and stood independent briefly as the Kingdom of Callaway, when federal troops deposed Governor Claiborne Jackson and established a provisional government in Jefferson City during the Civil War. Early in October 1861, 600 federal troops came to subdue Rebel Callaway County. Former state representative Jefferson Jones gathered 600 troops to defend the county from the federal invasion. Equipped with shotguns and hunting rifles, they tried to look like a trained army. They even painted logs black and hid them in the brush with wagon wheels to look like artillery. The federal commander, General John Henderson, agreed not to advance against this "well-trained force of men" and allowed Callaway County to negotiate a treaty with the federal government. The treaty recognized the county's independence and granted Callaway the right to govern itself. And so, Callaway County became "the Kingdom of Callaway." After the war ended, the "kingdom" still refused to be reconstructed and governed by outside forces.

The ***City of Fulton Walking Trail*** is a 3-mile walking and biking trail that connects three parks. The trail runs along Stinson Creek, crosses a covered bridge, and passes below "Lover's Leap" cliff.

The ***Fire Fighter's Memorial of Missouri*** (5548 Dunn Dr.; 573-642-7692) in ***Kingdom City*** features a bronze statue that is identical to the one donated to the city of New York after the terrorist attack of 9/11. Here tribute is paid to all the brave firefighters who have given their lives in the line of duty.

Summit Lake Winery (1707 S. Summit Dr.; 573-896-9966; summitlakewinery.com) in ***Holts Summit*** sits high atop a bluff overlooking US 54, the Missouri River, and Jefferson City. Try the distinctive Missouri wines on the bistro menu, and be sure to visit the tasting room. The winery is open year-round. In the summer enjoy the view in the outdoor garden terrace, or when the winds blow sit by the cozy fireplace. While ***Crane's Country Store (and Museum)*** (10675 Old US 40; 573-254-3311; cranes-country-store.com) in **Williamsburg** may look like an old-time general store, once inside you find it is a real working store. Many antiques and memorabilia are on display. Have a sandwich and an ice-cold bottle of pop while you browse. Open 8 a.m. to 6 p.m. Mon through Sat.

The tiny **Marlene's Restaurant & Antiques (and Old-fashioned Ice Cream Parlor)** (10665 Old Highway 40; 573-254-3356), a few steps from the Country Store, has only 6 or 7 tables. Marlene Crane is the co-owner of the Country Store with her husband, Joe. This place is small but mighty. If you are traveling with a busload, just call ahead and they will make it happen. Somehow they can seat up to 30 people comfortably using space from the museum.

From the Kingdom of Callaway, thence hie thyself back east along I-70 to **Graham Cave State Park** (573-564-3476) near **Danville.** (Oops, this royalty stuff gets to you!) Graham Cave is a huge arch of sandstone that dwarfs its human visitors. This rainbow-shaped cave is shallow, so the tour is a self-guided one. Spelunkers, don't let that put you off. Although this is not a deep-earth cave with spectacular formations, artifacts were found here dating from the area's earliest human habitation, some 10,000 years ago. Before the Native Americans formed themselves into tribes, Graham Cave was an important gathering place. Spear-type flints, made before the bow was invented, were found here, along with other signs of human use. The dig itself is fenced to prevent finds from being removed, but you can admire these fine examples of the earliest Show-Me State inhabitants in the small museum in the park office. Take the Danville/Montgomery City exit off the interstate and follow Outer Road TT 2 miles west; it dead-ends at the park, so you can't go wrong. Check in at the park office to pick up a map to the cave. Check the park's website for the cave's seasonal hours at mostateparks .com/grahamcave.htm.

Places to Stay in Northeast Missouri

HANNIBAL
Quality Inn & Suites
120 Lindsey Dr. Highway 36
(573) 221-4001
Inexpensive

COLUMBIA
Holiday Inn
2200 I-70 Dr. Southwest
(573) 445-8531
Inexpensive

LOUISIANA
River's Edge Motel
201 Mansion St.
(573) 754-4522
Inexpensive

ST. CHARLES
Red Roof Inn
I-70 and Zumbehl Road 3
(636) 947-7770
Inexpensive

MOBERLY
Best Western
1200 E. Hwy. 24
Junction of US 63/US 24
(660) 263-6540
Inexpensive

KIRKSVILLE
Days Inn
3805 S. Baltimore
US 63 South/Route 6
(660) 665-8244
Inexpensive

Super 8 Motel
1101 Country Club Dr.
(660) 665-8826
Inexpensive

MACON
Super 8 Motel
203 E. Briggs Rd.
Junction of Highways 36 and 63
(660) 385-5788
Inexpensive

MEXICO
Budget Inn
1010 E. Liberty
(573) 581-1440 or
(800) 528-1234
Inexpensive

KINGDOM CITY
Super 8 Motel
3370 Gold Ave. (I-70 and US 54)
(573) 642-2888
Inexpensive

KEARNEY
Super 8 Motel
210 Platte Clay Way
(816) 628-6800
Inexpensive

BETHANY
Family Budget Inn
4014 Miller St.
Exit 93, Highway 1351
(660) 425-7915
familybudgetinnmotel.com
Inexpensive

MARYVILLE
Comfort Inn
2817 S. Main
(660) 562-2002
(800) 528-1234
comfortinn
.reservation-desk.com
Inexpensive

CAMERON
Econo Lodge
220 E. Grand
(816) 632-6571
Inexpensive

Places to Eat in Northeast Missouri

HANNIBAL
Lula Belle's
111 Bird
(573) 221-6662
lulabelles.com
Inexpensive

COLUMBIA
Booches Billiard Hall
110 S. 9th St.
(573) 874-9519
Inexpensive

Shakespeare's Pizza
9th and Elm Streets
(573) 449-2454
shakespeares.com
Inexpensive

KIRKSVILLE

Rosie's Northtown Cafe
2801 N. Baltimore
(660) 665-8881
Inexpensive

KINGDOM CITY

Iron Skillet
3304 Gold Ave. (I-70 and
US 54)
(573) 642-8684
Inexpensive

KEARNEY

Outlaw Barbecue
129 W. Washington
(816) 628-6500
Inexpensive

MARYVILLE

A&G Restaurant
208 N. Main St.
Business 71
(660) 582-4421
agrestaurant.com
Inexpensive

FINDING HELPFUL VISITOR INFORMATION

Kearney
kearneychamber.org
(816) 628-4229

Kirksville
visitkirksville.com
(816) 665-3766

Marceline
marcelinemo.us/tourism.htm
(660) 376-3528

Paris
parismo.net
(660) 327-4450

Plattsburg
plattsburgmo.com
(816) 539-2649

Smithville
smithvillemo.org
(816) 532-3897

Index